A Little Bit of
MisChief

Christina Gillgren

SALINA BOOKS

About the Author

Christina was brought up on the island of Malta and was known for her high spirit and mischief making very early in life. The Nuns at the Girls' School she attended tried to channel her enthusiasm for life by making her prefect, which of course did not work.

Growing up in a large brood, her father encouraged all his children - with no excuse for gender - to take up his love for a sporty outdoor life; this saw her adopt sailing, diving, gliding and other high adrenalin activities. She represented Malta in the world championships for Mirror 10 sailing dinghies (Holland 1972) and has taken part in the Middle Sea Race.

Christina travelled extensively with her husband Bjorn, with spells in Switzerland, Sweden and Iran (during the revolution) before settling in Perth, Western Australia 1982. They have two children.

In Australia, Christina completed two degrees in History and Communication Studies, and then progressed to a PhD in social/political science. Towards the end of her career, she worked as a public policy advisor to the Premier of Western Australia, running an office on active citizenship and good governance.

After a successful life and professional career, she decided that enough was enough and it was time to go sailing around the world.

Reviewer Comments

'*A Little Bit of MisChief* is a great read full of memories of an unforgettable trip. Most of all it depicts how anyone can take the challenge and make the dream their own.'

The Cruising Helmsman, Phil Ross

'…a particular sailor's journal entwined with a good dose of humour, equally peppered with sweetness, and bold, clever risks …'

Times of Malta, Nadine Muscat Cini

'Christina's tales of heart pounding moments with pirates and swimming with whale sharks and dolphins in exotic waters, among many others…'

The Malta Independent, Marie Benoît

'A trailblazing Maltese sailor …It was the sort of trip bound to bring with it adventures, positive and negative, as they edged their way across the oceans.'

The Times of Malta, Vanessa McDonald

On Authors Facebook page, Goodreads and Amazon:

'Fantastic good read. So vividly described that it feels almost like being there. No need to be a sailor to enjoy!' - Josianne Stottrup

'Great book, Great writer, loved her book. A Little Bit of Mischief is a good read, funny and interesting.' - Sharon Verry'

'I loved the book from the first page. Couldn't put it down. It was like being there, sharing the adventure.' - Nallen Karlsson

'An easy book to read about one couple's adventures that will inspire those who dream of a cruising lifestyle to get on and make it happen.' - Johannes Roggeveen

'So happy we met and shared some happy times with you, good luck with your book.' - Audrey Napier

'Loved the book. Loved the humour.' - Joanna Bonnici

'A tremendously enjoyable read which I could not put down until I had sailed around half the world together with Christina and Bjorn, in this delightful peripatetic account.' - Christine A

'Loved this book, learnt way more than I ever knew about boating !! It took me on such a ride I was wishing I could go too....it has opened up a whole new world for me.' - Karyl

'This is great read - an inspirational story of travel and a true partnership.' - Cec Broderick

'One of my favorite Christmas presents was "A Little Bit of Mischief" Looking forward to reading the next one.' - Nancy V. Jaderen

'Golly it's great. I cannot get my nose out of it.' - Lynne Newton

'I thoroughly enjoyed it… what an amazing journey you had.' - Clare Crusham

'The description is so natural I feel as though I'm living the moments.' - Josephine Gatt

'What an excellent read.' - Helen Corbett

A Little Bit of MisChief
Copyright by Christina Gillgren 2018.

The moral right of the author has been asserted.

All rights reserved. No part of this publication may be reproduced, stored in or introduced into a retrieval system, or transmitted, in any form or by any means (electronic, mechanical, photocopying, recording or otherwise), without the prior written permission of both the copyright owner and the publisher of this book.

Design and Layout by Bjorn Gillgren 2018
Cover Photo by Fab Lentz on Unsplash 2017

Edition 2 published 30 April 2019

Available in Print and as eBook.

SALINA BOOKS
email: salinabooks@gmail.com
Facebook.com/ChristinaGillgrenAuthor
Christina Gillgren g GOODREADS AUTHOR

*This book is dedicated to Bjorn
My husband
My Life Companion
And more…
…much, much more!!*

Acknowledgements

I would like to thank all our friends - sailors, cruisers and landlubbers - for unwittingly providing us with many treasured memories and making this journey a truly memorable one. With a maxim of *what goes around, comes around* that most cruisers live by, Bjorn and I came to love, appreciate and savour the friendship, helpfulness and warmth that characterises the sailing community and long-distance cruisers. In particular, I would like to thank Helen and Joe on *Dreamcatcher* for being our sailing buddies, and Birte and Jorgen on *Circe* for their wisdom and advice along the way.

Embarking on such a journey was made so much easier with the enthusiasm and encouragement of our children and their partners.

This book would probably not have been completed but for my sister Josianne roping me in to write academic articles with her. And it would not have found its way to publication were it not for the tremendous support, help and patience of my husband and partner, Bjorn. He is also my first editor, publisher and collaborator. Bjorn roped in his brother Dan to help with technology. Thanks Dan! A big hug and thanks to family and friends who gave me the confidence to progress to publication.

Many came to the party with their encouragement and support. I would like to give a special thanks to my editor, Sam Treble for painstakingly going through the manuscript and for her feedback. I absolve them of all responsibility for any linguistic quirks in the book.

It would be remiss not to mention the invaluable resource of the "OpenStreetMap Foundation" on which we relied to cobble together our simple maps for each chapter. These maps are intended only to give an indication of our travels and locations mentioned in each chapter. The OpenStreetMap Foundation's material is made available under the "Creative Commons Attribution-ShareAlike 2.0 licence" which can be found at www.openstreetmap.org/copyright. We encourage you to go to OpenStreetMap to follow us, and for greater clarity and accuracy.

We must also give credit to "Unsplash" that provides beautiful, free images gifted by the world's most generous community of photographers. The cover of this book is clear evidence of the quality of material to be found there.

A final word of thanks to cruisers who travelled before us and left behind a treasure trove of anecdotes and information handed down between sailors via emails and sailing blogs. Our journey has been made so much richer by their contribution.

Just before leaving Fremantle

*"Live in the sunshine,
Swim the sea,
Drink the wild air's salubrity."*
                    Ralph Waldo Emerson,
                    Merlin's Song

Contents

Chapter 01: .... Launching a Dream
Chapter 02: .... A Fishy Start
Chapter 03: .... First Crossing: A Lively Welcome
Chapter 04: .... Bali to Sebana Cove, Malaysia
Chapter 05: .... The Malacca Straits
Chapter 06: .... Thailand and Ship Repairs
Chapter 07: .... Second Crossing: Thailand to the Maldives
Chapter 08: .... Third Crossing: Maldives, and then to Oman
Chapter 09: .... Down Pirate Alley
Chapter 10: .... Yemen: Land of Contrasts
Chapter 11: .... The Red Sea
Chapter 12: .... An Egyptian Escapade
Chapter 13: .... Finally the Med
Chapter 14: .... Turkish Delight
Chapter 15: .... Winter in Finike
Chapter 16: .... Idyllic Greece!
Chapter 17: .... The Corinth and the Ionian
Chapter 18: .... Finally, Malta
Chapter 19: .... Cruising in the Adriatic
Chapter 20: .... With a Taste of Italy
Chapter 21: .... Sea Change: Malta and Scrumptious Sicily
Chapter 22: .... And Everywhere Else!
Chapter 23: .... The Caribbean
Chapter 24: .... Dream the Dream

The Weather Gods
The Weather (For The Nautical Among You)
The Boat: SV Mischief
Glossary of Nautical Terms
Vessel List
Map

1
Launching a Dream

It all started one Australian summer evening when Bjorn, my husband, was surfing the net. Here we were, both in our early to mid-fifties, bogged down with work, long hours, high stress jobs and mobile phones constantly ringing: Bjorn even had two work phones, one of which we referred to as the 'death' phone, which was when he would receive notification of fatalities in a work place. Being in charge of occupational health and safety in Western Australia, where we lived, was no joke and we often wondered about the toll the working hours were taking on our health.

It did not help that I worked for the State Premier running a small Office as a public policy advisor. I was entrusted with the task of empowering citizen participation and making public policy decisions more inclusive and accountable. We valued living in beautiful, sunny Perth, Western Australia, the land of the sandgropers with their love of the outdoors. Sandgropers, incidentally, are tough, resolute insects closely related to grasshoppers and locusts. This moniker is the colloquial name for Western Australians and their laid-back but tenacious approach to life. Yet here we were, stressed out and running around with mobile phones to our ears. So where did we go wrong? Surely there was an alternative to this madness.

"Wouldn't it be lovely to leave all this behind?"

"Yes, but can we afford it …and what would we do instead?"

Discussions on a lifestyle change had become a frequent evening topic, as we sat on our balcony with a glass of vino in hand, chilling out after a long day: the dreaming, we used to call it! Our sanity was called *Salina*. She was a Sparkman and Stevens (S&S) 40-foot sailing boat, just right for the stiff sea breezes that blow, often at 25 knots and more (Force Six), along the Perth coast all spring and summer. No boat, either before or after, has ever come near the way our *Salina* cut through the water. Much as we loved her, though, we knew she was not our choice for long term cruising. She was built along more traditional lines with a narrow stern and little storage space. *Salina* was a gorgeous boat to sail and race in, but if we were going to make it our home for a few years at least, there was not much room for comfort.

Our dreaming involved conjuring up the ideal boat, with a variety of names from *Water Music* to *Anchor Song* and finally to *Salina 2*. The boat Bjorn saw listed on the internet was a Moody, a 43-foot sailing boat built in Britain for serious ocean cruising. And very comfortable with lots of room for the long-term cruiser.

"Come look at this, Chris."

In our frequent discussions on what we would do and where we would go, we had narrowed down the type of boat that suited our purpose to a couple of brands. A 'Moody' was close to the top of our list. She also had the one prerequisite from my point of view: a lovely detached queen size, centre line bed accessible from both sides, with loads of headroom. Not for us the squashed berths where you have to climb over each other, with hardly any room for a good bonk! We had a healthy love life and we certainly wanted to keep it that way.

What made her even more attractive was the fact that this particular boat was fully equipped for going round the world. She was a sturdy boat, tried and tested. The Swiss owner had sailed her from Spain across the Atlantic and the Pacific Oceans. But then he got impatient waiting for good weather in Tonga. The result was a horrible crossing to New Zealand when

A Little Bit of MisChief

he ran into a terrible storm. That was the end of sailing for him. For us, the boat was conveniently located in the Bay of Islands, tied up from freedom, awaiting a new owner and some more adventure.

It was just by chance that the following week I was scheduled to fly from Perth to Canberra for work. Luckily, Bjorn was flying to Sydney on another work-related trip at the same time. Auckland, New Zealand, was a stone's throw away for us both, and from there we proceeded to Opua in the Bay of Islands.

Talk about love at first sight! She was a typical Moody. As she swayed jauntily along the pier, I could already picture her and her playful 'mood' and the name just came to me: *Mischief*, spirited and free, and ready to sail off and sprinkle our path with fun and adventure. She was just the right size, one I was able to handle singlehanded if necessary. I wanted a touch of cheek, laughter and friendships to be the hallmark of our future - and a smile to be the first response of those who crossed paths with us.

Due to Australian importation and tax laws, it became more feasible to purchase the boat in Australia. Our helpful boat broker arranged for the boat to be sailed across the Tasman Sea to Brisbane, where ownership would be transferred to us. And so *Mischief* began her new life.

Jomaro, as the boat was then called, was in a 'tired' state when we flew out to welcome her in Brisbane. I had negotiated with Julie, a veteran sailor who was to become a good friend, to sail her to Fremantle, the seaport to Perth. Here we would work on her and prepare her for her new cruising life. With an all women crew, Julie sailed the boat from Brisbane to Fremantle over the top of Australia, a trip of almost 4000 nautical miles. A few glitches along the way reflected once again the sorry state that *Jomaro* had fallen into. I flew to Darwin in August, getting away from mid-winter in Perth, to help sail her down the Western Australian coast.

"This is exciting! I'm so looking forward to this trip, but I confess to being a bit uneasy. I really do not like crocodiles." I had heard so much about the vast, untamed northern coast of

Western Australia with crocodile infested waters, king tides that can reach up to 11 metres and above, and a wild desolate coastline with little habitation.

Julie soon put an end to my speculation, however. "We'll be sailing in two to four day hops," she told me. "This way we will get to Perth faster, and won't have much problem with the tides, as we will be well away from the coast. Hopefully, it will be a smooth run."

On our first day at sea, a coast guard plane approached and swept down to fly past our stern. Soon they were calling us on the radio.

"Sailing vessel with white hull and blue canvas. This is the Australian Coast Guard. Please identify yourself."

"Australian Coast Guard. This is sailing yacht *Jomaro*: Juliet, Oscar, Mike, Alpha, Romeo, Oscar…."

"Sailing yacht *Jomaro*: Last port of call and destination, please?"

"Last port of call was Darwin, we left one day ago. We are making our way south having come round all the way from Brisbane. Our next port of call will be Dampier."

"OK, *Jomaro*. Have a good trip."

…And they came back the second day, and the third…. Suddenly the world had grown smaller. The feeling of isolation dissolved. There was no way we could be lost here.

On our second day at sea, a large pod of whales caught up with us off the coast at Wyndham.

"Hey, guys. Look at that!" I marvelled, awed by the sheer number of whales, spouting water, breaching and turning the sea into a maelstrom of froth. "There must be close to a hundred."

Julie immediately got up, looking anxiously around, and I soon realised why.

"Shit, what the hell is that!" I shouted, startled and worried at the same time. I was at the helm keeping a lookout, and a whale had breached right next to us, so close that I could almost reach out and touch its enormous tail.

"That looks like a calf." Julie warned. "Make sure you don't get between her and her mum!"

A Little Bit of MisChief

"And how am I going to do that?" I muttered to myself. The whales had overtaken us and all we could do was hold our breath and hope for the best. Luckily, they swam past and moved on without incident, though not without a spectacular splash or two to show who the masters of this marine universe were.

We had terrific weather with just the right amount of wind to propel us south. The rest of the trip was uneventful. We spent some lovely mornings getting to know each other, appreciating the serenity of the boat cutting through the water. We chatted away happily on everything from sailing and cruising to politics. Julie was an excellent skipper, always unruffled and yet, ever watchful and ready; she was an excellent role model.

One evening, as sunset approached, Julie introduced me to the 'green flash' phenomenon.

"Watch the sunset, as the sun hits the water," she started out. And sure enough, as the sun ducked into the horizon, a brief tinge of green appeared on its upper rim.

"What causes that?"

"Not sure…"

"Perhaps it's the combination of the blue water with the yellow sun?" I wondered. I found out later that this was a visual wonder that came about in certain conditions.

Another amazing sight was the 'cat eyes'. As the moon set one evening, a pair of cat eyes stood out on the horizon. Again, Julie pointed them out to me.

"That's really strange; almost unsettling," I started out. The twin tips of what was left visible of the setting moon shone eerily over the horizon. This only happens when the waxing or waning moon crescent is lying horizontal.

We enjoyed a stopover in Broome where we had to tackle the tides for the first time. Julie set the anchor a good distance from the shore, ensuring we would still have enough depth as the tide receded. We took the rubber dinghy ashore, laden with diesel cans and shopping bags, to be greeted by an old friend who lived in the town. It was great to be able to stretch our legs and walk about after almost two weeks on board.

"Hey, what happened to the water?" I said as we returned to

the beach, much to the amusement of Julie and Margaret. Our dinghy lay stranded a good 50 metres from the water's edge.

"Now you see why I wanted to consult the tide tables." Julie smiled at me, as we vainly tried to drag the dinghy with outboard motor on the stern - and four jerry cans full of diesel - down the now exposed beach.

Not one to give up easily, I took hold of the bow, turned the dinghy around so that the stern was towards the water, lifted and pushed, and let the large wheels on the back of the dinghy do their work.

"*Voila*!" I said triumphantly. But I had also learnt my lesson: never mess with the tides.

It was with great sadness that I waved goodbye to Julie and Margaret at Carnarvon, our next stop. Three weeks had flown past, and I had to return to work. The trip had strengthened my resolve to set off and sail the boat westward. *Jomaro* was a sound and steady boat, ideal for cruising. She behaved well with a following sea. Even the two to three day passages keeping watch night and day had not put me off. Rather, they simply confirmed that sailing was indeed the right antidote to our current mad life.

It took a turn of events at my workplace to push us past the dream stage. Following a change of State Premier, my office underwent a series of transformations, with the new leadership looking to change our focus. There was no love or enthusiasm for the work my office was doing, and I had had enough of the political spin. It was time for a change. I was well positioned to branch off as a consultant, and did so to start with. However, the zest and interest were lacking. I craved the freedom to embrace a life of adventure. It was in this context that the plan to set off sailing in about four to six years' time got thrown out of the window, together with caution to the wind. A formal departure date was set for Easter 2008, six months hence.

Our initial thoughts were to sail to Southeast Asia, and get our sea legs before setting out to cross the Indian Ocean. We then hoped to sail up the Red Sea to the Mediterranean, and finally to the island of Malta. This is where I originated from before coming to settle in Perth with my Swedish-born husband,

A Little Bit of MisChief

Bjorn, some 35 years ago. We estimated our journey back to Europe would take a couple of years and then we would see how things evolved.

Six hectic months followed in which *Jomaro* was stripped, and every bolt and rivet checked. With Julie's help, the interior was sanded and varnished. I spent a great deal of time chasing 'tradies' to do the work, and I can also now confirm that WA stands for 'Wait Awhile', as some of the trades gave us the run around.

Work involved replacing the 'crazed' acrylic glass and rubber seals in all the portholes and hatches to ensure they were watertight. With Bjorn's help, we removed the ceiling in the main cabin, which was stained yellow with cigarette smoke and re-sprayed it. To complement the renovation, I ordered new upholstery foam and covers throughout. I even had a queen size mattress made up. These were complemented with fresh fitted carpets and curtains. Meanwhile Bjorn took the galley apart, installed a new fridge/freezer. A shipwright helped rebuild the galley, to replace the worn timber and surfaces.

Within a couple of months, *Jomaro* was transformed. Soon it was a case of putting it all together again in readiness for a new life. Bjorn went through the electrics changing most of the wiring to the tinned copper wiring type that better withstands the salt-water environment. Then he turned his attention to all things mechanical, including the wind generator. And finally, we checked all the sails and ordered a new storm jib. Luckily for us, the rigging and the instrumentation were fairly new, as *Jomaro* had been struck by lightning in the Caribbean and everything had been changed as a result.

One of the wonders of owning a Bluewater, ocean-going cruiser is that life can be so self-sufficient. We could generate our own power with the aid of the wind and the sun, and make our own fresh water with our inboard water maker. We were eager to test them out to see how they would serve us once we were out and about, away from civilization.

Of course, being sailors, the boat underwent a de-naming ceremony: champagne, and a solemn thanking of the boat for having carried all aboard safely during its life as *Jomaro*. A week later, as is customary in boating circles, the newly refurbished *Mischief* was christened in a lovely welcoming ceremony and yet another bottle of champers. Not to put too fine a point to it, I performed the ceremony - amidst a host of friends, sailors and landlubbers - with great gusto: a swig for me, and a swig for the bow; another swig for me and one for the stern; and so it went on, for port and then for starboard, with my swigs in-between. I was soon swaying about merrily, even though we were still on dry land.

After this thorough drenching to ensure she was appropriately launched, we had a moment of solemnity as I beseeched *Mischief* to deliver us with 'fair winds and following seas' to exotic places in safety. It proved to be a very cheerful occasion as the champagne flowed freely and our guests matched each of my swigs, charging their glasses to toast our new boat.

Watching the goings-on, my daughter quipped, "Yes… hmm… 'Miss Chief' at it again, I see!"

There was sadness at leaving our daughter Annika, her partner and Chika, that beautiful half-human dog of hers. But her encouragement and enthusiasm drove us on.

"I'm so proud of you," she told us. "We'll definitely come and join you somewhere!"

Our son Mark and his wife were living in London at this stage. Being globetrotters and adventure lovers, they were thrilled about our plans, and did not hold back in encouraging us to follow our dreams and make them reality.

"Send us your itinerary," Mark told us. "We'll join you wherever we can."

A couple of weeks later we faced the challenge of moving from a large house onto a boat. Whilst we did not sell our home, which we intended to lease out to fund our trip, we had to deal with the contents accumulated over a lifetime. With packing up house, arranging to auction off most of our furniture, and organising our affairs whilst overseas, we were soon running around ragged.

I couldn't help but compare dealing with our worldly goods with winding up the estate of dear adopted grandparents of ours

A Little Bit of MisChief

two years previously. It seemed weird that we were now doing the same with our possessions: "this stays, this is for auction, this goes into storage …and this is for the bin!" Except, of course, that we were still well and truly alive.

Hectic though it was I felt charged with energy. This was a pivotal moment in our sea change.

Bjorn and I moved on board just before Christmas 2007 to start our lives as live-a-boards. It was an awesome moment. *Mischief* was now our home, and we found her welcoming and cosy. We did not neglect the comfort items. We purchased a flat screen television and DVD player. At one of the boating and camping shops, we acquired a wonderfully compact washing machine, the envy of many sailors. Even more useful was the gas barbecue that Bjorn set up on the pushpit, the railing on the back of a boat, for all the fish we intended to catch and feast on all the way to the Mediterranean. This was apart from the stereo system with indoor and outdoor speakers. To power it all there was a large battery set, with battery to mains power converters for kitchen gadgets.

At this stage, Bjorn had not yet sailed the boat once. Something had to be done about this. Therefore, on Boxing Day, we set off with fellow sailors from the Fremantle Sailing Club on the two-week shakedown cruise to Quindalup, south of Perth. This was a good opportunity to check everything out, commission the water maker and generally ensure that the boat was self-contained enough to keep us going between ports.

We spoke to as many long-term sailors as we could find but they were thin on the ground in Fremantle. The few who had made it round the world, like Jim and Margaret, were very supportive. My friend Julie, a long-time sailor, helped organise ship's stores and sea charts. For the booze, I have to confess to being an aficionado of long standing, though in moderate quantities and always in company. They say 'shared sorrow is sorrow halved and that shared happiness is happiness doubled'. May I also add that with a bottle of good red this works even better.

Our first destinations in Asia were predominantly 'dry' countries, and so we stocked the boat bilges with eight dozen bottles of red and white wine plus about another 50 litres of cask wine. The boat was bursting at its seams with an endless supply of canned tuna, pasta, rice, sauces, and a variety of canned fruit. This was in addition to the 400 litres of water and 460 litres of diesel we carried. No wonder the waterline on *Mischief* sank by about 10 centimetres.

It's funny how we would go out sailing in practically all weather and never worry about anything when based in Fremantle. Then suddenly we were leaving on this big cruise and the nerves kicked in.

One of our wisest decisions was the plan to have Admiral Julie, as we now called her, accompany us for the first couple of weeks, sitting quietly in the background enjoying the sail, exuding calm. This turned out to be a prudent choice, especially as Bjorn had yet to learn so many of *Mischief's* quirks.

Julie introduced us to cruising guides, covering almost all sailed parts of the world. These guides are similar to the *Lonely Planet* type of guides for land travellers, but contain valuable information for sailors: weather, local customs, visas, permits, port entry requirements, and of course safe anchorages and harbours. The *Western Australian Cruising Guide* enabled us to draw up a rough plan for our passage up along the west coast of Australia. Cruising guides also provide details of facilities available at different destinations, such as laundries and types of shops available. In addition, Jimmy Cornell's *World Cruising Routes* offered essential advice on the best passages between locations, and especially across oceans. All were necessary, as our knowledge of passages at this stage was pretty close to abysmal.

We set the departure date for 24 April 2008, heading north to the Abrolhos Islands outside Geraldton for around 10 days before continuing up the Western Australian coast. Our club, the Fremantle Sailing Club, organises a cruise up the Western Australian coast to the Abrolhos Islands every year. This seemed a good spring broad to start our passage north. From there we would take off on our own and continue up the coast as far as Broome. We would check out of Australia at this location and head to Indonesia, probably to Kupang or to Bali.

A Little Bit of MisChief

The plan was to spend six months in south-east Asia, gently making our way northwards to arrive in Thailand by the end of the year, as this was the best time for crossing the Indian Ocean in a westerly direction. We expected to be able to visit Sri Lanka, the Maldives, and the Seychelles along the way, before going up the Red Sea to the Suez Canal. This would bring us to the Mediterranean around April or May 2009.

As the start of our cruising adventure loomed closer, Bjorn and I were run off our feet with last minute checks: not a bad thing, given the cocktail of excitement and nerves. It didn't help when my wrist played up. After months of sanding and varnishing, I had aggravated an old condition and now needed surgery for carpal tunnel syndrome. I hoped this would only leave me out of action for a couple of weeks, during which time I could concentrate on the passage preparation and stocking the boat.

With many countries now asking for sailing qualifications, Bjorn and I turned to the paperwork. Bjorn was a certified ship's master from his days in the Marines in Sweden. He was registered to handle boats up to 300 tons (*Mischief* was twelve tons). Meanwhile, I immediately signed up with Yachting Australia for an Offshore Yacht Master's course, to complement the Coastal Skipper's certification I already held.

Next on our list were the radios on board: *Mischief* was equipped with a short wave radio for talking to other boats, marinas, and any ports or harbours we approached; there was also, more importantly, a HF Single Side Band (SSB) long-range radio for when we were out in the middle of nowhere. With this, we could always access weather forecasts, so vital especially when traversing an ocean.

"We need a licence to operate this," Bjorn informed me, referring to the SSB radio. And so, we enrolled in the appropriate course at our sailing club and got our licences. The next step was to register the HF radio with the authorities in Australia and we were allocated our call sign: WAN3065 (Whiskey [appropriate, given my love of this golden liquid], Alpha, November 3065) which would identify us in case of emergencies.

"I'm a free man," Bjorn hugged me as he returned home from work for the final time after having handed in his resignation a month previously. It was the 28th March, and not a moment too soon for Bjorn to get used to being on the boat 24/7. Slowly things started falling into place. After three months on the leasing market, our house looked set to go as we signed up some good tenants for a couple of years. This would be our main source of income during our travels, leaving all our savings intact.

The reality of this incredible sea change was gradually sinking in. At this point, we were in an almost trance-like state and did everything on automatic pilot. As our sailing friends realised we were serious about sailing away into the horizon they became very supportive: we ended up with three doctors offering to advise us on a comprehensive first aid kit for sailors. I will always remember with fondness a lovely neighbour of ours, a renowned surgeon, showing us how to do sutures using a raw chicken breast to practice on.

Our land-based friends were just as caring and helpful, although somewhat concerned. We were touched at how they ensured we would be kept in mind whilst we were away on our escapade. Our bi-monthly dinner group consisted of five couples, all of whom - except for us - were great Footy (Australian Rules football) fans. They had a medal cast that they called the "Gillgren Medal" in our honour. This was awarded at the end of each season to the person who scored the highest in the footy tipping.

We had done our best to ensure we prepared as well as we could: *Mischief* was a serious blue water cruiser and could handle tough conditions. We needed to ensure that we were also up to the task as best we could. And then as D-Day drew close, so did the panic, with scribbled lists and last minute suggestions.

"How about a first-aid course" Bjorn proposed.

"And a 'survival-at-sea' training course would also help," I added.

We were lucky to be able to enrol for these courses at the last minute. Boat and dinghy engines were serviced with the

A Little Bit of MisChief

help of professionals. Bjorn went through as much equipment as he could; for example checking the inflation cylinders to the life jackets. Flares were updated, a new emergency EPIRB (Emergency Position Indicating Radio Beacon) was installed and registered with the appropriate maritime authorities, and life jackets examined and tested. We took the life raft in for an inflation test and had it re-equipped with emergency rations. It was then down to the last shopping spree, loading the boat with as much fresh food as we thought would survive.

However much you achieve, you still end up with this long list. But we felt we had the basics right and the time had come for our departure. The panic was gone. In its stead there was elation, excitement and anticipation. We were practically chafing at the bit to take off on our adventure.

We motored out of Fremantle harbour on the 24th April 2008. We proudly set the Australian flag on the boat's stern and the Fremantle Sailing Club burgee on the spreaders. It was a sunny day with light, variable winds. Friends lined the breakwater, waving us off as we set sail to Andrea Bocelli's 'Time to say Goodbye'. Accompanying us to help us, especially Bjorn, adjust to the boat's quirks were Julie and her friend Margaret.

"Now, where's that sunset!" Bjorn quipped. To which I responded "Hey-Ho! And away we go. This calls for a drink!"

We popped open the first bottle of champagne at sea. Mind you, this broke our agreed rule of no drink while under way. But then, rules are made to be broken, aren't they?

Christina Gillgren

Boat Christening

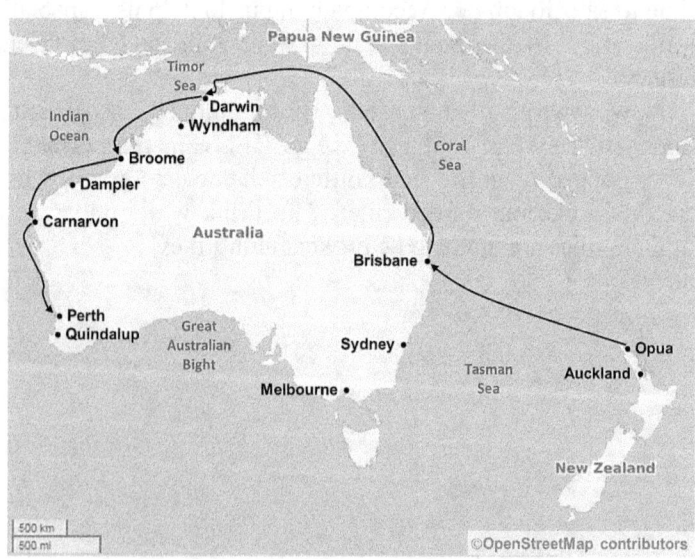

Boat Delivery Route: Opua to Fremantle

2
A Fishy Start

After the hectic running around to get ready for departure, it was heaven to sit on the boat and watch the world go by.

We were lucky in that the forecast north-easterly winds were delivered in gentle doses, enabling us to motor-sail up the coast. It was a case of testing the engine out, as we made our way to Mindarie in the Perth northern suburbs - and onto our first minor mishap as we tried to tie up to the jetty in Mindarie Marina. A slight miscalculation with a strong current pushed the boat onto the quay, which resulted in our losing the port navigation light.

"Dammit! Is it a write-off?"

"'fraid so. We'll have to replace it. Hope we can get a matching one, as this one looks like it was part of the original boat." We had sensibly taken a chandlery catalogue with us, so we could identify any boat parts we would require and order them wherever we found ourselves. A quick check and Bjorn told me "I think we are in luck. This looks similar to what we have."

We had officially left Fremantle, but we had not left Perth. Our children plus in-laws joined us for a final farewell dinner, more hugs and kisses. Then we spent a restful night at the quay without further mishap.

The next morning, the promised easterly winds arrived. We

left the marina nice and early for our first overnight trip to Port Dennison. Averaging a decent five to six knots in the light to moderate wind, we headed out to sea, but our relaxation was short lived. Before long, we found ourselves winding our way through a nightmare of cray pots. Avoiding them in the daylight was not too problematic, but what were we going to do if one of them got tangled around our propeller during the night?

To make matters worse, at around 4.00am the wind veered to the north-east which was right on the nose. Trying unsuccessfully to get some sleep down below, I heard Bjorn mutter as we brushed against yet another craypot in the increasingly bumpy seas. Not a good first night out.

It was not long before the wind blew up to around 22 knots. The waves built up, making the ride uncomfortable. We continued tacking northwards, but then we had to turn on the motor for the last five miles to reach the shelter of Port Dennison and get out of the swell.

We spent a few days waiting for better weather, checking everything out, glad that all seemed to be working well. We passed the time swimming and exploring the surrounds. Admiral Julie introduced us to fish trawling: driving around in the dinghy at low speed with a line out the back. But we had no luck.

Our next stop was Geraldton, and we had a pleasant day at sea, sailing into the harbour in the afternoon. We called in at the fuel jetty to do some shopping for fresh goods. Then we motored around to the north of the harbour to anchor overnight in preparation for a very early morning start to our trip across to the Abrolhos islands, a small archipelago west of Geraldton.

We had to leave at 2.00am to get to the archipelago at midday, which is always the best time to approach reefs. It was a bumpy night with thunderstorms and squalls, but as morning rolled on the weather calmed down and the sun came out in all its glory. This was a bonus as, with the sun directly overhead, you can see the reefs more clearly and navigate through them safely.

As we approached the atolls, we were confronted with a fascinating, magical sight: a line of low-level buildings, which

A Little Bit of MisChief

like a mirage over the horizon, seemingly floated on water. These were fishermen's huts, occupied all year round, with the fishermen evacuated whenever a cyclone threatened in the southern hemisphere's summer months (November-April). You could not see the beautiful, flat coral atoll they stood on until very close. The scene was bizarre, with surf exploding over the invisible atolls.

Of course, whoever said that sailing was dull! Just as we approached the northern entrance to the atoll, our motor started playing up, coughing, with air in the system. It seems that *Mischief* decided to have some mischief of its own.

"!*#!*!^? ...not again!" Bjorn rushed down to check all the fuel hoses and to tighten clamps wherever necessary. The engine had this uncomfortable tendency to start 'coughing' - a sign of air in the system. Meanwhile I made my way to the southern entrance, which had more legroom. It didn't help that there was a mussel farm in the way, but finally the engine held out and we entered the calm waters behind the atoll, heaving an almighty sigh of relief. We put down our anchor and tested it for holding, ensuring that the anchor had bitten into the small patch of sand properly. With the strong winds blowing, we needed to be sure we would not drift back onto the reef.

The reef fringe consisted of about 20-40 centimetres of coral above water. Once inside the reef, the contrasting image of a four-metre swell breaking on the outside whilst we sat in perfect calm is permanently stored in our memories. It is strange to look around you at huge waves, with no land in sight, while you bob calmly at the anchorage. Bjorn did yet another thorough check of the engine without finding anything obvious.

"There really is mischief aboard! I can't figure this out. It's like there is a *hustomte* on board," he muttered. Bjorn was born and raised in Sweden, and Swedish folklore encompassed a variety of mystical beings.

"You know," he continued, "these little folks that lurk in your house and are known to be house protectors. However, it is said that they occasionally get bored and play pranks."

"I like the idea of a protector, but this is one prank I could do without."

A few other boats had made it into the anchorage behind the Morley Island Easter group. Soon, we were exchanging information. It seemed that there was an even more beautiful anchorage in the northern group of the Abrolhos. So the next morning we made our way to Turtle Bay in the northern Wallaby group of the atolls to spend a few more days of rest and relaxation with many of our Fremantle Sailing Club friends.

It was here that we met Leighton and Julie on their boat *Downshifting*. They were keen divers and fisher folk. Anchored right next to us they tried to entice us into the water, tempting us by diving in three to four metres of clear water under our boat and practically throwing live crayfish on board, and straight into the pot!

"Eukkkk! I can't bear to hear the crays as they hit the boiling water." Crays have no vocal cords so we knew that they could not 'scream': what you hear is possibly the escaping air bubbles trapped in their shells when they boil. We knew that the best way was to freeze them first, but they were our lunch so there was no time to waste.

With stories of vicious tiger sharks in the area, Bjorn and I plus our crew of Julie and Margaret decided it was safer to stay on board. After a few days of crays for lunch, we longed for some good steak, which we had vacuum packed in our fridge.

They were a pleasant few days, surrounded by beautiful clear waters and magnificent coral. Sundowners were obligatory, and we cheerily helped ourselves to the wine store, making the most of having the company of other cruisers.

The time had come to say our final 'goodbyes'. At 8.00am on the 6th May, we headed out from Turtle Bay. Bernie, Roger and Dennis plus partners on *Jacqui Mac*, Rob and Kaye on *Pegasus II*, and Lynne and Ralph on *Jandanooka*, with whom we had sailed on a number of cruises, waved us off, blowing their fog horns in salute. It was almost more poignant a moment than when we had sailed out of Fremantle harbour. We were now on our own to continue our passage northwards …well almost on our own. *Downshifting* had also decided to sail on and explore the northern parts of Western Australia. And so it was that we resumed our cruising up the Western Australian

A Little Bit of MisChief

coast in pleasant company.

Another overnight trip took us to our next destination: Shark Bay. We approached the spectacular entry with its threatening wall of cliffs with waves crashing relentlessly against them, looking for the narrow 'cut' that would take us through to the large bay beyond. Perth has very little tide but as we ventured further north, the tide was increasing and would reach about 14 metres around Broome. We had timed our arrival at the entrance of Shark Bay for when the tide was slow but the churning waters were somewhat scary. Julie tried to reassure us, as we entered the cut and approached the over-falls with wind fighting current. With my hand on the throttle, I gingerly steered *Mischief*, trying to keep to the middle, following *Downshifting*, just ahead of us. We both made it through safely. I am sure you could hear our sighs of relief as we rounded the bend and entered the beautiful and peaceful waters of Shark Bay. What an amazing transformation! That evening we celebrated our first leg beyond the traditional Western Australian cruising grounds with our travelling companions in true cruising fashion.

Shark Bay, so-called by explorer William Dampier some 300 years ago, is an extraordinary inlet with unique natural features that led to it being included as a UNESCO World Heritage Site. The name Shark Bay is not accidental as it is a shark nursery with tiger sharks being the most common species. The beaches were decorated with warning signs pointing out that these fish are 'indiscriminate' eaters. Swimming was definitely not recommended. The bay is also home to a plethora of marine life including dugongs, dolphins, sea turtles and the largest fish in the world, the whale shark.

We spent almost a week cruising around various anchorages, having a lot of fun with the tides that were getting stronger the further north we sailed. I vividly remember trying to tie up in the cosy little harbour of Denham, inside Shark Bay, with a tide flowing at about five knots, and boats bobbing all around us, swaying with the current.

Admiral Julie and Margaret were by my side. I approached the jetty on the leeward side of the wind so that the boat would be blown off the jetty rather than on to it, which would make getting away very difficult.

"We only have one try, Bjorn. Get ready to jump ashore with the ropes."

"Don't panic. If you fail the first time, we can always go around again!" …came the response.

I shook my head… this was going to be tight. I managed a perfect turn to bring the boat alongside, but Bjorn, hesitating, was too slow jumping off. Ever the engineer, he sometimes wanted things to be too perfect - a good quality when we were about to cross oceans, but somewhat frustrating at times like these. Luckily, Julie and Margaret both jumped off before the tide swept the boat too far off the jetty, took the lines and before you knew it we were neatly tied up.

We explored several bays and anchorages, met other sailors, seafarers and landlubbers of course. We shopped and provisioned the boat, and did our laundry. It was also here that we celebrated Bjorn's 55th birthday with our friends. I cooked up a lovely Chicken Mediterranean dinner with garam-masala, almonds and raisins, followed by a delicious New Norcia nut cake.

Undoubtedly, the most poignant memory is the sea life: turtles, dolphin pods galore, tuna and mackerel, sometimes jumping clear out of the water as bigger predators chased them. The water teemed with life all around us as we navigated through the sandbanks.

"Just hold the frying pan over the side," I called to Bjorn. I felt sure the fish would just land in there ready for us to cook. We had enough flying fish littering the deck and could not keep up with putting back the ones that survived being knocked out. It was a pity that they are so bony and inedible.

There was a downside to the magical Shark Bay: all this beautiful water and we dared not swim. Not after the tales that everyone we came across revelled in telling about tiger shark attacks. They seemed to be everywhere. In fact, it only took five minutes for our intrepid fisherman friend Leighton, fishing from his inflatable dinghy, for a two meter shark to come, start circling him and unnerve him enough that he pulled his rod in,

A Little Bit of MisChief

started his outboard motor and got back onto their boat.

We left Shark Bay with some regret. It had indeed been a wonderful couple of days exploring such areas as Monkey Mia with the semi-tame dolphins. We returned to the open sea and made our way up the coast to Carnarvon. This was the first time I was navigating up a river to our destination. I recalled the ease with which Admiral Julie had steered the boat on our delivery passage south. I had done my homework, but was still grateful to have her on board as I tackled the ever-shifting sandbanks at the entrance. We proceeded up river with caution and made it to the Fascine in the centre of the town without incident.

As we came around the final bend to where we intended to put down anchor, a number of other sailing boats came into view.

"Look who's here!"

"There's *Westward II*, *Eloise*, and look, there's *Sailaway Too* here" - all from our sailing club.

"Come for a sundowner this evening," shouted Selena on *Westward II*. This was the start to a 'wet' week of sundowners, which marked our stay in this peaceful anchorage.

Whilst relaxing at Carnarvon, a number of other cruisers called into the Fascine, also headed north.

I also clearly recall a father and daughter on a catamaran. "The crocs took our rubber dinghy... we have to head south to replace it; this time with an aluminium one."

As they had now missed the weather window to sail to Queensland over the top of Australia, they pledged to have another go the next season.

Stories were rife about crocodiles being lured by the lapping of water and attacking rubber dinghies, which were aptly called crocodile teething rings in these waters.

We were finally settling down to the leisurely pace of cruising life. We set off to explore Carnarvon town, which has an interesting history and a variety of graceful heritage listed buildings. Admiral Julie introduced us to some of the local cruisers at the tiny yacht club, where we could also do our laundry. In the early evenings, we would meet up with friends for a gentle stroll along the boardwalk on the oceanfront to admire the coconut and cotton palms that line the path. Julie also pointed out the mangroves as we came to the beach.

"This is where you shelter if there is a bad storm or cyclone forecast. But do beware of the snakes," she warned.

The warm, blissful sunshine was a bonus as we reflected that Perth, now some 600 nautical miles to the south of us, was experiencing awful wintry weather.

The time had arrived for Bjorn and I to head off northwards without our sailing mentors.

"Fair winds," Julie told us as we hugged. "We look forward to hearing about your adventures. Keep us informed."

Bjorn and I were now on our own. We turned our attention to the next leg of our journey, and to becoming more self-sufficient. Leighton and Julie on *Downshifting* had watched amused at our pathetic attempts to catch fish along the way.

"OK guys, time we made fisher-folk of you," Leighton told us.

The following morning, we caught up for a trip to a fishing tackle shop in Carnarvon. Soon, we were equipped with a sturdy fishing rod, lures and all the paraphernalia that goes with catching fish, down to a filleting knife and board. We also stocked up on the cheapest vodka available. Never mind the quality - it was not for us, but to stun any fish we caught into submission. It seemed that we had to spray the vodka into the gills of the fish. Now this certainly sounded like a 'fishy' story.

On checking our email account via radio, we found that the cruising permit for Indonesia had arrived. Sailors rely heavily on word of mouth and experience of others to find out about what is going on in different countries. The word was that the Kupang authorities, which would be the first Indonesian port of call if we made it up to Darwin, were imposing a hefty import and cruising tax, thanks to some corrupt officials. Instead of heading up to Darwin and across to Kupang, on the eastern end of the Indonesian archipelago, it seemed more prudent to amend this part of the sailing plan to cross over to Indonesia from Dampier to Bali.

There was another aspect that enticed us to this plan. We were now approaching crocodile territory. On our sail south

A Little Bit of MisChief

when delivering the boat from Brisbane to Perth, we had largely avoided crocodile infested waters as we were passage making: travelling south as fast as possible to get to a destination. Now we were cruising, taking it easy, and only doing overnighters when necessary. This meant we were closer to the coast and stopped wherever we could along the way.

The thought of being in warm waters, surrounded by crocs, without being able to jump in for a swim was not inviting. In addition, sailors were warned not to pee over the side of a boat in the same place two days in a row, as the crocodiles were known to keep watch and attack. Another tall tale? Who knows? But I was not game to find out. I noticed that Bjorn varied his habits, especially as we knew the 'training' that went on: On tourist boat excursions, crocodiles' athletics are demonstrated by hanging a dead chicken off a fishing pole two to three meters above water.

Crocs were not the only menace. Dangerous jellyfish and poisonous sea snakes competed for attention. Julie had told us to check buckets for unwelcome visitors every time we splashed water over the decks to keep them clean.

Another good part about the change of plans was that we would have more time to cruise gently to Dampier, and perhaps to Broome. We could pick the right time to cruise around Western Australia's best kept secret, the Ningaloo Reef. The Montebello Islands were also on our to-visit list, depending on weather conditions.

We had another reason to prolong our stay in Carnarvon. The alternator on the motor suddenly stopped charging. Bjorn reckoned our resident *hustomte* was playing up again. In addition, the new port light for the boat to replace the one we had broken in Mindarie Marina had not yet arrived. A local mechanic fixed us up with a new alternator. Luckily, it was a common tractor model and easily replaceable.

We felt proud to be self-sufficient on *Mischief*. We had to be. We generated our own electricity, via wind, sun and, on those occasions both failed, by starting the main engine. We were so proud of our minimalist environmental footprint. I'm happy to report that, over the first month, we had only resorted to the engine three times for short spurts. That included running not only all our 'household', including washing machine, but also the water maker, with the water tank in a healthy near full position most of the time. The experience with the alternator, however, prompted us to buy a rattlebox two-stroke Chinese made generator in Carnarvon. Thanks to the wonders of modern marketing, this was cheaper than a spare alternator.

Admiral Julie had done her work in introducing Bjorn into all the quirks on board, particularly with regard to the engine, and its unnerving habit of suddenly spluttering to a standstill. Neither Julie nor Bjorn had been able to figure out what was behind this mischief. Bjorn checked hoses and connections tirelessly, but could not find any air leaks, so we decided to push on regardless. It was a sailing boat after all.

The next stage of our journey northwards along the West Australian coast took us along the world heritage listed Ningaloo Reef, with the first stop at the magical Coral Bay, a place you have to visit at least once in a lifetime. Here we caught up again with fellow cruisers Leighton and Julie on *Downshifting*.

Our first foray ashore, with magnificent coral reefs all around us, was unforgettable. As we jumped out of the dinghy onto the sand cay, about half a dozen lovely spangled emperor, a good third of a metre in size, came to greet us, nibbling at our legs. We were amazed. The ever-present park rangers explained that, since the introduction of a fishing ban in the marine park, this had become the norm.

We swam and snorkelled along the pristine waters in all shades of blue. The abundant marine life darting about through the colourful coral graced every anchorage we stopped at along the inside the reef. In fact, we were pleasantly surprised at how far you could travel north protected by the reef.

At one stage, we had to navigate through a very narrow channel and realised we had a visitor. A large shark, probably about four meters in length, was shadowing us. It seemed to be contemplating eating our propeller. The shark continued in tow for quite a while, until it finally disappeared before we got to an anchorage called Norwegian Bay. We heaved a sigh of relief as

A Little Bit of MisChief

we were looking forward to a quick refreshing dip.

Norwegian Bay was another beautiful spot we shared with *Downshifting*. Going ashore one afternoon, we walked into a turtle 'resting' ground full of turtle shells at the back of some sand dunes. It felt disrespectful to intrude on what felt like a sacred site. As we explored further we found numerous turtle nesting places. Though turtles were all around us, we never succeeded in taking a photo of these shy creatures, which dive the minute they spot you.

We did try fishing when we were out at sea. Leaving an anchorage, our routine was to put out a heavy-duty fishing line with a sizeable lure at the end. Before long, there was an enormous tug as the line spun out.

"We've got one! we've got one!"

"Quick, release the main sail."

"Haul the line in."

Bjorn got the reel going. Suddenly an enormous fish, a sail fish at least three metres long, jump clear out of the water.

"What on earth!" I shouted to Bjorn. There was no way we could - or even wanted to - land such a fish on our boat, stunning vodka at the ready or not!

There was nothing for it but to cut the line.

It was not the only incident either. Unfortunately, there are a number of fish now swimming the ocean with our lures attached. We once hooked a shark that broke an 80-kilo line; the second one split a lure open and took off with the hook; and the last big fish snapped the line again. What were we doing wrong? The cost of the lost fancy lures now exceeded the price of fish per kilo.

We never landed anything worthy of mention. Happily, Leighton and Julie on *Downshifting* proved incredibly successful fishermen and kept us going with a supply of fresh fish. We repaid their generosity by introducing them to a versatile card came called 'Frustration'. We still have to finish it.

At one point, as we were heading north, some excited voices came on over the radio, and soon a helicopter was hovering overhead.

"There seem to be whale sharks in the area," Bjorn said, having caught some of the chatter. He twiddled the radio knob to get a clearer signal.

"Listen, the helicopters are directing the tourist boats."

"OK, changing course. Bring in the foresail."

As we slowed down, a whale shark breached right in front of us. We hurriedly put our sails down, and came to a standstill. I got into my bathers.

We could only go in one at a time. It was foolhardy to both leave the boat when we were not at anchor. In I went, swimming up to join a group of tourists. What an incredible experience! Can you imagine being in crystal-clear water and watching this wall of fish - a full ten metres long - swimming gently by. Time stood still. The whale shark, with its distinctive white spots, lifted its tail, which then came down with a splash that caused a minor tidal wave. As it twisted to turn, it showed off its white underbelly.

Whale sharks are of course harmless, interested only in plankton. In my excitement, I had forgotten all about all the other dangers lurking around.

Our first brush with strong winds came at Tantabiddy, near Exmouth, where we were stuck for about 10 days. It was a good thing we were not going all the way up to Darwin as the winds were impeding our passage northwards. We met many 'grey nomads': retirees who buy a caravan and drive up north during the Perth winter months, or those going exploring round Australia.

With Leighton and Julie, we hired a car so we could get to Exmouth, collect our mail, do some shopping, see some sights, and chase the endless bits and bobs that need attending to on a boat.

The time had come to wave windy Tantabiddy and our friends on *Downshifting* farewell. After hanging on for dear life as the howling 35-45 knot winds really tested our anchors, they decided they had had enough of some of the very dubious shelters along the way.

We were now truly on our own. There were only tiny enclaves of civilization between here and our next destination at

A Little Bit of MisChief

Dampier. We had gained confidence as sailors, felt relaxed about our plans and were encouraged by our travels so far.

From Tantabiddy, we had a delightful five-hour sail averaging a good seven knots and reached Serrurier Island in early afternoon. I immediately fell in love with this islet and its beautiful crescent shaped beach and aquamarine waters. The reef was in good condition, and the fish plentiful, as were the oysters along the shoreline. We had the place all to ourselves for the first two days. Swimming and sunning ourselves in our birthday suits, with a glass of wine or two on the beach watching the sunset made this our own idyllic little island paradise.

Walking along the shore one afternoon, we came across a resident shovelnose ray about three-quarters of a metre in length. It had a long triangular snout with a peculiar wedge shaped disc. The fish was right at our feet, practically on the beach. When we got back on board *Mischief*, we looked it up in our fish book. This type of fish is usually only found on the east coast of Australia.

On the third day, a powerboat called in, and we decided to move on. With favourable winds blowing, we headed off to Onslow, leaving behind the clear coral waters as the sea turned a muddy, greenish colour and mangroves surrounded us.

Onslow is an interesting old town that services the local salt works and surrounding mines. Again, bad weather held us there longer that the planned two days, but a good restaurant on shore more than made up for our stay there. All week we were regaled by strong wind and gale force warnings. Fortunately, we seemed to have found a wind hole at Onslow as the winds did not exceed 20-25 knots.

One afternoon we heard a very low rumble and wondered if a thunderstorm was on its way. However, the skies were cloudless. As sunset approached, we witnessed a spectacular kaleidoscope of colours, with a glowing red core. Something had happened. When we went ashore the next day, the locals told us about a huge explosion at the gas pipeline at Barrow Island.

One of the pleasures of cruising is the circle that develops on

HF radio. We had two radios on board: the VHF that has a range of about 50 nautical miles, usually used for ship to shore and ship to ship exchanges. This radio should always be turned on, in case of emergencies in the local area. The HF radio was useful over longer distances, similar to the way BBC radio operates on short wave. With this radio, we usually establish a time and frequency, one of the boats acts as a host, and we all report in at scheduled times. With two radio schedules a day, morning and evening, we could keep up with who was doing what and where. So despite being completely on our own, we were in touch with cruisers up and down the coast and even as far afield as the Cocos Islands.

Talking via radio with Selena and Steve on *Westward II* in the Montebello Islands, they told us how they had been caught out by the strong winds. They had sheltered behind the reefs with gale force winds howling around them. These winds had also played havoc with our plans and our delay at Onslow meant that we had to give up our rendezvous at these islands. We continued on our passage north towards Dampier with a three day trip through the Mangrove Islands passage, past Sholl Island for a sleepover, and then on to the Dampier archipelago.

Just five miles south of Dampier, we again hit strong winds, which turned northerly. We had to put on the engine for the final run into Dampier Harbour. Once again, the engine decided to play up. We continued sailing in the strong winds, tacking furiously as we navigated the narrow passages. Crossing our fingers, we put the engine on for the final approach into the inner harbour, cosily tucked into the small bay overlooked by the Hampton Harbour Boat and Sailing Club.

"We have to do something about the engine problem," I told Bjorn. "Some days there is no problem. Other days, it seems to fix itself."

"Bloody English engines," muttered Bjorn, frustrated. He could not fathom the problem. "I'm really getting to hate the smell of diesel."

"Maybe it's your little mischief maker from Sweden!" I replied, trying to lighten the moment.

We decided to change all fuel lines and filters immediately,

A Little Bit of MisChief

but the problem would plague us for another half a year.

Dampier was a strange place. All around us was deep red-brown sand, soil or dust very rich in iron oxide. Every rock was this colour and it was not long before our boat started turning this shade. Guarding the entrance to the port lay the stunning Dampier archipelago, with some lovely islands and anchorages.

We had been incommunicado with our family for a few days, and the first thing we did was to contact our children.

"Where the hell have you been? We've been worried sick!" our son Mark bellowed at my husband.

"There was no mobile phone signal north of Onslow, and then we had to wait for some weather to go past."

"Not good enough, dad!" Talk about role reversal.

The yacht club was a real bonus as we caught up with many cruisers that were sailing in the area. It was thanks to them that we discovered 'Sailmail', a service over the HF radio which allows boats to send and receive emails, including the weather reports. We immediately subscribed. From that day on, we sent an email twice daily with our exact location, whether near land or out at sea. Family and friends could follow our progress on an internet website (linked to Sailmail) which would position the boat name and call sign on a world map that updated automatically daily. This way they could track our progress and we could document the good anchorages to pass the information on to others.

Dampier was our last stop in Western Australia after two and a half months cruising up the coast. At the local yacht club we were meant to track down a veteran sailor to give us more tips about Indonesia. We never met the person, but caught up with a number of other cruisers, one or two of whom were also heading to Bali. Unfortunately, we just missed our friends on *Eloise* who had left a day or so before we arrived. Another boat, *Imagination*, was leaving a few days after us.

Thanks to *Eloise*, with whom we kept in touch over the radio, we learnt we had to make our way to the south of Bali and avoid the channel between the islands of Bali and Lombok. It seemed that as they approached the Indonesian coast, they had headed for Lombok and then for the gap between the islands of Bali and Lombok. Because of the trade winds, the sea to the north of Bali at this time of the year can be about a third of a metre higher than the Indian Ocean, and so the water rushes south between the islands at a fast rate. This, compounded with the tides, resulted in an incredibly strong current that our dear friends Tristan and Jas on *Eloise* ran into. They spent a full 18 hours in a sea that was churned up like a washing machine, terrified and praying for their lives, with engine going at full speed ahead trying to get out of it.

Finally we had the right weather conditions, with a high pressure system moving over Western Australia providing us with easterly winds to drive us northwards until we picked up the east/south-east trade winds that would take us to Bali. We checked out from Dampier and from Australia on the 10th July 2008 at a friendly Customs and Immigration office, where they wished us luck on our adventures!

This was it: our first proper crossing!

A Little Bit of MisChief

Spangled Emperor at Coral Bay

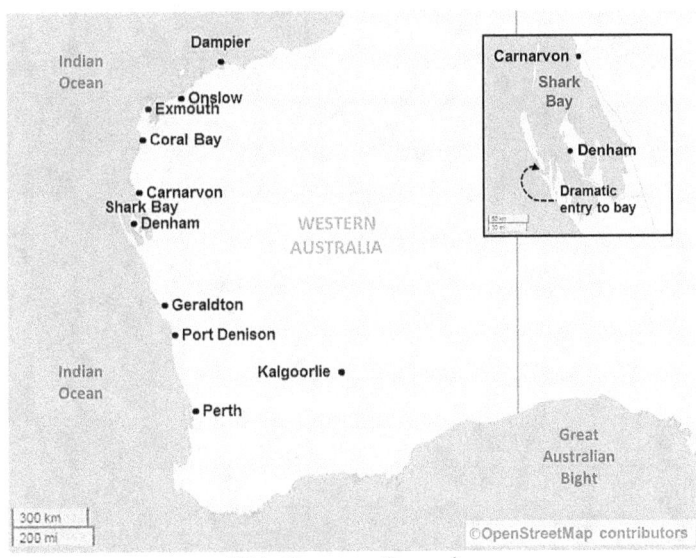

WA Coast to Dampier

Christina Gillgren

3

First Crossing: A Lively Welcome

We motored out of Dampier harbour at 6.30am for an early start. No sooner were we clear of the archipelago that we got the first easterly breeze blowing at around 12 knots, an ideal start to the day. Up went the sails and off went the motor. Using a computer program called 'Passage Planner," Bjorn had worked out the best course to take to maximise winds, tides and currents. Then, taking into account the experience of our friends Tristan and Jas on *Eloise*, Bjorn and I had moved our waypoints to make landfall further west of the strait between Bali and Lombok. We set our autopilot accordingly.

By 10.00am, the wind was up to around 17-18 knots and we were flying northwards with a comfortable six to seven knots on a relatively smooth sea. We had our mainsail and number one genoa (our largest foresail) out and *Mischief* was handling the sea and the wind really well.

Our first day gave us the chance to organise ourselves. Right from the start, Bjorn and I had decided that we would have all meals together, and commence the 'watch' system from 6.00pm. This was because most sailors live by the sun, rising at around 6.00am and then retiring at around 9.00pm - the sailor's midnight. In many ways, it was like going back to pre-electricity times. We did have power on board of course, but the aim was to conserve it and make maximum use of the natural daylight.

That first evening was special. Bjorn and I were treated to a spectacular 'green flash' as the sun set. We then enjoyed a lovely supper of chicken cacciatore under the stars. Being our first night out, we waved aside our rule of no alcohol whilst at sea and had a glass of vino to celebrate our first passage together.

"It's finally a reality. We're off; living our dream," I reflected to Bjorn, sitting back and enjoying listening to the wind whistling along the deck, and the waves rushing past the hull, a 'whooshing' lullaby, as *Mischief* glided through the gentle swell.

"It's been a good first day of perfect sailing. There should be no surprises tonight. I think our little Swedish guest is settling down, doing his job of looking after us and finally behaving. And even better, the weather files promise more of the same gentle easterly."

It was a moment to give each other a cuddle, a hug, and to appreciate each other (hint! hint!) under the stars. We both knew we were very lucky to share a dream.

Bjorn took the first watch from 8.00pm to midnight, as we sailed at a more leisurely pace of between four to five knots on a gentle 10-13 knots of wind. The sky was cloudless, but lit up with the millions of stars. The 'milky way' stood out, like a twinkling brush stroke against the dark skies. I spent the first hour of his shift with him, trying to work out the various constellations, but soon got sleepy and went for a nap before my shift from midnight to 4.00am. The four hourly watch schedule worked well for us. It meant that Bjorn and I got only one full night watch every night, between 8.00pm and 4.00am. As it gets dark around 6.00pm when you are close to the Equator, we would have an early dinner and then I would join Bjorn for breakfast at around 7.30am.

We had an uneventful first night, and did not see or hear anything. The second day dawned with the same wind blowing us gently northwards. I woke up to Bjorn cooking eggs, bacon and baked beans to celebrate our first 24 hours at sea, a

A Little Bit of MisChief

departure from our usual muesli and yoghurt breakfast.

It was not long before the wind eased a bit more and we put on the motor and motor sailed until well into the afternoon, charging our battery bank and making fresh water at the same time. We were having some fun mucking about and 'christening' the cockpit in our birthday costumes when we suddenly heard an engine noise, quickly followed by someone calling us over the radio.

What the heck!

"Oh no, it's the Australian border control again! I forgot all about them. They had seemed to follow our every movement when we had sailed *Mischief* down the coast from Darwin. And then, they had called us up every day for about four or five days to identify ourselves and where we were headed. Well …here they are again."

A good hundred and fifty miles away from land we just did not expect anything to suddenly appear on us. Bjorn immediately jumped down into the cabin and threw up a couple of towels, whilst I handled the radio call.

"Sailing vessel with white hull. This is the Australian Coast Guard. Please identify yourself."

White hull??? They must have been colour blind. After our two week stay at Dampier our boat had turned a reddish brown tinge.

"Australian Coast Guard. This is sailing yacht *Mischief*."

"Sailing yacht, please spell name, Registration Number, last port of call and destination."

"This is sailing yacht *Mischief*… Mike, India, Sierra, Charlie, Hotel, India, Echo, Foxtrot …last port of call was Dampier. Our registration number is Oscar November (O.N.) 858529. We checked out of Australia yesterday and are making our way north. Our next port of call will be Bali, Indonesia."

"How many people on board?"

"There are two of us here," I giggled. To Bjorn I whispered "should we mention our mischievous boat guest from Sweden?"

"OK. *Mischief*. Have a good and safe trip."

We spent the next 30 hours motor sailing gently at around five knots before we hit the south-east trade winds. Off went the motor, and silence returned. We relaxed on cushions along the cockpit, reading a book as the winds did their job and blew us steadily northwards for a couple of days. We were progressing well averaging about 140 nautical miles a day. Our second night had also proved uneventful, but we sighted our first freighter, which meant we were approaching the sea traffic channel.

It took me until the third night to really settle into my midnight to 4.00am watch. I had been used to getting up around 2.00am every morning in my working life and going over problems, writing speeches and the like. Being awake at this hour was no big deal. Mind you, I did have a fascinating book *The History of Venice* and a red night light, which allowed me to read without ruining my night vision.

We did not see any more shipping for the rest of the trip, and only encountered fishermen during the last 20 miles, when we got close to Bali. The crossing itself had turned out to be quite pleasant - it took us five and a half days to do the 734 nautical miles. But it was not all without some last-minute excitement.

We were on our fifth day out and expecting to land at Benoa harbour in Bali at around mid-morning. Then, around 25 miles south of Bali, we ran into the dreaded strong current we had been warned about. Our passage planning precautions had not been enough.

We were flying at eight to nine knots according to the log and suddenly realised we were only doing one to two knots over ground on the GPS. This was incredible as it meant that the current was about seven knots in strength. Within an hour, we grew alarmed, as the current got stronger. Despite the fact that we were literally flying through the water, the GPS was showing that occasionally we were losing ground, going backwards. To add to it, the sea had turned into a veritable washing machine, with the current running south hitting the south-easterly's waves going northwards.

"Shit! That wave is higher than our davits. It's going to break over our stern."

"Chris, put the engine on at full speed ahead."

"Hell, we may be here all day. I'm a bit worried as we are so close to land. We will have to both keep a look out tonight."

A Little Bit of MisChief

"It's still early morning, Chris. It looks bad but this current does not seem to be as strong as the one described to us by Tristan. They were going backwards, and so far we are still making at least some progress."

An hour and a half later of trying to steer by hand, we gave up and put the boat back on to autopilot. Incredibly enough, the sophisticated autopilot was paying dividends, steering and managing the turbulent seas much better than Bjorn and I had done. Thankfully, *Mischief* took the waves well and seemed unbothered with the confused seas. We changed course to crab sideways out of the current without having the turbulent sea side-on, not unlike what you are advised to do with a rip on the beach.

"The log is up... we have gained another half a knot. We are now making two and a half knots over ground. There's hope yet." Bjorn gave me a reassuring hug.

The worst of it lasted about five hours, and then even though we still had a very strong four-knot head current, the sea eased more and more as we reached closer to shore. It had taken us about eight hours, which wasn't bad considering our friends' experience on *Eloise*.

We continued north, hugging the coast as is usually recommended to maximise on the weaker current along the shoreline. We dodged through the local fishing boats which increased in number as we drew nearer, and this way we made it up the east coast of Bali and around into the estuary which took us to Tanjung Benoa (Benoa harbour). It was now 4.30pm. We called the marina office on radio and were lucky enough to secure the last available berth. I guided *Mischief* first to port into the compact marina, acknowledging the welcoming waves of a woman on one of the boats. To frantic signals from the quay, I then took a sharp turn to starboard to steer *Mischief* into a pen. Bjorn threw the lines ashore and *Mischief* was tied up once more.

Judy, as I found out she was called, and her husband Ray immediately came over and introduced themselves. "A woman skipper! And the way you brought her into the pen... so impressive!"

After our recent ordeal at sea, these were indeed welcome - and flattering - remarks. Little did they know how nervous and 'green' I had felt just a few hours earlier. It had been a natural decision for me to steer the boat as I had a 'bad' knee; Bjorn was more agile and looked after the anchor and the rope work, jumping ashore to tie up when necessary. We had also heard from other cruisers that they were often hassled and given a hard time by authorities overseas, but these authorities did not quite know how to deal with a woman. We thought we would have some fun with this. I was therefore the official captain, responsible for all the passage planning and navigation. Bjorn, meanwhile, was the chief engineer, and complained that it meant he was in charge of anything that needed fixing. He would say that I only claimed ownership of anything when it worked (he still does).

We also had an agreement that whoever was at the helm or on watch was in charge of the boat and all orders were to be acted upon.

"Ah, here comes Bjorn." I said to Judy.

"The Immigration guys are on their way. Time to open a bottle ...or two!"

"Come ashore to the yacht club. You can wait there. You've got to taste the local beer. It's great," said Ray.

"Woah!" I cried as I stepped ashore, swaying as though drunk! I still experience the giddy feeling whenever I go ashore after being out at sea. The world is inverted and 'terra firma' does not feel so firm but sways as though you are still on a boat.

Bali Marina was small but the facilities were pretty good, with showers and bathroom facilities to one side and a lovely resort-style bar and restaurant overlooking the boats. Before long, I was sipping my first Balinese cocktail, whilst Bjorn tried the local *Bintang* beer. It compared very favourably with other international beers, and the price was enticing. So we sat, chatted to our newly found friends from *Nereid* (Alaska, USA) and waited for the local authorities to turn up.

A half hour later, two lovely and friendly Balinese officials arrived to fill in the customs, immigration and quarantine forms. We noted their look of surprise when it was revealed that I was

A Little Bit of MisChief

the boat captain. And then awaited their reaction, which was to hand all the documents to Bjorn who then passed them on to me for signing. Checking in, producing our cruising visa and other relevant documentation proved to be a breeze. Thanks to the assistance of the Marina management, the formalities were over in a couple of hours. The whole process would have been even faster if we had a boat rubber stamp, so the marina manager kindly offered to order one for us, which had the boat name, port of registration and Australian boat number. Then, after contacting our family to say we had arrived safely, off we went on our first walk on foreign soil to stretch our legs after six days at sea.

It was a hectic first day ashore. We found out where all the supermarkets, chandlers and other useful shops were and familiarised ourselves with the surroundings. Having internet access at the marina, Bjorn and I checked our mail. We were gratified to see the many wonderful messages of encouragement from friends. These messages were precious to us.

That evening we caught up with an American and a Dutch couple and had a delicious and incredibly cheap dinner at the Marina restaurant. We organised to share a minivan to go around the island together and explore.

Bali was our introduction to Indonesia. Frankly, the beaches did nothing for me - but then I'm not a surfer. Bjorn and I preferred the highland areas. Unfortunately, we also had to put up with the endless hawkers in the touristy areas.

"Come, come …look only… only one dollar," begged a little girl, desperately trying to sell her wares.

The bombings that had occurred on 12 October 2002 in the

tourist district of Kuta had killed 202 people, including 88 Australians, many of whom were from Perth. These terrible incidents had dented the Balinese economy, and we empathised greatly with the mostly gentle locals. We could therefore understand why the south and east coast of Bali sprouted endless souvenirs and hawkers wherever we went.

Once we got away from the tourist areas and drove up into the northern mountainous region, we saw another beautiful side to Bali. We drove through lush vegetation up and down mountain ranges, with terraced rice paddies on their slopes. We explored attractive towns like Ubud, and visited some of the Hindu temples and shrines dotted around the island. Wherever we went there seemed to be some form of artwork, and we appreciated the friendly, creative and industrious Balinese. On our third day at the marina, a local man in his mid-30s approached Bjorn and asked for some work.

"Only 100,000 Rupiah for day. I do anything. I have young family. Please mister." This was under 10 dollars.

"What can we give him to do?" Bjorn asked me.

"We still have to wash off all the red dust from Dampier."

"But I had better do that myself. I can go up the mast this afternoon and we can rinse the boat down. I don't want anyone else climbing the mast, as we know what we are doing, and whilst there I can give everything a check."

I went down to the cabin and rummaged around until I found the tube of stainless steel polish. "Is tomorrow OK for you to work? You can wash the decks and the hull, and polish the stainless steel."

"Chris, we only have one other tube left after that one, and it is very expensive at 17 dollars a tube."

"No problem" said our new Balinese friend "I can buy here. I come back soon."

"Bjorn, we have to give him some money. We cannot leave him to fork out more than a day's wage."

"No problem. No problem," he quickly argued back. And off he went round the corner to return five minutes later with an identical tube (and make) of polish. The difference was that it cost the equivalent of fifty cents.

A Little Bit of MisChief

This was our first lesson in the inflationary prices that are charged in some countries, including ours, around the world. Price has nothing to do with cost of production but rather how much the local economy will pay! Needless to say, we stocked up with stainless steel polish which prolonged the life of the steel and kept them free from rust in the harsh marine environment.

Our stay in Bali was a very enjoyable one, interspersed between doing work on the boat and exploring this gorgeous island. We got to know our lovely Balinese friend well. He invited Bjorn to visit his son's school to speak to the students in English, which of course, Bjorn did. In appreciation, he then invited us to meet his family and we enjoyed a typical Balinese dinner with chicken, rice and the most delicious peanut sauce ever.

A week later, we welcomed the boat *Imagination* (Australia) which we had met in Dampier prior to our departure. "How did your crossing go?" I asked, over a *Bintang* at the marina bar.

"We had quite a scare! One night we ran into a sleeping whale. I don't know who was more scared, us or the whale, but we thought we were going to sink. The huge whale panicked and almost capsized our boat."

Later that evening, back on our boat before we retired for the night, I said to Bjorn: "Maybe we do have some sort of guardian angel, or perhaps your *hustomte*. They are meant to protect you, aren't they?"

'Why do you say that?"

"Well *Eloise* left a week before us and ran into an almighty sea and current, and *Imagination* left a week after us and ran into a whale! Both incidents were very scary. We got off lightly by comparison." We hugged!

"Hmm!" Bjorn mused, grinning wickedly. "Perhaps they should get a T-shirt printed 'We got bumped by a whale'."

Our 10 days ashore flew by, and soon it was time to leave. After chatting to a local fisherman, we found that the dreaded current ran up all the way between the islands of Bali and Lombok. It seemed that as long as we stayed within the 10 meter depth line, close to the shore, the current was much weaker and allowed better progress northwards. Our next destination was to visit Lombok and the Gili Islands, where we hoped to catch up with *Eloise* and then go east towards Komodo, where the famous Komodo dragon hails from.

Our new friends on *Nereid* were headed the same way, and so we decided to cruise Indonesia in company. We set off on the morning of the 24th June, ready to take on our new adventure and try and live up to our boat's name.

A Little Bit of MisChief

Bali Rice Fields

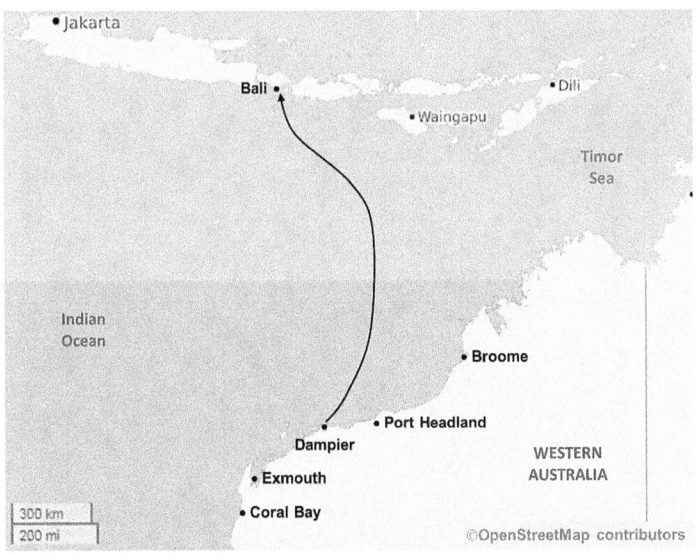

Dampier to Bali Route

Christina Gillgren

A Little Bit of MisChief

4
Bali to Sebana Cove, Malaysia

We sailed out of Bali Marina and found that hugging the coast did indeed help us avoid the immensely strong southerly current. In company with Judy and Ray on *Nereid*, we motored all day to reach Padang Bay, which was about half way up the eastern Bali coast, and anchored for the night. This was a spectacular anchorage with the 1700-metre peak of the active Mount Agung volcano as a backdrop. It was a good thing the volcano was behaving at the time, with only a thin streak of smoke spiralling up peacefully.

The next morning we left early to complete our run to the top of the island of Bali. Suddenly, ahead of us we saw literally dozens of small narrow craft, each with a colourful, triangular sail. If I hadn't known better, I would have guessed they were windsurfers. But as we approached them, we saw that each craft was crudely carved out of timber and had an outrigger, with lines hanging off the stern: obviously, local fishermen. These vessels looked like giant crabs.

Around mid-morning, the wind started to pick up. All at once, the little boats turned towards shore. It was disconcerting to see so many craft suddenly come whizzing towards you. These fishermen must have trained as Kamikaze pilots. They seemed to be vying with each other to see who could sail closest past our bow, narrowly missing us by a metre or two, if not centimetres. Bjorn and I were horrified. What if we hit one of them? It is not as though we could take any evasive action with the numbers of them around us. In Indonesia, if you hit a local boat and damage it or the owner, you have to pay retribution for loss of income to the family. It was no joking matter to have to tackle the local authorities.

We looked back over our stern and saw *Nereid* faced the same problem.

"What's going on!" Ray said into the radio.

"They seem to have bets on who can cut across our bow with the least margin. Either that, or a death wish!" I replied.

As suddenly as the show had started, it was all over. We were happy to see the end of them, although I can still vividly recall the colourful fleet darting right and left. Perhaps it was some fishing tactic we never cottoned on to.

We continued motoring up the eastern Balinese coast and then crossed over to the northeast of Lombok to Teluk Kombal, just south of the island of Gili Air. Here we finally caught up with Tristan and Jas on *Eloise* (Australia). Over a sundowner, they recounted their terrible ordeal south of Bali when caught in the current. Also at the anchorage were Dorothy and Ed on *Prism* (USA) and together with *Nereid* we spent a pleasant week on moorings provided by young Mohammed, from the local village.

Lombok was unspoilt by tourism and the island somehow felt more authentic. However, we wondered how long this would last because, with development progressing at an incredible pace, it was destined to become the new Bali.

On our first evening at the anchorage, Mohammed invited us to his village to see a wedding. We walked through bush and into the jungle to his village, which was where the bride came from. Heralded by the music, we came into a large clearing, where a ceremony was being held for both bride and groom to the accompaniment of drums and loud trumpets. As this part of the ceremony came to a close, the new bride was practically bundled onto the back of a pick-up and then driven away over a dirt track. We watched amused, and with some concern, as she was thrown all over the place. Another pick-up followed suit,

A Little Bit of MisChief

carrying all the musicians. Meanwhile the rest mounted motorbikes, the main means of transport on these islands. As they disappeared in a cloud of dust, Mohammed explained that the next phase of the ceremony would take place at the groom's village, where they would formally welcome the new bride.

Our second night was even more surreal. We were in the midst of a classical movie, *Tea with Mussolini*, telling the story of a young Italian boy's upbringing by a circle of British and American women who were trying to maintain a normal life in Italy during the Second World War. Suddenly, the evening call to prayer rang out loud and long, the calm waters amplifying the sound. We were transported from Italy into our current reality: we were now in Muslim territory, Bali having been mainly Buddhist.

"We really are the willing 'victims' of our own fantasy or illusion, aren't we?" I said to Bjorn.

"We are the fortunate ones, though. We can choose to stay or to stop the show."

Every morning, Mohammed stationed himself on shore, ready to help and to address our needs, such as supplying water and fuel. Other members of his village had collected near a makeshift tent, selling wares made at their village. Mohammed proudly explained that the revenue from the moorings and services went to their village for the local school. We were impressed with the entrepreneurship of the village community and the way they included their younger community members, entrusting them with responsibility.

At our request, Mohammed organised a tour of some of the highlights of the island, taking us to see monkeys, forests, a volcano, a traditional village where locals still lived in huts with all sorts of farm animals roaming about, and some beautiful bays and vistas.

"Thank goodness they have mini busses," I told Bjorn. "I was a bit worried we would be travelling in the back of a pick-up, as they all seem to do."

"Yes, and it is clean, comfortable and air conditioned. I think tourism is starting to make headway here too."

We took the opportunity of visiting the Gili Islands.

Following Mohammed's advice, we did so with a ferry rather than taking our own boats across. When we got there and saw the incredibly strong currents sweeping around and between the islands we understood why.

The Gili Islands were definitely on the tourist maps. We chose to visit Gili Air, which has the strongest local character and an appealing mix of buzz and bliss. Lounging on cushions on a cosy, elevated bamboo veranda and sipping cocktails with our friends, we discussed our next destinations. It was here that Bjorn and I decided it would not be practical to go further east along the Indonesian archipelago for two reasons: one was the time constraint; we were working with the monsoons and had a three-month window to get to Malaysia. The second was that we would be struggling against the current.

After Lombok, we sailed to the Kumai River via the island of Bawean where we spent six days in company with *Nereid* and *Eloise*. The island was off the tourist track, so we were quite the novelty. We had hardly put down our anchor and tested it for holding when we saw a man waving a towel and signalling us to come ashore. Amused but alert, Bjorn lowered our dinghy into the water, picked up Ray and Tristan along the way, and made it to shore. We had been warned to watch out for some young thugs who try and charge you extortionate fees for anchoring in the bay. This was no young 'thug', though. It turned out to be the local English teacher, excited that three boats had called in, all flying flags from English speaking countries. He asked us to visit his school and talk to the children in English, telling us he would arrange transport for the following day.

"You go, and I will take you into the beach. I prefer to stay on board and keep a look-out!"

"I'll keep you company, Bjorn." Tristan offered.

Imagine our surprise the next morning when the teacher and a group of children turned up with their version of transport. Judy and Ray looked at each other, shrugged and decided to go with the flow. The young boy on the high-powered motorbike I was to ride pillion on was not a day over 11 or 12 at the most.

A Little Bit of MisChief

These intrepid kids plus teacher, all on oversized motorbikes on steroids (namely, powerful bikes), drove us uphill. The road meandered through jungles, across some dicey bridges, one very obviously in need of serious repair. We were driven along cliff edges, rice fields with farmers cutting and thrashing the rice, and through a number of villages. To our amusement, locals lined the streets cheering and waving to us as we were driven past.

For a day, we got to know what it felt like to be a movie star!

We had a wonderful day at the school, drawing clumsy maps on the blackboard to show where in the world we came from and where we were headed. Everyone was so excited. The children would mischievously come up to us and quickly touch us. Then each would retreat giggling amongst their classmates. It was a co-educational school, with the boys and girls in uniform, the latter also wearing a *hijab*, a veil which usually covers the head and neck but not the face.

Judy and Ray wanted to return the hospitality and so invited the teacher and the headmaster for afternoon tea onto *Nereid*. The locals had never been on a sailing yacht before, and were amazed at the interior organization of the boat. Judy also kindly and thoughtfully provided some *National Geographic* magazines for the school.

"Did you see the superb stainless steel railings along the way?" Ray remarked, the next morning. "Perhaps I can get my wind self-steering unit fixed. I need to have some welding done to repair it."

"Yes. It looks really odd to see 21st century materials tacked on to houses that belong to another era,' Bjorn replied.

"There is so much of it. There must be some local guy who works stainless steel."

"It looks incongruous! They are not delicate pieces of work, but heavy tubes, more resembling the kangaroo bars on four-wheel drive vehicles in Australia. There seems to be some wealth on the island. Did you notice all the guys wearing their orange boiler suits?" Tristan added.

Some of the men on the island worked for shipping

companies in Singapore on a fly-in, fly-out basis. The orange company boiler suits were a status symbol. Also, fortunately for Ray, one of these was a stainless steel welder.

On this island of contrasts, the problem was to get the sheared wind steering unit to the welder. This was solved again using the motorbike method. Bjorn and Ray set off, each riding pillion on a bike, with a third bike used to transport the boat parts. And yes, the wind steer was fixed and they did a great job. The cost was negligible, in fact around five dollars, although I am sure the locals thought they had made a killing.

We enjoyed our stay at Bawean. Every night we all ate ashore at a small 'restaurant' on the beach, taking one of the two refectory tables. Each delicious meal cost us around two dollars per person, and that was with a soft drink included.

We were set to depart the island when some fishermen came up to us and warned us, using charades, of huge waves coming in our direction. It seemed prudent to let whatever weather system was out there pass by prior to resuming our journey. Gradually a number of large local boats entered the bay, seeking shelter. They put down anchors using only rope and no chain. The boats looked ungainly, almost grotesque, with high stern structures, not unlike how we imagine pirate ships to be. They were built of wood and bobbed up and down crazily. Of course, with the wind picking up, they kept dragging their anchors. It was not long before one of these monstrosities was bearing down on us, threatening to smash into our boat. Our calls for them to move away went unheeded. I lost my cool and swore at them in Maltese, which luckily no one could understand. Bjorn took me by the arm and told me to calm down. "Remember we are guests in their country," he told me.

We quickly hauled up the anchor and moved out of the way. It was not easy to find another spot with the number of boats that now crowded the bay.

◇◇◇

We needed an overnighter to get to the Kumai River from Bawean. With the weather having now settled, we set off in the early morning, with *Eloise* and *Nereid* following. With a gentle

A Little Bit of MisChief

10 knots of wind we made slow but pleasant progress and settled in for another quiet night at sea. We had not taken into account was the unusual Indonesian fishing methods: bamboo tower frames on rafts with lines hanging off them. This was fine during the day, as the frames could be seen from a reasonable distance. On a night with not much moon to guide us, it was another story.

The waters between Bawean and Borneo were full of fishing activity. You could spot the squid boats from afar. They carried enormous floodlights to attract the squid, which were then scooped up by two swinging arms with a chain loop with hooks. Other fishing methods included two trawlers, sometimes as much as a kilometre apart, dragging a net between them, and you had better not get caught in the middle. Other trawlers just dragged a huge net behind them. This was apart from the bamboo structures that seemed to differ in construction from one area to the next. With all this activity, the night watches kept us on our toes.

We were sitting in the cockpit, during Bjorn's evening watch, when he suddenly saw a flicker of light. The next minute it was gone. Then it came on again.

"Chris, come and see this!" He called out.

I couldn't believe my eyes. A fisherman was standing on a small bamboo raft, using a lighter to indicate his presence. He was perhaps five meters away from our boat, eyes wide open in fright. There was no time to warn *Eloise* who were right behind us. They almost ran the poor guy down.

We did try and put a line out, but there was no fish to be had. "All these boats and fishermen, and no fish. It must be hard on them," I mused.

"There is so much poverty around!" Bjorn reflected.

That same eventful night, we also had a close shave with a medium sized tanker. With the fishing boats and their odd lights all around us, I did not immediately pick out the freighter lights until it was almost upon us.

"Bjorn! Quick, help!" I shouted into the cabin. Bjorn was out like a flash.

I put the engine on, released the foresail and turned 90

degrees to starboard.

Bjorn tacked the sails and we motored as fast as we could to get out of the way.

We were relieved to welcome daybreak that morning. We were leading the group, with *Eloise* within sight and *Nereid* a little further back from us. As the winds continued to die down, on came the motor. We made our way slowly up the Kumai River delta in south Borneo, the water turning a putrid green with algae, as we tried to avoid the sand/mud banks. *Nereid* was not so lucky and, missing one of the river route markers, ended up aground. They had to wait until the tide was back in, to float again and get off the mud bank. Fortunately for them, we had not gone up river at full tide.

We motored about three nautical miles up-river to where the town of Kumai was located and then dropped anchor along the mangrove lined bank. Once *Nereid* had caught up with us, we all went ashore to the highly industrial and dirty township. The purpose of our foray up-river in Borneo was to visit Camp Leaky, the renowned orang-utan sanctuary and nature reserve.

We had dinner ashore that evening. Tristan was good at scrutinizing the street vendors for the 'safest' ones to dine at. He picked a stall, which only had one table to accommodate diners. We had to wait a few minutes for the stall keeper's children and husband to finish eating before we could sit down. We ordered the local fare, which was some version of *Nasi Goreng*, or fried rice. When one got bored with this dish, there was always *Mie Goreng*. You guessed it, fried noodles. They were both reasonably healthy with lots of vegetables and tasty. And they usually included your choice of protein: chicken, meat or prawn. Ray insisted on paying. We laughed at the 'expensive' bill, which came to the equivalent of eight dollars for the six of us, soft drinks included.

The next morning, we were all up early for our trip to Camp Leaky. Getting there was as exciting as the actual encounter with the apes. Seated in two motor boats with Tristan, Jas and us on one boat, and Judy and Ray on the next one, we were driven at breakneck speed for about three hours. We zoomed along one of the tributaries that took us right into the heart of

A Little Bit of MisChief

the jungle. In some places, the overgrowth was so dense that there was hardly any space for the motor boats to pass through. At times, I could almost feel the foliage on my face.

It was exhilarating but also dangerous. Bjorn and I held on for dear life. It would take one branch hanging out over the water or indeed in the water itself, a miscalculation at a corner and surely we would be thrown clean overboard. As if that wasn't enough, you also had the boats returning from the camp hurtling round the bends in the opposite direction. With crocodiles in the area, this was not an endearing prospect.

Luckily, we made it up to Camp Leaky with no mishaps. Still dazed from our petrifying experience, we struggled out of the motor boats and staggered onto the pontoon.

"Wow! That was something else,' Tristan started out.

"I felt as though I held my breath all the way. I certainly had to hold on to my hat," Bjorn added.

"We kept thinking that one error was all it would take. We would end up either in your boat, or in the jungle," Judy said.

We had a packed lunch on the landing station, surrounded by small monkeys, birdlife galore and all the noise that emanates from a jungle. It gave us time to collect our thoughts and prepare ourselves for our encounter with the primates. We were warned not to take any food as the primates could become quite aggressive. We followed a ranger through a narrow, winding path that led to a feeding platform in the middle of the jungle. The orang-utans were impressive, one or two even cheekily walking right by, extending their 'hands' as though they were humans. I felt privileged to be in their natural habitat, watching them at such close quarters. It was a timely reminder that we have so much natural wealth on this earth. We needed to work harder to treasure, protect and conserve it.

We spent a few days in Kumai town, exploring the surroundings and then we were off again. On our way down river, we stopped on a sandbank at the mouth of the river. We hauled our dinghies out of the water and gave the bottom a good scrub. They had become totally fouled up with weed in the dirty but nutrient-rich river waters.

We bade farewell to Judy and Ray at this juncture. They had

to sail across to Malaysia to catch a flight back home to Alaska for a break from their round the world trip.

Mischief and *Eloise* were now headed via a number of islands to the Riau Archipelago, south of Singapore, and to our final Indonesian destination at Noongsa Point. As we approached the Archipelago, we started encountering thunder squalls, which were rather intimidating to begin with. We were slowly getting closer to the Equatorial Line. Light winds interspersed with thunderstorms are a hallmark of this zone. Bjorn kept complaining that we always made it to an anchorage just in time for the customary afternoon shower, as thunderstorms struck. Of course, he got drenched every time, whilst I stayed nice and dry, under cover, at the helm, guiding the boat into the anchorage.

In some of the bays, we tried fishing off the back of the boat, but with no luck. At Pulau Kentar (*Pulau* meaning island), we were approached by a dugout canoe with an elderly man and a young boy, both wearing clothes so tattered we wondered how they held together. The man pointed to some tiny fish in the bottom of their canoe, offering them to us.

"There's not even enough for a meal over there; they'll just about fit in a sardine can," Bjorn whispered to me.

"They look so poor though. We have to buy some." I pointed to three or four of the few fish and got some money out.

The fisherman shook his head and opened his hands to signal that money was no good. An exchange of sign language followed, and the fisherman gesticulated to show his and the boy's torn tops. A quick rummage down in the cabin quickly yielded a couple of tee shirts and a cap, and the exchange took place. A beaming fisherman took off, beaming. It was not the same for us. What would we do with fish I would hardly feed to a cat, if there were one on board, that is? We therefore returned our purchases to the sea, in the hope they would nourish some other ones.

We crossed the Equatorial line on the three-day trip between Nangka Point and Pulau Kentar, at the southernmost end of the Riau Archipelago. Out came the champagne bottle. Crossing the equator is a milestone for sailors as we bid farewell to the

A Little Bit of MisChief

southern hemisphere and greeted the northern one.

We had a particularly nasty thunderstorm which struck when we were about to put down our anchor at Mesanek, also in the Riau Archipelago. Looking back to see how far behind us *Eloise* were, we watched in awe as we saw the most amazing, humongous waterspout forming. It came down from the dense clouds, dancing in the air as it headed towards the sea, and then as it hit the surface there was this eruption of water being sucked up as though a giant vacuum cleaner had struck.

All around us the rain was pelting down. Trying to keep a cool head, I took our bearing in case we had to evacuate the mooring in a hurry; at least we would know which direction was away from land. The next thing we knew, we were surrounded by another three waterspouts. It was incredible watching how fast they formed and changed shape and direction. How did one avoid them when they were so close?

There was not much we could do about it. We downed sails, stored everything on deck securely, went into the cabin and opened the bottle of scotch. If this was it, at least we would go in style!

We spent an anxious hour on the radio with *Eloise*, trying to keep each other calm. Finally the storm abated. The rain was still pouring down. The visibility was so poor that even though *Eloise* was anchored some 50 metres from us, we could not see each other's boats. This was another anchorage we were happy to leave the next morning and we headed into the Riau Channel, where better shelter was available.

We spent a pleasant two weeks going from one anchorage to the next in this area. It was during this passage that we had a scary moment with potential pirates.

We were motoring at a leisurely pace in calm seas with little wind when a fishing boat approached us. They started waving, and tried to get close to us. I waved them away and called to Bjorn who was below in the cabin. He came out on deck and signalled to them to keep their distance. I increased boat speed, but there was no way I could outrun this big vessel. We had heard of pirates in the area, especially on the east coast of Sumatra. For this reason, we had chosen to keep closer to the

Riau Archipelago where most sailors usually cruised. These potential pirates kept following us for about an hour, sometimes gaining on us, sometimes falling behind, as a guy strolled the deck watching us all the time. We don't know what did it but then luckily they gave up and went their own way. They could have been honest fishermen after some free cigarettes for all we knew, but it was an unsettling experience none the less.

We made our way to the final port of call in Indonesia at Noongsa Point Marina for a few days of rest before running the gauntlet of the Singapore Strait. It was good to be back in a marina and give *Mischief* a well-deserved fresh water rinse. Checking-out of Indonesia was an experience as we tackled the bureaucratic paper war where we had to declare Captain and Crew and everything on board; and I mean everything, including booze and spare parts lying in the nether regions of the boat.

We had finished cruising in our first overseas destination, and all was well. In hindsight, I think Indonesia needed two visits: the first to get to know the peculiarities such as weather and currents, people and customs and the like of each area; and the second to be able to explore the place in a more relaxed fashion. We fully intend to return there one day.

Singapore lay just across the water from Noongsa Point. We were headed to the south-eastern part of Malaysia going up river to a place called Sebana Cove. This was one of the safest marinas in the area. To get there we had to tackle our next challenge: cross the incredibly busy Singapore Strait. And this *Eloise* and *Mischief* undertook a few mornings later.

We headed out into the Strait and started timing the ships going past. There were two commercial traffic corridors, the closest to us heading westward, with a buffer zone in the middle and then there was the eastward bound channel. We approached as close as we deemed safe, motoring along the shipping lane. Just as one super-tanker drove past, *Eloise* and *Mischief* quickly turned in behind its stern. We were almost too close as the wake was still very troubled waters, and this slowed the boats down.

A Little Bit of MisChief

Keeping our fingers crossed we made it into the buffer zone before the next tanker came hurtling along. With a lesson well learnt, we attempted the next corridor. It felt a bit like trying to run across a busy freeway: it took more than just nerves and a bit of craziness.

Once on the Singapore side of the Strait, we heaved a huge sigh of relief. We had successfully crossed what must be the busiest shipping channel in the world. Now it was an easy motor up river, on the east end of Singapore, and into brown murky waters once again. Sebana Cove Marina, some three miles away with its accompanying resort hotel, luxury pool and amenities, was indeed a welcome sight.

We spent the time alternating between lazing away and busy activity over the next six to seven weeks as we waited for the monsoon to change. The heat and humidity took their toll, slowing us down. Relaxing at Sebana Cove took on a new meaning: some work during the early part of the day, the lovely and inviting tropical pool which was part of the resort hotel in the late afternoon, then hand exercises with a glass of vino or a gin and tonic to keep the 'mozzies' at bay.

One morning, early in our stay there, I saw what looked like a head just beneath the water's surface, swimming across the pontoons.

"Bjorn, there must be crocodiles here!"

"No. Definitely not. Where are you looking?"

"There! Look, just beyond the pontoons. Whatever it is, it's big."

We followed its passage across the water to the pontoons at the far end. There climbed out this enormous lizard, about one and a half metres in length.

"That's the Komodo dragon," Bjorn explained. "They are also called Monitor Lizards. They grow to a couple of metres. This one is a baby. They are carnivores and can be dangerous. It seems that they love wildlife, especially monkeys - and the occasional tourist if you get too close."

The humidity and the incessant heat in Sebana Cove resulted in some funny habits. One of these was that we noticed many sailors in their underpants instead of their bathers when on board or rummaging about on the jetties.

"Well, what do you expect, it's hot and humid!" one neighbour told us.

I soon knew all the brands of underwear everybody wore. There was a good reason for this, namely personal hygiene. The lycra used in bathing costumes does not allow the body to breathe the same way cotton does. We all eventually succumbed to the 'brief' temptation, which is one other reason why one always calls out when visiting another yacht.

The other tip we picked up during our stay here was to wipe the interior down with vinegar to stop the mould from building up due to the high humidity.

The Sebana Cove resort and marina were a great place to do some of the work that we had identified needed attention on the way; one definition of cruising is that of fixing your boat in exotic places, and this was certainly true of our stay there.

The resort was situated around 20 minutes from the nearest town site, so the hotel organised twice-weekly trips to town for cruisers to do their shopping. Even though Malaysia is predominantly Muslim, there was a significant Chinese population. As a result, we found that one could buy pork. Every Tuesday, when the shuttle bus took us into town, a Chinese guy in his blue van would be parked around the corner waiting for us. He had a good selection of fresh pork, and the price was unbelievably cheap.

It is also a custom of 'yachties' - that's us, cruisers - to buy anything exotic to locals in bulk.

"Look Chris, they have tonic water here! Mind you 'FN'…hmmm, never heard of this brand before." There were two whole pallets perched precariously outside the shop.

"Good. We've run out on board. I can now revive the gin-and-tonic. Shall we get two slabs? And we can get some limes from the vegetable vendors".

"Let's get half a dozen bottles first; see what they taste like."

Of course, out came the gin bottle that evening!

We went back a few days later to stock up, only to find they had completely run out. Back at the marina, we found that all

A Little Bit of MisChief

our friends had bought about half a dozen slabs (cartons) of the stuff. This was another lesson for us: when you find an item that is usually hard to get in a country, better stock up - especially with yachties around.

The resort hotel was able to supply us with exotic goods such as French cheeses and a variety of fresh bread. This was at a small premium, but well worth the price. The charm of this place included the friendly and polite marina ladies, all wearing *hijab*. The hotel restaurant was well priced and provided a welcome alternative to cooking on board, catering in both western and Asian cuisines.

Entertainment varied greatly. Sundowners were the norm, as we all tried to get to know each other. Sometimes we got together for a jetty party or a potluck dinner. On other occasions, the resort organised special theme evenings with food and music to match.

Along one of the shores of the marina inlet were a number of bungalows with their own landing, cum mooring jetties. One of these was owned by the son of the one of the Malaysian sultans of the district. For his birthday, he invited the whole marina to his bungalow to a great celebration where he also hosted an incredible firework display. Mention a party, and all the yachties turn up.

Part of the fun of cruising was going into the local towns, both in Malaysia and Singapore, and trying to find all the parts and bits & bobs that you need: this was an adventure in itself. You will find that it is a bit of an obsession and cruisers can often tell you where the local boating 'hardware' store is before they know where to get food. We went across the river into Singapore a couple of times as, conveniently, a ferry from the marina went across three times a day. In this way we got to explore not only the beautifully done-up parts of Singapore, but also the back streets.

"I think it is wise to get a new set of batteries for the boat," Bjorn said, checking the battery cells with the hydrometer. This was a weekly love affair of his.

So it was that on one of our Singapore excursions, we bought four batteries to take back with us on the ferry to Sebana

Cove, all 140kg of them. Getting them to the ferry was a bit of an adventure, with a perplexed driver trying to convince his aging car not to collapse under the load. We were very lucky that we were allowed to take them as 'hand luggage', as they are normally considered 'dangerous' goods - something we had not taken into account.

Bjorn attempted to fix our air problem in the fuel system again during our stay at the marina. Apart from going through the system looking for air leaks yet again, he emptied the diesel from the fuel tank, cleaned out the tank, added an extra fuel filter so that we now could switch from one filter to the other at a moment's notice, and purchased a dozen spare fuel filters, just in case.

I made a quick dash to Perth to catch up with our daughter Annika, her partner and her gorgeous half-human Kelpie-cross dog, Chica. This was a time to do tax returns and totally ignore investments, as the global financial crisis had just struck and we had seen our savings going so far south that it was scary. The way the stock market was going actually had us thinking about whether we should proceed to Europe, where it was reputed to be so much more expensive.

I spent the better part of my short time in Perth chasing exotic boat parts from an endless list Bjorn had drawn up. I had to acquire a suitcase just to haul back the boat bits, and only managed a corner to squeeze in some Italian salami and a few kilos of cheddar, so hard to come by in Asian countries.

Sebana Cove had been our first stopover in a marina filled with cruisers, and we learnt so much about cruising in these waters from those around us. Another bonus was being able to practise languages learnt as a child and hardly ever practised as an adult. It was here that we met and got to know Marie-Christine and Yves on *Blue Marine* (France), Frances and Bill on *Tulameen II* (Canada), and Birte and Jorgen, on *Circe* (Denmark) among others. Like us, they were headed to Thailand and across the Indian Ocean to Europe.

In our last week at Sebana Cove, we welcomed dear friends Gus and Gabbi on *Pampero* (Australia), also from the Fremantle Sailing Club.

A Little Bit of MisChief

"I hear you had an exciting time in Kupang," I told Gabbi. They had joined the Sail Indonesia Rally to obtain their Indonesian cruising permit and to cruise in company. This annual yacht rally departed from Darwin, Australia for a three-month program of linked events across Indonesia.

"You can say that again! The authorities there wanted to charge all the yachts a hefty cruising tax. Of course, we refused to pay, and were not allowed to leave. The Rally organisers finally contacting the President of Indonesia, and in the end the President turned up, sacked the corrupt officials and we were finally free to continue on our way."

In the same week, Ray and Judy from *Nereid* arrived back in Sebana Cove after a trip back to the US. We expected we would be seeing quite a lot of them as we were both sailing towards the Red Sea and the Mediterranean. This was very much an integral part of the story of cruising: hellos to people who become dear friends and, at some point, farewell.

And soon it was our turn to leave the flock and wave goodbye once again.

Christina Gillgren

Camp Leaky Dash

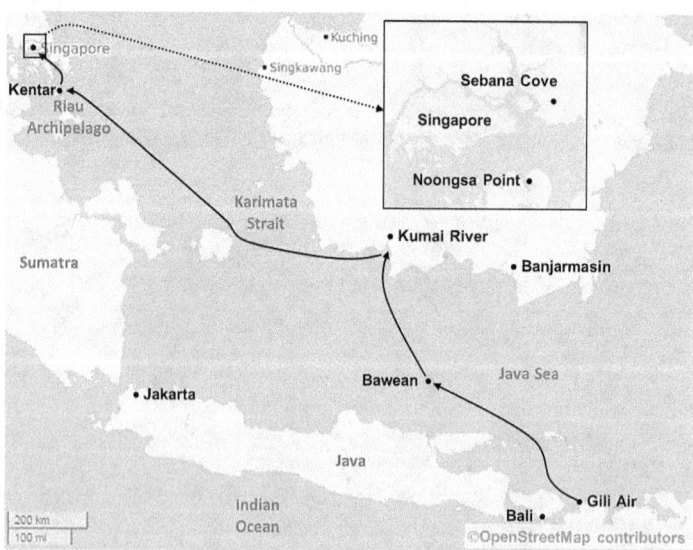

Bali to Sebana Cove Route

5
The Malacca Straits

We left Sebana Cove in eastern Malaysia in mid-October. Our first task was to anchor just outside the river mouth, where the water had turned clear again. Here we dived into the water and gave the propeller and shaft a good scrub: very necessary after almost two months in the marina. There was so much weed that we were hardly moving. This would not only slow us down but could potentially cause damage. It took us over two hours of free diving to get the job done.

We resumed our journey around lunchtime and rounded the island of Singapore, dodging all the shipping traffic. We gently motored in light winds to Pulau Merambong, which was on the west side of the island of Singapore.

The next morning we made an early start, rounded Tanjung (Cape) Piai and entered the Malacca Straits. The Straits proved to be an interesting passage with some good winds that saw us sail most of the way. It was a place of contrasts, with an ever-changing landscape. We noticed that the islands became more exotic the further north we travelled.

We had been told of the *Sumatra*: thunder squalls that appear out of nowhere, when winds would suddenly be whipped up to around 35-45 knots, followed by heavy rain. After our experience with the thunderstorms south of Singapore, we were apprehensive. The *Sumatra* was particularly prevalent in the southern end of the Straits.

We made our way northwards and were quickly introduced to fishing methods in this area. The sea was covered with nets, and you had to strain to identify the beginning and end of a net, usually signalled through the use of similar colour 'flags' on bamboo sticks. Some of these nets stretched for a couple of miles and we carefully dodged our way through them. We had gotten used to customs in the Indonesian waters, but the Straits were unsurpassed for the number and range of fishing methods. It therefore made good sense to try and stop at an anchorage every night where possible, usually at one of the small islands along the coast, ensuring that our anchor was secure.

At our second anchorage, at Tanjung Tohor, we encountered our first thunderstorm around sunset. We had set our anchor and gently reversed on it to test it for holding. The winds increased and the rain came bucketing down, but it was mild compared to what we had anticipated.

The following morning we proceeded to Pulau Besar on the Water Islands, outside the town of Malacca. We had anchored about a kilometre away from the shore, as the water around us seemed shallow.

"Sailing yacht approaching Pulau Besar anchorage," came over the VHF radio. "This is sailing yacht *Envy*."

Out came the binoculars. "It's an Australian registered boat," Bjorn said to me.

"Sailing yacht *Envy*, this is sailing yacht *Mischief*."

"*Mischief*, this is *Envy*, Bruce and Audrey on board. We are anchored up ahead of you, closer to the island. There is a way in to get closer for more protection."

"That's great. How do we get there?"

"Go to waypoint 02 06'427N by 102 20'584E, then head towards the water tower to about 500 metres from the shore. From there, aim for the end of the jetty behind us, and you can anchor in about eight metres of water."

"Thank you, *Envy*. Will do so! By the way, we note you are flying the Aussie flag. So are we. Christina and Bjorn, on board *Mischief*. We are heading north towards Langkawi."

"So are we. Your next stop is probably Admiral Marina at

A Little Bit of MisChief

Port Dickson. We shall be there for about a week and hope to catch up with you."

"We look forward to that. And thanks once again for the tip about the anchorage and the directions."

We made our way closer to the shore and safely made the anchorage. We were increasingly finding out how truly friendly and helpful cruisers are to each other, especially to newcomers to the area.

We spent an extra day at the Water Islands, encountering mild thunderstorms every evening. As we motored off in the morning, we passed by an enormous, seemingly brand new resort on the western end of the island. It appeared to be abandoned. This was puzzling, as it was not the first one we had seen. We had come across a few of these resorts in Indonesia, well kept, clean - but totally empty. Yet none had come close in size to this resort.

With light north-westerly winds we sailed gently up the coast, again, dodging the fishing nets and trawlers, and before long we had this crazy squid boat following us and drawing closer. We were uncertain of their intentions and felt uncomfortable.

"Keep clear… do not approach." I shouted out, gesticulating wildly. I switched on the engine, engaged the gear and sped up. It was to no avail. At least they stopped coming closer, and motored practically alongside for a further ten minutes. Then suddenly they turned away. We never found out what their intention was, but it had been an uncomfortable half an hour.

No sooner had they left us, and we had resumed sailing, than another yacht came into sight, motor sailing past us.

"Allo, *Mischief*" It was sailing yacht *Mary Vorgan* (France), with Martine and Philippe, whom we had met at Sebana Cove. They were heading in the same direction. We went back to motor sailing, glad of the company, as we made our way to Admiral Marina in Port Dickson.

Envy was there to greet us when we called into the marina. They introduced us to the fun-loving Aussie - New Zealand cruising community, many of whom are based in south-east Asia. During the dry monsoon season on the west side of

Malaysia they would spend their time in the Straits going as far north as Thailand. Then when the wet season came along the custom was to head to the east coast, which had the opposite monsoon. Of course I am referring to the climate here, because rest assured, it was always wet season on board, especially after 'four thirsty!'

The one thing in common among cruisers is their love of the *dolce vita* especially when you get to a marina, where you can leave the boat with peace of mind. We cruised, explored, wined and dined, chatted, joked, laughed and compared notes, with one common goal: to have a leisurely good time. We collected much valuable information on what to see and where to go. As everyone was headed up the Straits to Langkawi, we had company wherever we chose to set down anchor. And what a merry crowd they turned out to be! Certainly one where I could practise our boat motto of 'mischief' as we went from one sundowner to another, joined excursions and generally became acquainted with this merry bunch of sailors. I loved playing practical jokes and pulling people's legs.

"I think you've had too much to drink!" I would start out.

"No way… just merry!"

"Well, let's check!" I would shake and show an open hand. "How many fingers?"

Of course, many would answer 'five'.

"Bah, drunk and disorderly." "It's four fingers and a thumb of course!"

At other times, I would get them to repeat after me: "Whiskey <u>when</u> you're well <u>makes</u> you ill; whiskey <u>makes</u> you well <u>when</u> you're ill."

Try it! Few people will get it even if you say it slowly. They will transpose the 'well' and the 'ill', whilst the correct version is to transpose the 'when' and the 'make'. A quirk of the English language I had picked up whilst teaching English as a second language in Perth to newcomers to the country.

◇◇◇

At this time of the year, Malaysia celebrates *Deepavali*, a religious festival of lights that feted the triumph of light over

A Little Bit of MisChief

darkness. Thousands of Hindu families illuminate their homes with lanterns, exchange gifts, share feasts and perform prayers to deities. With our new friends, who knew the area and customs so well, we visited some of the colourful festivals around Port Dickson, joining in the spirit of optimism and fun. We also took a number of inland trips, one of which was a three-day overland trip to the city of Malacca.

Malacca is a colourful, multiracial city. We fell in love with the narrow streets of the historic old town, full of doorways into worlds of by-gone days. We hired one of the colourful bicycle rickshaws for a tour of the town. Our driver was no spring chicken. As we started on an incline, it was obvious that he was struggling. Bjorn and I jumped out of the rickshaw so that the driver would not have to peddle uphill with us on board. You should have seen his look of bewilderment - and relief!

The cuisine in Malacca was to die for: a mix of Malay, Indian and Chinese cultures. Complementing this were the layers of Dutch, Portuguese and English history, which made it an extremely interesting place. The town had just been declared a UNESCO world heritage site, and deservedly so. Out for an evening stroll, we witnessed a Komodo dragon fight in one of the canals, though these ones were the smaller variety and not as dangerous as their Indonesian cousins.

Among the cruisers we met in Port Dickson were Sue and Wayne on their boat *Court Jester* (Australia). Wayne was a diesel mechanic and Bjorn discussed with him the 'air in the fuel' problem that still plagued us despite all our efforts. One look at the engine and the location of the tank, and Wayne had the answer.

"You have a fuel pump on the diesel tank. Just run it whenever you run the engine."

It was as easy as that. The fuel pump on the engine was not strong enough to keep up a steady flow of fuel from the tank to the engine. The previous owner of our boat had installed an extra pump on the fuel tank, which he only used to purge the system of air after changing filters. Bjorn now rewired the electrics for the pump to the starter key so that the pump would come on at the same time as the engine. He cussed and cursed himself for not having thought of this, as it would have saved us many nervous moments along the way.

"Hurray! Finally! This particular 'mischief' is finally put to rest." We could only hope our little boat guest would now concentrate on keeping us safe at sea, and leave any other mischief to us.

We love you Wayne. Thank you!

Bjorn was not too sure of my mischief though. After one very merry sundowner, as he guided me back to our boat, he began: "Chris, limit yourself to two glasses of wine. You do get carried away."

"So does everyone else. Relax, it's all harmless fun."

"Some might be put out with your 'naughty' language and antics."

"What! the cruisers we have met so far? You must be joking! We are naughty-cal people, aren't we?" I retorted. "Ahhh, do you object to being called my 's-crew'?"

I used to joke about the fact that since I was the skipper, Bjorn was my s-crew. I think he preferred it when I referred to him as the chief engineer. Quite honestly, without his persistent and thorough efforts with all technical parts of the boat, we would never have had the peace of mind of sailing in such exotic places. Peace of mind that would come in handy when we came to cross the Indian Ocean.

"No, that part I like," he grinned wickedly, "but do you have to tell the whole world?"

"Well, it's your fault really." I added mischievously. "Isn't it you who told me about the origin of the word 'crew'? How does it go? Yes, 'people acting or working together'. That's the late Middle English definition from the Old French word *creue* meaning 'augmentation, increase'. Gives it a new slant, doesn't it?"

Port Dickson proved to be a turning point in our cruising life. We met many cruisers who were going to cross the Indian Ocean and become lifelong friends, among them most notably Helen and Joe on *Dreamcatcher* (Australia). We also reconnected with Birte and Jorgen on *Circe* and Frances and Bill on *Tulameen II*, whom we had first met in Sebana Cove.

A Little Bit of MisChief

A week at Port Dickson flew by, and soon we were on our way again. The big worry of the *Sumatra* had never eventuated, apart from the few mild thunderstorms at the lower end of the Straits.

We sailed up to Port Klang, a busy, industrial port, and on to the island of Pulau Pangkor outside Lumut. The humidity decreased, and the water was getting clearer by the day. At Pangkor, we followed fellow cruisers into a brand new abandoned marina.

"We keep seeing pristine, yet abandoned resorts. And now this marina! They can't all be 'white elephants' - and costly ones at that."

I am not sure who it was that explained the practice of money laundering thus: "magnates would build or buy a resort, then claim full occupancy for a couple of years, during which time the resort is just maintained but never functional. Tax would then be paid on the imaginary 'profit' making the money legitimate. After a few years, the resort would then be sold on as a fully functional business" - or so the story goes. Go figure, as we say in Australia.

We set off to explore Pangkor Island, which had been one of the strategic stops on the trading route of the Dutch East India Company in the late 1600s. Tourism had arrived here, which was understandable given the pristine beaches, coral reefs and turquoise waters.

We discovered one particular island with a spectacular beach and not a soul in sight. As was usual wherever we put down anchor or moored, we would take the dinghy to explore the surrounds. It is amazing that we left the dinghy on so many shores and always found it there on our return. On this occasion, we had pulled up the dinghy on shore as usual, and went off to explore. When we came back, a few hours later, it was to discover that the waves were now pounding the beach and had started to drag our dinghy into the water. It was completely swamped.

"Quick Chris, into the water and let's grab hold of it before it goes under," Bjorn yelled at me.

"Where has the bailer gone to?" We had a cut up plastic

orange juice bottle, which we used to bail out water. It was tied to the dinghy with a string.

"Here it is… but let's try and drag the engine round so it does not get flooded."

It took us almost an hour to empty the dinghy with nothing but the pathetic little bailer. It was a struggle to hold on to the dinghy with big waves crashing in all around us, often sweeping me off my feet. To begin with, as much water was pouring in as we were bailing out.

"Another hour and we would have lost the dinghy."

"I'm completely drenched." I complained. I got no sympathy as Bjorn was very much in the same water. I did hear him mutter something about wet t-shirts however, accompanied by a cheeky grin.

One of the pleasures of travelling up the Malacca Straits was that we rarely made it to an anchorage on our own. We spent many an evening exchanging boat yarns, comparing notes of our travelling experiences and generally getting to know each other.

One of my favourite proclamations was to shock cruisers we would meet for the first time by stating, "We are a 'dry' boat." I would get some funny stares, sometimes with couples exchanging looks of disbelief or incredulity.

"We do not carry alcohol for boozing," I would explain to newfound friends. "The alcohol on board is only for medicinal purposes. We make our own water - it is very pure but contains no minerals. Therefore, the beer is for the minerals; the gin to go with the tonic to protect against malaria; rum against the cholera; whiskey as anti-rust with all the water we were drinking; wine to keep my eyesight centred.

"Without glasses I am the opposite of cross eyed, and one, two, three glasses of vino keeps my eyes looking straight ahead… ah yes, it also avoids the problem of glasses as they get wet with sea spray."

"And finally brandy for the shock of being alcohol free - aka, a 'dry' boat!"

"Phew! Let's drink to that" was one response, amid the laughter.

A Little Bit of MisChief

At the island of Penang, we spent a lovely week at the Tanjung City Marina right in the heart of George Town. Penang was an island of contrasts, and certainly the place with the greatest 'western' influence we had come across. Mountains contrasted with surrounding low lands, and gorgeous beaches dotted the west coast. The food was a mix of so many cultures and inexpensive, and we enjoyed many an evening savouring the tastes and the quasi 'carnivalesque' atmosphere in downtown George Town. In the evenings, the Indian quarter of the port city was transformed into a noisy, raucous street party. Bollywood music blared through the streets and locals came out in force, enjoying the cooler evening temperatures. There were some interesting pieces of architecture, but these were slowly being swallowed up by the spread of high rises.

We were enjoying a sundowner when someone broke the news that a couple had inadvertently sailed their catamaran between two trawlers hauling an enormous net between them. They had got trapped. As a result, they had been dragged by the net in the wrong direction for hours before the trawlers realised the problem. Then it had taken quite a bit of bartering before they were released from the tangled mess - and with some hefty compensation, if rumour was true.

We headed northwards once more, intending to overnight at the southern islands outside Langkawi before heading there. We stopped over at a place called 'the Fjord', with a majestic sheer cliff face in a narrow channel sandwiched between stunning islands. We found that *Circe* had also chosen this anchorage, and others soon followed. We loved it so much that we ended up staying for three days and had a terrific time running around in the rubber dinghy exploring caves and coves.

Our Malacca Straits cruising had come to an end and we headed to the small island of Rebak, on the west of the island of Langkawi. Rebak Marina was a fully-fledged marina with boat lifting capability. It was time for boat maintenance and general repairs in preparation for our Thailand visit, and for the start of the Indian Ocean crossings before Christmas. Our list of things to do, check, repair or add had grown to a couple of pages. It reflected our 'quiet' anxiety at the upcoming first major crossing of the Indian Ocean.

Once again we encountered an incredible mix of cruising nationalities. The local wisdom was to purchase all materials and requirements in Langkawi, do routine work such as antifouling in Rebak, and get any detailed professional work done in Thailand.

We got hauled out of the water the next day, and then it was down to sanding and antifouling the bottom, during which process I turned into a 'Smurf', blue all over. The boat had been in the water for well over 12 months. We had spent an appreciable amount of time in places like Benoa Harbour and Sebana Cove with quasi-stagnant waters adding to the growth on the hull.

I hate boat lift-outs: often, you still live on board, but without the ability to use the amenities. We resorted to a bucket for overnight and early morning needs and you had to be careful going up and down the ladder. Happily, most marinas have excellent shower and toilet facilities. And in Asia, many of the marinas had luxury resorts attached to them. The Rebak Resort was not as easily accessible as those in other marinas but was a welcome break anyway.

We met with an Aussie who ran a small chandlery at the marina and he helped with some of the more minor repairs. On his advice, we had a new cutlass bearing installed made from a new space-war material called 'Novasteen'. This enabled the propeller shaft to spin more evenly without getting too hot. It certainly worked for us.

New anodes, a propeller zinc and then two coats of antifouling, including a special propeller antifouling called 'Propspeed', a freshly waxed hull and *Mischief* was looking very good indeed. What was not so good was a check of the interior. We lifted the floorboards and checked where the keel bolts were. There was the same hairline crack under the mast foot that we had first spotted in Fremantle - but perhaps slightly more marked than previously.

All boats move, but we had been used to our previous boat

A Little Bit of MisChief

Salina, a Swan 40, which had been built like a battleship. This little crack worried us. Probably more so than usual, seeing how we were about to embark on a number of long crossings through territory where it was difficult to get a boat repaired. With this in mind, we approached our good friends on *Circe*. They had cruised in this area for some time and knew their way around.

"What's your view? Should we get someone to look at it? Is there someone in Phuket that can help us?"

"We do know of a Danish shipwright who operates out of Boat Haven Marina in Phuket. Get him to have a look." We would follow up on this advice in due course.

We now turned our attention to shopping and took the daily ferry service from Rebak Marina to Langkawi. This island was a cruiser's paradise, with a range of chandleries. It was also a good place to re-stock our boat for the Indian Ocean crossing.

"Mr Din. We would like to hire a car for the day. We are coming on the nine thirty ferry."

"Yes… what is your name?"

And that was it. No questions, no paperwork, no insurance. We arrived at the ferry landing on Langkawi and were handed the keys to a small Japanese car in quite good condition. Armed with long lists and 'granny' shopping trolleys, we went off to explore and to shop 'til we dropped.

I recall the small shop where we were able to obtain the courtesy flags for all the countries that we would be visiting on our way to the Mediterranean. The shop also contained cruising guides, sea charts and any other paraphernalia that a cruiser required in order to be able to navigate these waters.

We also visited many alcohol wholesalers. It took us about two boat trips to purchase enough wine, beer and alcohol. This was to replenish our depleted stock for the next six months, until we reached the Mediterranean.

◇◇◇

We were excited about cruising in the incredibly majestic and stunning Thai waters, which we had heard so much about. Four weeks was perhaps not enough time to do it leisurely, but at this stage, the plan was to be leaving for the Maldives just after Christmas.

Stories of significant pirate activity operating out of Somalia had us concerned. Instead of heading from the Maldives to the Seychelles and then up the African coast to the Red Sea, as planned, we decided to follow the bulk of cruisers crossing the Indian Ocean that year. We opted to head from the Maldives to Salalah in southwest Oman and then along the Yemeni coast to Aden. This way we would keep away as far as possible from Somalia and the notorious island of Socotra, from where it was rumoured many of the pirates operated.

A Little Bit of MisChief

Malacca Rickshaw Bikes

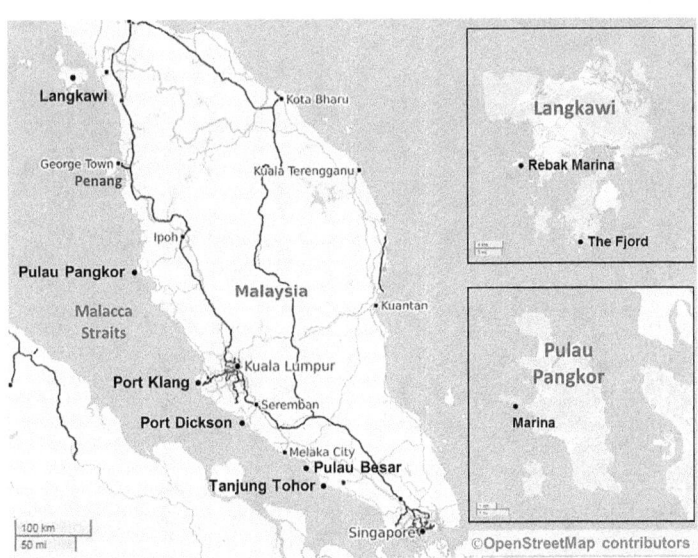

Malacca Straits Route

6
Thailand and Ship Repairs

We left Rebak Marina at the end of November and headed to Telaga in Langkawi. A cable car took us up to the top of the mountain overlooking the first of the Thai islands - looking north, the Ko Adang Archipelago to the left and Ko Tarutao to the right. Then it was a matter of checking out of Malaysia and heading to these islands. The scenery was majestic: the water on the outer islands was crystal clear, the reefs stunning and the weather warm. But at least it was not so humid, and it cooled down in the evening for a good night's sleep.

Ko Rok Noi was our first Thai anchorage, with brilliant beaches and good snorkelling. As you have probably guessed, *Ko* was the Thai equivalent of the Malaysian *Pulau*, meaning 'island'. This was our first encounter with pristine reefs since we left Western Australia, and it was indeed a welcome and beautiful sight.

We approached a cut between two islands and tried to make it across to where other boats were anchored. It was around midday, the best time to approach any coral anchorage or reef.

Bjorn was up on deck watching the water depth.

"There are 'bommies' all over the place. Go slowly," he shouted back at me. 'Bommies' were coral growth that sprouted sporadically throughout the seabed.

"The cruising guide says that you can get across," I

answered back, hopeful that we could find the path through the reefs.

We felt a sudden scraping on our hull.

"Steer to starboard. Full starboard!" Bjorn urged. Then he added, "I cannot see a path through this. I suggest gentle astern."

I reversed the boat and turned around. The depth immediately fell away quickly to over 20 metres. There were a few mooring buoys close by. We picked one up. In this depth we did not have the pleasure of a colourful reef view, but it assured us a better night's rest.

The next day we lowered our dinghy and went around to explore the coral cays and to have a swim. There was an abundance of fish of all colours swimming around the majestic coral. We never found the cut that would have taken us through to the other side of the islands.

Another 'must' pointed out by our cruising friends was Ko Muk. The name was not very inspiring, but we gently sailed across to the island and anchored at the mouth of a cavern.

It was high tide and the cavern was inaccessible, so we settled down with a cup of tea and a good book to wait for low tide. Around 3.00pm the tide had receded sufficiently for us to see more of the roof of the cavern, with a sliver of light now showing through from the other end. We donned our bathers, fins and snorkels, got into the pristine blue waters and swam to the entrance of Emerald Cave. We could only just have our heads above water, gently brushing the roof of the cavern. We swam for about 20 metres towards light, to reach the *hong*. A *hong* is essentially a type of secret garden accessible through a sea cave at low water. What a sight greeted us: a small lagoon within the island surrounded by high cliffs and lush vegetation. Very tall trees covered with climbers reached up to the top of the cliff face. The tidal waters lapped gently on the sandy shore. We came out of the water on to the fine sand and took in this magnificent sight - our own little private piece of paradise. I had never seen anything like it. It was stunning!

Our next stop was Ko Lanta and we visited a number of anchorages around the island. We were sailing past Pimalai Bay

A Little Bit of MisChief

when suddenly the VHF radio came alive.

"*Mischief! Mischief!* This is *Eloise*."

"*Eloise*, this is *Mischief*. Where are you?"

"You just overtook us. We were anchored up at the beach and have only just left."

"Where are you headed?"

"We are going to the top bay at Ko Lanta. There is a lovely little village that is worth a look."

"OK *Eloise*. We will go the same way. Dinner ashore?"

"Sounds good."

We put down anchor in about four metres of water, checked it for holding, and then lowered our dinghy into the water. We had davits at the back of our boat. This made lowering the dinghy an easy task and was usually the first thing we did as soon as we anchored.

"*Mischief*, this is *Eloise*. We are going ashore in half an hour. See you there."

"*Eloise* this is *Mischief*. We can pick you up on the way."

The town was quaint but somewhat touristy. In fact, it was a tad overrun by Swedish tourists. Bjorn, having hailed from there, had the opportunity to practise his native language. It was always amusing to watch the faces of others when we told them that we had sailed from Australia and were heading east towards the Mediterranean.

Thai cuisine is a particular favourite of ours and the food in Ko Lanta was well up to expectations. The usual Thai meal usually consists of a soup, and a curry dish or a spicy salad. Often there is a dip with accompanying fish and vegetables. I particularly like their spicy soups. Individual dishes often combine a harmony of flavours and textures that we like so much. Additionally, the food can vary in levels of piquancy.

The beach was full of resorts and restaurants so we had a wide variety to choose from. It was another wonderful, balmy evening. A bottle or two of wine later, we made our way back to the dinghy, pulled up on the shore. As had been the case wherever we had been, it was still there, safe and untouched.

Tristan and Jas on *Eloise* were headed north to Phuket much faster than we were. They were leaving the boat in Phuket, flying back to Australia and then on to Canada. We had enjoyed each other's company and shared a number of experiences together. It was time to part and we would miss them.

◇◇◇

There seemed to be no end to the majestic Thai islands, rising out of the water to great heights and covered with rainforest. In addition, the Thai waters were strewn with the most incredible caves, caverns, beaches and the mesmerizing *hong*s.

The approach to the Phi Phi islands was stunning with dramatic sheer cliffs rising out of the water, sometimes with dazzling white sand at their feet. The bay on Phi Phi Le (Maya beach) was another beautiful location where the movie, *The Beach*, was filmed. We anchored overnight at Ko Phi Phi Don. It was obvious that this was once quite the place to be, but frankly, ad hoc and unfettered tourism expansion have totally ruined it.

"Let's get one of the local boats and go explore," I suggested.

We took our dinghy to shore and bartered with one of the local guys driving their 'long tail' boats. The 'long tail' referred to the converted car engines with a long shaft reaching into the water over the stern. We took off to explore even more of the surrounding islands and beaches, visiting a number of places that were not accessible with our sailing boat.

It is customary to make the first port of call into any country the place where one completes the formalities for visa and formal entry. In the case of Thailand, the local authorities are aware that many of the boats are sailing up from Malaysia. We were told that they usually turn a blind eye to boats stopping along the way as we had done. This was as long as the time between checking out of Malaysia and into Thailand is not more than a week or two.

We called into Ao Chalong, Phuket for our formal entry to Thailand. We anchored the boat among many others, and hastily made our way ashore before the checking-in queue got too long. When our turn came, I was once again amused by the reaction from officials when they found out that I was the registered captain. Yet again we went through the charade where they would hand the paperwork to Bjorn, and tell him where I was to sign, communicating to me via him. We were given a month's visa that we thought would see us through our visit in this country.

With the formalities over, we headed north along the Phuket coast to Yacht Haven, a marina where we were scheduled to meet the Danish shipwright that our friends on *Circe* had recommended to examine the crack in the flow coat in the bilge. The verdict from the preliminary inspection was not clear and the problem needed further investigation.

"If *Mischief* needs taking out of the water again, and the mast taken off to examine the issue, then surely it would be best if we just presumed that there is a problem," I argued.

"I think it is just a stress crack: boats and buildings get that. I do not think it has worsened, even after the heavy seas we encountered outside Bali," Bjorn replied. Ever the engineer, he had marked the extent of the cracks to be able to see what was happening.

"Yes, but the shipwright wants to check the cross beams to see if water has seeped through and rotted the timber inside the beam."

"Well, that is just a drill hole... you can see whether the shavings come out dry. But if you are so worried - and if we are going to haul her out again - then I think we should go the whole hog. Let's check everything out, keel bolts and all. We will be out at sea for the next six months until we reach the Med."

And with that we headed south again to another marina, where the work was to be carried out. The entrance channel into Boat Lagoon was all silted up. We timed our arrival for close to high tide, and called the marina on radio. Two young men came out on a dinghy to guide us in through an ever-shifting silted passage.

With the boat on dry land, we moved into a marina apartment, hoping it would only be for a couple of weeks. In the hot, humid conditions, it was a lovely break to be in an air-conditioned apartment. There were all sorts of restaurants just round the corner, with a good selection of traditional Thai meals at hand.

Meanwhile, tests were carried out on *Mischief*'s cross beams. To our relief, the wood came out nice and dry. However, since the mast had been removed, it seemed sensible to go ahead and check the boat out thoroughly.

The interior was taped up and the contractors set to work sanding down the flow coat to the fibreglass. Poor *Mischief* turned into a sea of white. Yet every cloud has a silver lining. The contractor doing the work was a pleasant young Thai by the name of Oh. Oh set a high standard and was a pleasure to work with. He closely followed the instructions given by the shipwright. The steel bolts that hold the keel came up as good as new, and as dry as a bone. Everything was then replaced and re-fibreglassed, with a couple of extra layers on Bjorn's insistence, and we now had the cleanest bilges in town.

We found the Thai tradesmen to be professional and so took the opportunity to do some engine and boat maintenance work. The engine overhaul included installing new fuel injectors, checking the gearbox and investigating the engine oil seals, where there had been a slight leak. Before any work was started, Bjorn checked that spare parts were available for our unusual engine. Being an English engine meant that it took imperial size nuts and bolts instead of metric sizes. We were assured that all was available in Phuket, and so the work began.

We expected to be back in the water in eight to ten days. Soon this extended to two weeks, and then to a third week. But we still anticipated that the boat would be back in the water by Christmas.

Impressed by the quality of work in Phuket, I got new boat cushions for the cockpit done. They looked stunning in blue and white stripes. With time on our hands, we took up Oh's suggestion to inspect the chain plates that held the stays for the mast. This involved cutting round holes into the cupboards in the main saloon to get to the plates. We were delighted to find that all was in top condition.

It was not all work. At the marina, we got to know Annie and Tony on *Sunburnt* (Australia) who were also having work

A Little Bit of MisChief

done on their boat before setting out across the Indian Ocean. Our friends on *Blue Marine* introduced us to long-term cruisers Katie and Kurt on *Interlude* (USA).

With the protracted time on land, we hired a car for two days and drove around the island, including visiting the big Buddha. It was so much fun that we rented a scooter for a week or so. That was an experience in itself as all motorbikes drove on the shoulder of the road, dodging cars. But it got quite tricky at intersections.

Most of our friends were berthed at Yacht Haven and the scooter made it possible to catch up frequently. The day before Christmas, all the work was completed, except for a tiny rubber oil seal to the engine. Countless trips into Phuket town had yielded no success. Nobody could track down the seal with the correct imperial dimensions.

"So much for assurances that all parts are available here!" Bjorn grumbled.

"Oh hell... and its Christmas!" I moaned. "All the businesses will be closing down over the festive season."

"Thank goodness for the time difference. It is still morning in Europe. I'll phone my contact at Moody's in England and source the part."

We did succeed in getting through to our contact who pointed us in the right direction. Several frantic phone calls later and we had tracked down the part that now had to be shipped out of the UK. With the seasonal factory shutdown, we could not get the parts sent out immediately. We were getting anxious. Our friends intended to leave Phuket in early January; and we wanted very much to sail off in company with them. However, there was nothing else to do except sit and wait.

It was our first Christmas away from family. We spent hours on the phone catching up with our daughter back in Perth and our son and his wife gallivanting around the world. Then it was time to get on our motor bike and head north to meet with our friends on *Circe* and *Dreamcatcher*. They had organised a table at a local restaurant in Yacht Haven for Christmas dinner. Surrounded by cruisers, we left our worries behind and settled into having a great time.

Christina Gillgren

The New Year arrived and still no sign of our rubber seal. Our plans to set out on *Mischief* to explore the Ao Phang Nga National Park fell apart. Instead, we hired a local boat and went exploring. We had heard much about the area, characterised by limestone cliffs and rock formations, as well as mangrove forests.

Phang Nga Bay did not disappoint. This fascinating area is full of spectacular scenery: unique rock formations, mangrove forests, exotic islands, caves and caverns, and coral reefs. We did the tourist round and visited Ko Tapu, known as James Bond Island, with its iconic phallic rock jutting out of the water. We also travelled on canoes through numerous caverns, entering at low tide to emerge into the most fascinating inland bays and *hongs*.

Back on land, it was a frustrating time as we continued to wait for the spare part. One tiny rubber oil seal and here we were - trapped! We watched enviously as our friends got ready to leave for Sri Lanka, hoping we would catch up with them somewhere along the way. Our Thai visa was about to expire. There was no choice now but to extend it. This involved a trip outside Thailand. For this reason, we put our names down for a visa run to Myanmar (Burma).

We were picked up in a mini bus at 5.30am for the six-hour drive at break neck speed to Thailand's northernmost border with Myanmar.

"Do they always drive like this?" Bjorn asked.

"It is a long way, and there will be quite a crowd doing this trip. Don't expect to be back in Phuket until very late tonight." - This from one of our fellow passengers, Georges.

It was a pretty ordinary trip. When we got to the Thai harbour, we could see that there were at least 18-20 buses full of people on the same quest. We were herded into queues and stripped of our passports, which were stamped for exiting Thailand. Then we had to await our turn to hop across boats moored alongside one another to the boat, which would take us across the water to Myanmar.

"Is that thing sea-worthy?" I asked.

Before us was a 30-foot narrow boat with a big sign that said

A Little Bit of MisChief

"Visa Run" on its cabin. It looked like it was ready for the scrap yard. The engine started and a big puff of black smoke blew all over us… charming: if we did not drown, we would suffocate!

The boat chugged along out of the river mouth and into the open sea, which thankfully was calm and flat. It was an hour's crossing before we made land at Myanmar. Here we disembarked and were asked to queue once again. Passports were collected and these were duly stamped with entry into, and then exit from Myanmar. Back onto our ferry we trouped. We hardly had a chance to glimpse the town we had landed on; with no local currency, we could not even afford a drink.

The return trip was again unremarkable except for the Thais touting duty free before we re-entered Thailand. There was only one thing for sale - little trademark blue tablets: Viagra. Phuket has a reputation as the sex capital of south-eastern Asia. I am sure that a large number of the people doing this visa run were here for that reason, seeing the way the Viagra sales were going. For our efforts, we were given a two-week extension to our visa.

In the end we were delayed for the full two weeks, and almost had to do another visa run, which we thankfully managed to avoid.

The spare seal duly arrived, was fitted, the mast remounted, the rigging checked and reset. All ropes, which I had cleaned and stowed away, were brought out again. The halyards (up the mast), sheets (from the sail to the cockpit), or other lines such as the forestay furler were laid out through all the sheaves, and up the mast or affixed to the sails. The canvas in the cockpit was draped and secured over the stainless steel frames. *Mischief*, looking as new with polished topsides and hull, was finally ready for relaunching.

Catching up with Katie and Kurt on *Interlude*, we worked out that we were leaving Thailand at roughly the same time.

"We will be heading directly to the Maldives and giving Sri Lanka a miss." I said to Kurt and Katie.

"So are we," said Katie. "We are then heading straight across the Indian Ocean and up the Red Sea direct to Egypt as fast as we can."

Kurt volunteered to do the radio net, which meant that twice a day - morning and evening - he would call us and other vessels in the vicinity doing the crossing of the Indian Ocean. This was done on a pre-agreed HF frequency. We would then exchange positions and information on a daily basis.

If we could not sail in company, this was the next best thing. It meant we would be in contact with others all the way across to the Maldives.

We were now on a timeline to get out of Thailand before our extended Visa expired. Phone calls to our family and friends became a tad emotional. This was our first major crossing and the ideal conditions of sailing in company had not eventuated.

We made our way gently out of the river mouth at Yacht Haven and sailed *Mischief* down to Ao Chalong Bay to check out of the country. We checked and tested everything out as much as possible. All being well, we then sailed down to Nai Harn, at the bottom of Phuket Island. Nai Harn is also called 'Christmas Bay' among cruisers. This is where the yachties gather after Christmas to await the right conditions to commence their crossing of the Indian Ocean. We got there by mid-afternoon. Catching up with other cruisers, we checked the weather files to select the right weather conditions to undertake our first major crossing: 1562 nautical miles to Uligan Island in the Ihavandhippolhu Atoll, the northernmost atoll in the Maldives.

A Little Bit of MisChief

Maya Bay Phi Phi Le

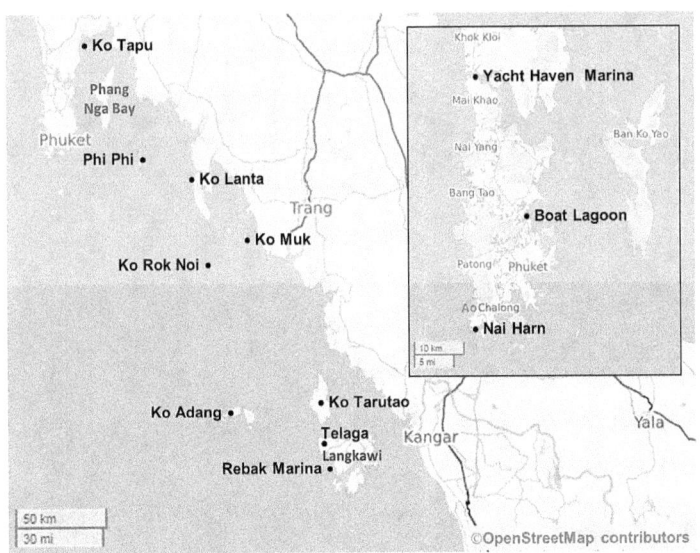

Langkawi to Phuket Route

Christina Gillgren

7

Second Crossing: Thailand to the Maldives

We did not have to wait long at Nai Harn Bay in southern Phuket. The weather files showed a good weather window with steady north-easterly winds. This meant that the monsoon had established itself with the promise of steady 15-20 knot winds for the next few days. The trick with monsoons is not to be too early in the monsoon season, to ensure that the steady winds have set in. But also not to wait until the monsoon is well established as the winds then become stronger, with a greater likelihood of wind surges over 30 knots.

Our timeline was that we would get to the Maldives around the end of January, spend a week or so there, then sail on to Oman to arrive around the third week of February. Then we would leave in the beginning of March to make our way down to Aden in Yemen before entering the Red Sea. With the delays we had experienced in Phuket, we were glad that we had decided to take this more traditional route. This way we would be sailing in company with the majority of the three hundred plus yachts that were crossing the Indian Ocean that year.

The night before our departure, we went for a sundowner with Malcolm and Linda on *Mr Bean*. We had met Malcolm at Langkawi and he was quite a character, besides being an experienced sailor. He knew that we were nervous about the forthcoming crossing. He was full of words of encouragement, filling us with anticipation for the adventures ahead.

We headed out of Nai Harn Bay at about 7.00am, waved off by Malcolm and Linda. We were ready for the start of our daunting Indian Ocean crossing, with about 5000 nautical miles to go before we reached our ultimate destination: the Mediterranean.

We did not have to motor far at all before we hoisted our sails - full main sail and the number 2 'Genoa' foresail. With a steady 13-18 knots blowing from astern, we tried goose-winging the sails, which means having a sail out to port and the other to starboard to maximize our speed. However, the swell made this a bit uncomfortable. Therefore, we opted to 'tack' downwind, first on a starboard broad reach for two hours and then switch to a port one. In this way, we increased our speed, but without the discomfort of a stern swell.

'Thank goodness for our beloved autopilot," I told Bjorn. "It certainly beats sitting for hours on end behind the helm, steering. And if these conditions prevail, we will have a very pleasant sail."

"I think the wind will lighten up tonight - at least that's what the GRIB files are showing." Bjorn replied. 'GRIB' files are weather files with prediction models that show wind, rainfall and swell among other information. They included global models of weather systems. We could narrow the information down, in our case, to what was happening across the Indian Ocean. This way we could anticipate the weather coming our way.

I am always amazed how once we were out at sea and settled into sailing it did not matter how far from land we were. The boat sailed as it does anywhere, steadily with that wonderful rhythmic motion along the waves, whooshing along, the mast and boom creaking gently as the wind filled the sails and as the boat adjusted to the gently rocking motion.

We never lost sight of the fact that this was an ocean crossing, but the nerves and the anxiety were gone.

"OK how about some ground rules for this journey. I liked the shift we adopted from Dampier to Bali. The midnight shift

A Little Bit of MisChief

suits me fine."

As is obvious, it is dangerous to leave a boat unattended - even for a short time - in open seas. With the speed of freighters nowadays, a cargo ship spotted on the horizon will be on top of you in about 15 minutes. If the paths collide, you can be in serious trouble. There are enough stories of close shaves to make one wary. I could still vividly recall the near miss we had with a cargo ship in Indonesian waters.

On the Dampier to Bali run, we had tried out four-hour shifts, hoping this would not be too long during the night hours. This allowed for a couple of hours of restful sleep for the person off watch. In the tropics, the day light hours tend to be 12 hours, from 6.00pm to 6.00am. During my working life, I had become used to retiring to bed around 10.00pm and then waking up at around 2.00am to do some work. I had hated the mid sleep interruption. It was probably due to the stress of my last job that I had developed this tendency. I would then go back to sleep at around 4.00am. It seemed a natural progression to do this night shift.

As it worked out, Bjorn and I would have dinner at around 6.30pm and do the shift to 8.00pm together. Then Bjorn would do the first night shift to midnight, when I would take over until 4.00am for another change. Often, I would then join Bjorn at around 7.00am to have breakfast, and this way we managed to have all meals together.

I had my night light with white/red light during my shift, and my iPod to keep me company. The red light ensured that I did not lose my night vision as I worked through a collection of books, music and even the occasional video clip.

We had agreed that on night shifts we would each wear a life jacket and always be tethered to the boat. Should one of us need to go on deck, even though secured, we would wake up the other person to stand by, in case of need such as a sail change.

We had some other rules as well: No booze whilst we were out at sea. After our last six months, this was a tough call at first.

The first night out was balmy. The wind slowed down to around eight to ten knots, our speed decreased to around four knots, probably about as fast as most of us go jogging at. On our first 24 hours, we only managed 115 nautical miles.

By 8.00am however, the wind picked up, as we knew it would. With 18-20 knots from the north-east, we came round the Nicobar Islands which belong to India. In the lee of the islands, with hardly any swell, *Mischief* just took off, surfing at eight to nine knots!

"Look at her go!" I cried out with delight. I could feel the fine sea spray all the way into the cockpit, and soon my hair was one wind-blown curly mop. I eased the mainsail and adjusted the foresail accordingly to ensure maximum efficiency. Cutting through the water up and down the gentle long swell, the boat seemed to groan with pleasure, and I wasn't far behind. "She is taking the sea so well," I said to Bjorn, "and this with one reef in!" For the landlubbers among you, reefing is a way of reducing the size of the sail.

To our amazement, we managed close to 200 nautical miles in the next 24 hours, a feat that has never been repeated.

Not long after, a sailing boat appeared on the horizon, astern of us. It was *Sailaway II* (USA) and we had a good natter on the VHF. Being a catamaran, they are usually much faster than a monohull boat like *Mischief*. With the ideal weather conditions we were experiencing, they were only a fraction faster and slowly caught up with us. We kept each other company for the next two days.

Via the radio schedule, we heard that our friends on *Interlude* had left a day later. Almost twice our size, they were bound to overtake us.

The next few days, the weather was true to form. We had a steady 12-15 north-easterly wind, a gentle rolling swell on the starboard stern, and ideal sailing conditions. We were just north of the main shipping line. All day and night, there was a stream of freighters and cargo ships passing just south of us. A few came up from the stern and we had to monitor their progress. One night a ship seemed to be heading straight for us.

"Cargo ship! Cargo ship! This is sailing yacht *Mischief*. Come in please!" I yelled over the radio.

No response.

A Little Bit of MisChief

Oh hell! I could see both the port and the starboard lights. This was not good!

"Bjorn, wake up. Wake up!"

Bjorn was on deck in a millisecond. "What's the problem?"

"There" I pointed dead astern. The vessel seemed to be some three to four nautical miles away.

"The starboard light is more visible …look the port light is occasionally blocked from sight."

I therefore tacked to starboard, to get further away. On came the motor to help us along. The ship passed within a half mile of us, and we both heaved a huge sigh of relief.

"They probably were not even aware of our existence!" I muttered.

"I think an AIS is definitely the way to go." Bjorn told me.

The Automated Identification System, or AIS, is a transmitter/receiver, which identifies ships in the vicinity by name, course, speed and even type of cargo. It is obligatory for ships to carry one. More importantly, it is illegal for a ship identified by name to refuse to answer the radio. It is a huge bonus to sailors. If we had had one on board, we could have identified the ship earlier, and called it by its name.

The daily radio schedules, morning and evening, were a welcome break to the routine. Kurt on *Interlude* was doing a fantastic job of keeping track of everyone *en route* to the Maldives. They finally overtook us on the fourth day, and brought with them decreasing winds. We used the slow period to run the engine and the water maker.

The next few days were uneventful. This crossing was turning out to be a dream run with the sailor's salutation of 'fair winds and following seas' bearing fruit. Every four hours, we logged our progress on a sea chart in the traditional manner, using our latitude and longitude from the GPS. We also sent twice-daily position updates so our family and friends could track our progress. We hardly needed to trim the sails, and could now appreciate the steady monsoons better.

Our eighth night was special. I came on watch as usual at

midnight to a good steady breeze that had us gliding over the water at just under five knots. Suddenly a pod of dolphins - there must have been about 15 - miniature in size and of a pinky-grey colour, swam up to *Mischief*. They frolicked around the boat, keeping me company for about an hour. I watched in delight, the sole spectator. This did not dampen their exuberant display. Some were riding the bow wave, whilst others jumped clean out of the water, and one or two of them even rose out of the water, swimming backwards on their fin.

There was magic in the air. The wonderfully playful friends gave me a water show to remember. It was accompanied by a dramatic light show. Their antics produced incredible phosphorescence that lit up the night. Looking astern, *Mischief* was also leaving her mark in the water with a chalky green wake.

I looked up to see the most stunning Milky Way, thankful and privileged to be able to witness such beauty. I was moved to tears one minute yet wanted to shout: 'Oh what a feeling!' the next. I stood behind the wheel, the wind in my hair. I swayed in rhythm with the boat movement responding to the gentle one-metre swell.

In many ways it was a culmination of the surreal days we had spent at sea. They had a calming, almost hypnotic effect: your time is spent between keeping watch, and dozing on and off to ensure you get enough rest. You experience a different sense of reality. Little things give you great pleasure: the wind whispering through the rigging, the boat and sails responding to the wind and waves, a bird that would land on the yacht, or even the odd flying fish that flew on to the deck at night. This was my enchanted evening that lasted well into the night.

As we approached the seas between Sri Lanka and the Maldives, we studied the weather charts carefully. Strong winds were reputed to blow in this area, kicking up quite a sea. Yet we need not have worried. Ever since we set out from Fremantle, this feeling of being watched over had grown. Whether it was *Mischief*'s Swedish folklore resident or something else I don't know. What mattered was that it was there.

On our ninth day out at sea, we suddenly heard our VHF

A Little Bit of MisChief

radio crackle and come alive.

"*Dreamcatcher*! *Dreamcatcher*! This is *Circe*."

Was I dreaming? …Up went the radio volume as we listened in.

"*Circe*. This is *Dreamcatcher*…"

Once their conversation was over, we identified ourselves.

"*Circe, Circe*. This is *Mischief*."

"Come in, *Mischief*."

"Where are you? We are about 120 miles south-east of Sri Lanka, on our way to the Uligan Atoll."

"We left Galle this morning at 7.00am and are now about 70 miles off shore on our way to the same destination."

There was only about 50 nautical miles between us.

We were delighted to have company to sail with once again. Over the radio, we said hello to everyone, absolutely blown away by the coincidence. During the night, as our paths converged, we occasionally caught sight of the masthead lights. At daybreak, on our tenth and last day at sea, we were within sight of each other. Everyone was almost at a standstill as the winds had deserted us. With motors on, we made our way across the final miles to our destination. At daybreak on the eleventh day, we could see the first signs of land.

By mid-morning, we were motoring into the Ihavandhippolhu Atoll group, and made our way to the island of Uligan. This was practically the northernmost island of the Maldives. We dropped our anchor in the pristine waters of the palm-fringed coral island.

There must have been about 20 other boats already at anchor. Soon, some of the cruisers came alongside in their dinghies to pass on information about checking in procedures, provisioning, customs and more.

We were in Paradise! And I am referring not only to the exotic surroundings, but also to the beautiful ever-growing yachting community which was now our extended family.

Christina Gillgren

Ihavandhippolhu Atoll Main Island Jetty

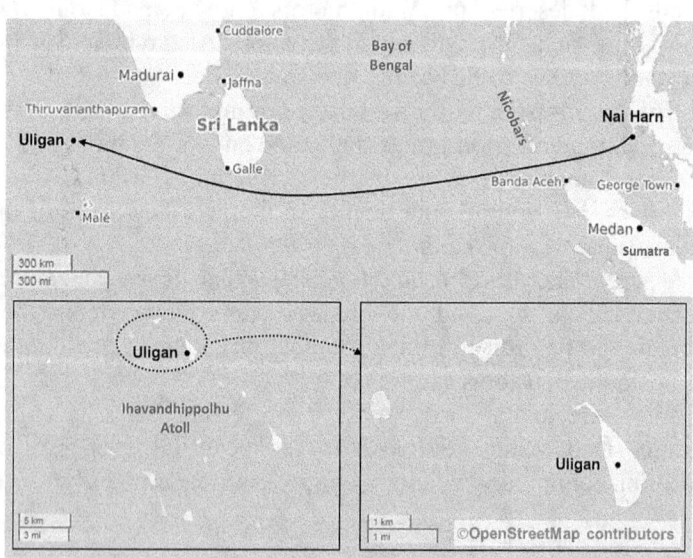

Phuket to Uligan Route

8
Third Crossing: Maldives, and then to Oman

The northern atolls in the Maldives were very peaceful. They provided a welcome reprieve between ocean crossings. We were impressed by the local organisation on the islands. Everything was basic, yet clean and efficient. The few roads on the island were made of crushed coral gravel, tidy and even. When we checked in, the immigration officials were friendly and welcoming. The charge for our short stay was around seven dollars. This contrasted sharply with the experience of our friends who had stopped over at Sri Lanka. Officials checking in the boats helped themselves to whatever they could lay their hands on inside the cabins, openly asking for alcohol and for bribes. One boat on the Vasco da Gama Rally had a couple of thousand dollars stolen. Only appeals at the highest level saw some of this money returned to the yacht owners.

All our contact on the Maldives was with men, who were efficient and helpful. They were somewhat protective of the locals, especially the women and politely told us we should not go ashore after 6.00pm without permission.

To compensate, the local Muslim community organised a number of events for the visiting cruisers. One evening they organised a buffet dinner for us. There was, of course, no alcohol. Instead, they provided fresh coconut juice and tea. To complement the evening, they organised entertainment that included a local band with drums and a number of games. All the visiting cruisers joined in. Then Katie and Kurt (*Interlude*) produced their guitars and we were soon singing along.

It was interesting to note that none of the women participated in the festivities. It had been left to the men and younger boys to serve and entertain us.

The locals organised an excursion to other islands in the atoll group, which we took up. The tour included visiting some of the coral cays and exotic islands. Wherever we went we found stunning, picture-postcard white sandy beaches, lined with plenty of coconut trees.

We stopped for lunch on Ihavandhippolhu Island, the main island of this atoll group. The main street, though unpaved, was lined with trees and as straight as any seen in first world countries. It was probably only one to two kilometres long, the length of the island. There was no rubbish. The coral sand was packed and swept clean of any rubble and debris. The buildings, also built out of coral, were of a high standard. Our tour guide, Mohammed of course, proudly showed us their local school, health and family centres that were well equipped and clean.

Rounding up a perfect day was an afternoon dive on the surrounding coral reefs; the warm, crystal clear waters teemed with fish darting in and out and between the colourful coral.

Our tour guide had become chatty by this stage. On discovering that Bjorn and I were Aussies, he started out, saying, "You are good friends. You are welcome!" Then he stunned us by adding "…in 50 years, when the global warming sinks our atolls, we will come to live in Australia. The government has arranged this."

Bjorn and I looked at each other. This was the first time we had heard of this. Yet our feeling was 'Good Luck to them'. They were a peaceful, friendly people.

With a mindset now on security at sea, the priority during our stay in Uligan was to order an AIS (Automated Identification System) for *Mischief*. We emailed our son in London to purchase one and send it immediately to the Holiday Inn in Salalah, Oman awaiting our arrival, as per the cruising guide advice. We had had enough close encounters with cargo vessels. With the leg to Yemen plus the 1,500 miles up the Red Sea still to go, we thought this was a wise investment.

As the week flew by, we started to plan for our next leg to Oman. We visited the one and only shop on Uligan: a five square metre room, with a couple of boxes of 'fresh' produce, some canned foods, dried biscuits and crackers. An outdoor freezer contained frozen chicken. Again, thanks to the cruisers' network we were well informed. The boat with fresh produce called in once a week, so the trick was to place your order for fresh foods a couple of days beforehand to ensure you did not miss out.

There was not a great choice, but the potatoes, onions, carrots, tomatoes, cucumbers, capsicums and apples and oranges were welcome indeed. I also ordered a bowlful of their tasty local version of *nasi goreng*, a rice based dish with chicken pieces and local herbs and vegetables. I managed to get my hands on two small chickens. These would go into the pressure cooker with whatever vegetables were at hand to make my trademark 'passage chicken' dish. We were ready for our next bout at sea. This leg would last between nine to twelve days, depending on wind.

Interlude, which had hosted the cruisers' radio network from Phuket to Uligan, was going to make a straight run up the Red Sea to Egypt to get through the pirate areas as fast as possible.

"We need a new radio net host." I told Bjorn.

"Why don't you do it," he suggested.

"Hmm, I'd enjoy that! ...Unless, of course, there is someone who is really keen. I'll bring it up with the cruisers tonight."

We had obtained special permission from the island to have a farewell gathering on shore that evening. I had identified a radio channel we could use, and passed on this information. It was thus that the first twenty or so cruisers put their names down on my list, as I commenced the morning/evening radio schedules.

At the last minute, we decided to postpone our departure from the Maldives by a day, in favour of another tour of the outer islands of the atoll. Once more, we would be setting out on a crossing on our own, as fellow cruisers on *Circe* and *Dreamcatcher* left a day ahead of us. This proved to be to their advantage, as will be seen later.

The crossing to Oman was about 1270 nautical miles, roughly 300 miles shorter than our first leg from Phuket to the Maldives. However, it took almost as long as the first crossing as we ran out of wind to begin with. On our third day out, I was down in the galley preparing lunch when Bjorn called me up on deck.

"Sailing boat, sailing boat," came across on our VHF radio again. "This is ?? calling."

We could not make out the name, but the vessel looked very much like a fishing trawler.

"Fishing boat; fishing boat. This is sailing vessel *Mischief*."

"Where are you going, where are you coming from?"

We were unsure as to how to reply. We were unsure of their intentions, but it was difficult to be circumspect in the middle of the Indian Ocean.

"We are on our way to Oman, sailing in company."

Then much to our surprise the response came: "this is incredible! Do you want any water or fuel? …or food? Do you need any assistance?"

Having declined all the invitations for assistance, we learnt that they were an Iranian based fishing trawler, on their way from their homeport to fish off the African coast. The conversation went on for a little while. They were obviously surprised to come across a sailing boat in the middle of nowhere - and bored.

Bjorn and I were chuffed. Here we were thinking the worst and that maybe our time had come. Instead, they turned out to be friendly and caring seafarers. However, the reality is that one should keep one's guard up in these waters. The stories about piracy were real and worrying enough.

On our fifth day out, our cruiser friends on *Dreamcatcher*, a day and about 120 nautical miles ahead of us, reported an extremely long fishing net.

"We had to steer about two nautical miles to port to avoid

A Little Bit of MisChief

going caught in the net," Joe reported.

We took down the position of the sighting, but luckily never came across this net. It was a quiet crossing. The sailing was generally much calmer and slower on this leg, with light northeasterlies. We still managed to average around 120 miles per day. When the wind lightened, we would put on the engine to help us along, and also charge the batteries and make water. We did not encounter many ships on this route until we got closer to Oman.

On the ninth and last day, we ran into a sand storm! I had just finished my morning schedule on the HF radio and *Sandpiper* (UK), about 80 nautical miles to our northeast, reported strong winds with bad sea conditions and no visibility. Meanwhile, our friends had arrived in the major Omani port of Salalah the previous day. They also reported strong winds and poor visibility in the harbour: not ideal conditions for approaching land.

Bjorn and I reefed the mainsail in anticipation. It was not long before the storm hit us. The wind and sea were whipped into a frenzy. We quickly reduced the foresail. What was quite scary was the incredibly poor visibility.

"Put the radar on, Chris!"

"Come and see this! Is this land or what?"

The sand was so thick that it showed up like an island on radar. It blocked out everything else rendering the radar useless. We were regretting not having ordered the AIS earlier. This piece of equipment would have still shown the location of vessels around us, and the direction they were travelling in. We were now barely fifteen nautical miles from Salalah. There were many large vessels in the area, some at anchor. Yet, without the use of instruments, we were technically blind.

We decided that the best thing to do was to sit still and so we 'hove to'. This tactic means backing the fore sail so that it counterbalances the main sail. As a result, the boat will gently drift to leeward at a greatly reduced speed.

We were in this position for about three endless hours: tense, and listening keenly for any engine noise that would herald imminent danger of a ship approaching. We noticed that the winds had eased. The visibility cleared sufficiently for us to see a large freighter sitting still about 100 metres ahead. We decided to do a run for it to reach the harbour. We cautiously made our way under engine around a number of large ships anchored outside Salalah.

We made it into the harbour at around 5.00pm, thankful to be out of danger. We put down our anchor in a tightly packed inner harbour, with everyone watching to ensure we did not snag their anchor. Before long, Mohammed, the local who looked after cruisers' needs, called by to advise us on checking in procedures and other useful information.

Checking in was more formal than in other places we had previously visited. Once again, officials, being all men as is usual in Muslim countries, spoke directly to Bjorn who had accompanied me ashore. We always made sure to wear appropriate clothing in each country we visited. In this case, I wore a long sleeved shirt over baggy trousers. It was still amusing - though of course I kept a straight face - to be handed the paperwork by Bjorn, sign and stamp them with our boat stamp, then hand everything back to him to pass on to the officials.

"Well, Bjorn," I grinned. "This tactic of me being the captain does throw them off. We never seem to experience the hassles other male skippers encounter."

The sandstorm kept us from exploring our first Arabian Peninsula landing. We only saw the port properly after three days, when the dust storm finally cleared. We could almost build sand castles in our cockpit with the sand that had blown in. The salt and sand had formed icicle-like formations on the lee side of our boom.

"Time to give *Mischief* a good clean," Bjorn called out, as he hauled buckets of seawater whilst I scrubbed the decks. There was so much red sand. Tired of emptying bucket load after bucket load of water, we tried out the seawater pump on the bow, usually used for rinsing the anchor. We almost burnt it out trying to wash off all the sand and salt from the boom and rigging.

In the evenings, we caught up with our friends on

A Little Bit of MisChief

Dreamcatcher, and *Circe* and met new friends John on *Blue Sip* (Finland) and Anne and John on *Sparrow* (Holland). Salalah is where sailors form small groups so that you cross from to Aden in Yemen in company. This stretch of water is notorious for piracy, and we were appreciative that this group of cruisers welcomed us into their fold.

We attended a number of meetings, always accompanied by nibbles and wine of course, to drink to another glorious sunset and to plan our journey to Aden. For practical purposes, we called ourselves the Tango Group. I also recall one other group composed of mainly Dutch and German cruisers who called themselves the Romeo Group. I had been asked to maintain my role of radio net host. With a growing number of cruisers, it was easier for me to note general positions of groups of yachts rather than individual ones, which numbered closer to 60 by this stage.

As Tango Group, we had decided that we would motor/sail as much as possible in a diamond formation, with the smallest yacht *Dreamcatcher*, out front, and *Mischief*, being the largest bringing up the rear. We acknowledged that it would be difficult to keep this formation under sail, but would try to keep as close to the other yachts as possible and trim our speed accordingly. Should we motor, then the designated speed was four and a half knots.

We selected four waypoints and called them randomly A, B, C and D. The strategy was that, in the event of sailing and getting away from the group, we would give our position (using the VHF radio, which had about a 50-mile range) as north, south, east and west of a specific waypoint. Any pirates listening in would not be able to have a fix on our location. This was not so much of a problem on the daily radio net, over shortwave radio. With its incredibly larger range, it was difficult for anyone listening in to first find the right frequency and then narrow down the area we could be in.

We also agreed that should any suspicious vessels approach, we would close formation to present a bigger obstacle to the potential pirates.

With the weather clearing in Oman, it was time to explore

and to party! Oman was a lovely surprise and a great introduction into Arabia. A comparatively wealthy Arabian Peninsula nation, we could provision for most things. Joe and Helen were celebrating their 39th wedding anniversary on St. Valentine's Day and invited the Tango Group to dinner at the Holiday Inn, just on the outskirts of Salalah. We were eager to get there as we also hoped to collect our new AIS for the boat.

It proved to be a great evening out, with good food, and lively entertainment. We were surrounded by well-heeled, elegant Omanis, the women clad in elegant black with *hijab* (hair cover), all made up, long nails lacquered, and showing off their bling.

Unfortunately, our quest to receive the package containing the AIS proved futile as the hotel reported that they no longer held parcels for cruisers. Then the hunt for our missing parcel started. With the help of the ever-resourceful Mohammed, we managed to locate it within two days. Mohammed was also great at helping us locate a mechanic who serviced our spare water pump for the engine.

Cruising in company has many benefits. One of these was that when we hired cars, again through the helpful Mohammed, we could share the costs and the fun. No mountains of paperwork for car hire here. Just a car left on the quay, keys handed from one set of cruisers to another, and money left under the carpet for Mohammed to collect.

We travelled in two vehicles as far as the Yemeni coast and went through varied landscape with *Wadi*s (valleys) and mountains. At one stage, we had to slow down to allow a herd of camels to cross the road, and they curiously leant right into our cars, drooling over Joe who was sitting in the window seat.

Of course, I could not pass by the opportunity of breaking into song, and regaled my friends with a naughty Camel's ditty about its love life (look it up!) I had come across in Malta decades ago.

"Great Chris," Helen laughed, "but don't give up your day job for singing."

Salalah was a strange town: quite open with a large urban sprawl but without a discernible centre. There were wide

A Little Bit of MisChief

avenues with sites of commercial activity, but it was also desert country. Shopping for provisions was excellent, the fruit and vegetables first class and welcome. The town exuded wealth with many modern buildings. Undoubtedly, one of the highlights of Salalah was the modern and well set out Frankincense Museum, which had one of the earliest maps of the world we have ever seen.

One evening, the local yacht club on the hill overlooking the harbour invited us to a barbecue. Also attending were the officers and crew of one of the coalition warships guarding the passage to Aden. It was an English warship, and we could not help but wonder at the tender ages of those entrusted with such a heavy responsibility. It seems they were as much in awe of us cruisers sailing in these waters. They advised us to announce our presence and maintain contact with the coalition forces.

The time was drawing near to move on again. Bjorn had proudly installed the AIS over the chart table. We fuelled up with the cleanest and cheapest fuel we had ever come across at nine cents a litre. We were now ready to embark on our most dangerous leg of the Indian Ocean crossing, from Oman to Aden, in Yemen.

Christina Gillgren

Camel Crossing - Humps in the Road

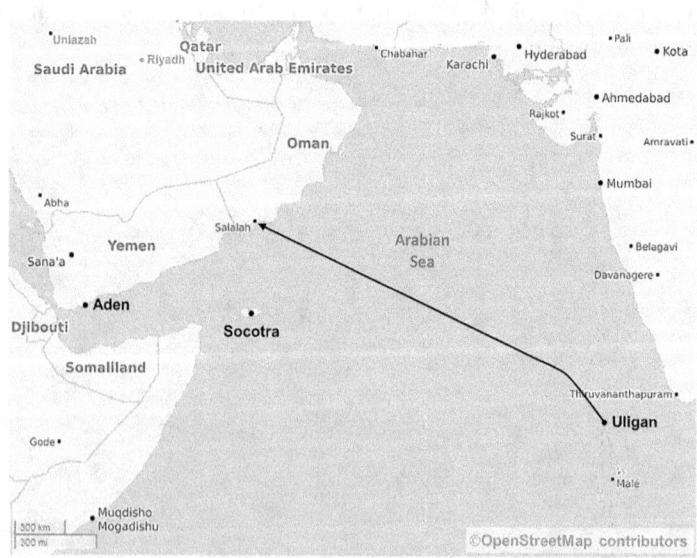

Maldives to Oman Route

9
Down Pirate Alley

Our departure from Salalah in Oman was not without incident. We left on a Saturday at midday after clearing customs and immigration. We were the third small convoy to head out to sea that day, only an hour apart. The first and second were two groups of three yachts each. Ours was a cluster of five yachts: our Australian friends Helen and Joe on *Dreamcatcher*, Birte and Jorgen on *Circe* and John and Petteri, English and Finnish farming neighbours in Finland, on *Bluesipp*, John and Anne on *Sparrow* and of course Bjorn and I on *Mischief*. Conditions were calm and there was no wind.

We were all anxious. The whole week, whilst we relaxed in Salalah, we had been hearing of a lot of activity in the shipping corridor from Oman to Yemen. There were many sightings of suspicious goings-on and warship intervention. The sundowners, with the medicinal wine or G&T, helped to normalise the state of affairs. Rumour was rife, and it paid to keep a cool head.

We had hardly left the harbour, when *Sparrow* came up on the radio.

"We still have propeller trouble; we have to turn back."

"What shall we do? Shall we all return?" *Circe* called in.

"No, please go on," John, on *Sparrow*, insisted. "We have to get to the bottom of the problems we have been having. We do not know how long we will be here." John had been struggling all the way from Thailand to fix the problem of an unbalanced propeller. This had entailed having the boat lifted out of the water in the most exotic places such as Phuket, Sri Lanka, and Salalah, including having divers look at the propeller in the Maldives.

"We will catch up with you or join another small flotilla," John told us.

The consensus was for the remaining four of us to go on as planned. And so we waved *au revoir* to *Sparrow* for the time being.

We had taken a number of precautions for this passage. Because of the pirate threat, the coalition forces - made up essentially of the USA and other NATO countries - were patrolling the area around two shipping corridors: one for vessels heading east, and the other for the opposite direction.

Based on previous experiences of other yachties, we decided to travel two miles north of the coalition forces' northernmost shipping corridor. This corridor was for westbound traffic, and was fifty miles south of the Yemeni shoreline. It was risky to travel without navigation lights, so we kept these turned on at night. We used VHF radio on low power for initial communication to alert our group (the Tango Group) to go to the HF on our pre-set channel 4069 in the event of any dangers. As an added precaution, we also participated in a cruisers' net, of which I was net controller, twice a day. This included other convoys going all the way up to Hurghada in Egypt, some 1800 nautical miles away.

We had pre-established an arrangement that any boat or group not reporting for two consecutive rollcalls on the cruisers' net would have the details relayed to the coalition forces. We had two satellite phones among the convoys, with emergency telephone numbers for the US Navy and the UK Royal Navy's Maritime Trade Organisation (UKMTO). This was over and above what each convoy would set into motion, the first being a call on Channel 16 to the Coalition Warships, as advised by them.

With little wind for most of the first day, we motored in

A Little Bit of MisChief

calm seas. We kept an alert watch at night because some cargo ships were reportedly travelling with their lights out. This was against maritime law and very dangerous, especially for smaller craft like ours.

On the afternoon of the second day, we started encountering fast skiffs and went on to full alert. We watched a few skiffs running in what seemed all directions. Further away, there was a much larger vessel with many smaller skiffs around it.

As the vessel in the rear of our formation, we were alarmed as some of the boats headed towards us.

"Tango Group! Tango Group! We have action on our stern." I reported, feeling uneasy. Was our time up?

Everyone in the formation closed ranks and waited to see what would eventuate.

One or two skiffs approached us. I had my hand ready to accelerate the motor. Meanwhile Bjorn pulled the box with flares towards him. If threatened, a flare fired into the vessel could cause quite a commotion.

"You want fish?" There were a number of people in each skiff. This seemed suspicious. One of the fishermen - if that is who they were - offered what looked like sardines for sale.

"You have coca cola?" another fisherman asked.

We had encountered fishermen asking for drinks and nibbles, so we gladly chucked over a couple of cans of coca cola and one or two packets of biscuits.

To our delight and infinite relief, their faces lit up. Maybe they were harmless fishermen after all. But it was so unusual to have four to five people in each skiff and so we remained wary. How they fished with so many people on board was a mystery. I did not realise how tense I had become, my hand squeezing the motor controls. More of the skiffs came close by and slowed down, waving away merrily. Then they slowly started moving away.

Bjorn headed down into the cabin and fetched the binoculars. "Look at them, over there," he said, gesticulating in the direction of where some of the skiffs seemed to be heading. "The dolphins are herding fish, and the skiffs are surrounding them. Ah! They seem to be dropping lines overboard, and hooking the fish on the perimeter."

It seemed to be a clever way of catching fish and accounted for the number of men in each skiff. This was the weirdest fishing tactic we had experienced so far.

On our third morning out, I heard a Coalition helicopter communicating with another sailing vessel in the vicinity. They checked on how the sailing boats were progressing and whether they had encountered any suspicious activity overnight.

I made contact with them, advised them of our small flotilla, and on our intentions to stick close to the shipping corridor. To their credit, they made two more follow up visits on that day and the next, which make us feel more secure.

"We've got company," Bjorn told me, as I came into the cockpit for breakfast. A bird had taken up residence on our pulpit, the stainless steel rail on the bow. Such a little thing, yet it made us feel better.

"Dammit, I knew we should have taken the birds of the world book with us. I'll take a photo."

We later found out that the bird was a 'Hoopoe', a species that inhabited this part of the world with the most delightful pattern of feathers on its wings and with a spectacular colourful 'headdress' that balanced out its sleek long beak. These birds were revered in Ancient Egypt, and often shown on the walls of tombs and temples.

Late in the evening on the third day, we heard the first interaction between a warship and a cargo vessel travelling with its AIS turned off. The coalition forces insisted that it identify itself. Then the ship was admonished, as both navigation lights and the Automatic Identification System should remain turned on at all times, despite the threat of pirates. It was otherwise too dangerous for general shipping.

On midnight Wednesday 25th of February 2009, my turn came to take the watch for the next four hours. This was our fourth night out at sea on our way to Aden. We had now entered the most active part of 'pirate alley'. Sure enough, a German warship hailed one of the four yachts in our small convoy. After ascertaining who we were, a disapproving voice reproached us: "These waters are full of pirates." The radio operator felt we were moving too slowly and strongly recommended that we proceed at maximum speed.

Well, sailing boats are just that. The engine is usually an auxiliary tool to get in and out of harbours and tight spots. Maximum speed for us was not much more than the five knots we were averaging. Our motors were no match against the high-powered motors that pirate boats were reputed to have. We were relying heavily on the fact that, in previous years, the pirates were not that interested in a small sailing vessel. They had been much more interested in the large commercial vessels with their millions of dollars of cargo or freight that they could hold to ransom.

With still no wind and a calm sea all around us - unfortunately, perfect conditions for pirates - we proceeded at full alert in close formation. But it turned out to be another quiet night.

As the next day dawned, we heard our first transmission between a merchant ship in potential trouble and a warship.

"Coalition warships! Coalition warships! We have many boats approaching us at high speed. There is a 'mother ship' in the distance," a highly stressed radio operator screamed over the radio.

The warship closest to the action advised the vessel to maintain speed but be alert and take precautions. "The boats could be harmless fishermen," they advised. "Just in case, prepare the sea pumps to repel any potential boarders."

We heard the very nervous exchange as the merchant vessel called again and again for more assistance. The warship advised that a helicopter was on the way. Then there was silence.

We saw two warships that morning, the first of which steamed close by and sent out a helicopter to scout us out. We chatted to them once more, reassured by their presence.

As the day progressed, we heard other calls from ships concerned with skiffs approaching at fast speeds and with a 'mother ship' around. Many of the merchant ships were on high alert, anxious and actually 'spooked' by anything that moved around them. They were successfully spooking us too!

We kept our fingers crossed and called on all the deities and other mythological beings to look out for us (more on adopted weather gods at the end of the book). In Oman, one of the rumours was that the pirates would approach small yachts to divert the coalition forces from the merchant shipping. We hoped we were not the target for the pirates. Who knows what goes?

Via radio, we actually followed one suspicious approach to a merchant ship about 20 nautical miles to our south-east. The distress call for assistance went out. The crew on board the merchant ship were understandably nervous and anxious. They hardly gave the coalition forces time to respond between calls for help. The ship was advised to proceed at maximum speed, and to prepare any water hoses to repel boarders if necessary. The suspicious vessel was only diverted away by the arrival of the helicopter and soon after, the warship, which then escorted the merchant ship.

On the fifth morning, we picked up more radio transmissions that indicated that pirates had boarded and taken over a cargo ship with a crew of 22. The events that unfolded were similar to those in the movie entitled '*Captain Phillips*'. However, we had not seen any other fishing boats or skiffs. Our nights had remained for the most part uneventful, save for one ship that seemed to be steaming towards us. Thanks to the AIS, it was simply a matter of contacting them on radio to alert them to our presence and position.

We finally got some wind and turned off the engine. It was heavenly to have quiet again, and we savoured the reprieve from the endless motoring. Our feathered friend decided that it was time to take off. Frankly, after looking at the mess it left behind, so did we.

After a day full of heightened emotions, excitement and apprehension, I felt that we needed a morale booster. Down into the galley I went, and cooked up a delicious chicken casserole. If you have to face pirates, it's better on a full and satisfied stomach! We would have succumbed to a glass or two of vino, but knew we were not out of danger yet, and needed our full wits about us.

The last night was only remarkable in one way, apart from

A Little Bit of MisChief

the dinner, that is. We had about ten knots of wind on a broad reach, and the sea was reasonably calm. It was a moonless night, but the sea was lit up as though covered with white caps. Coming up for my watch at midnight, it took me a few minutes to register that the white caps were not a sign of rough seas, but rather an amazing display of phosphorescence. We had experienced this from time to time, but I could not recall such brilliance. The boat wake was milky white, as was the bow wave. All around us, the breaking tops of waves twinkled as though lit up by fairy lights. Even our water maker's filter bowl glowed in the dark and flushing of the loo became quite a spectacular sight.

The approach to Aden was impressive with high mountains and cliffs all around. We reached the stunning cliff entrance to Aden Harbour at 6.00pm local time, safe and secure for the present, in time for a well-earned rest after all the tension of the trip.

Also memorable was the fact that our first major ocean crossing of the Indian Ocean was now well and truly behind us. We had successfully traversed 3,457 nautical miles of ocean, our first major ocean crossing.

Mischief with Navy Escort (Inset: Hoopoe Bird)

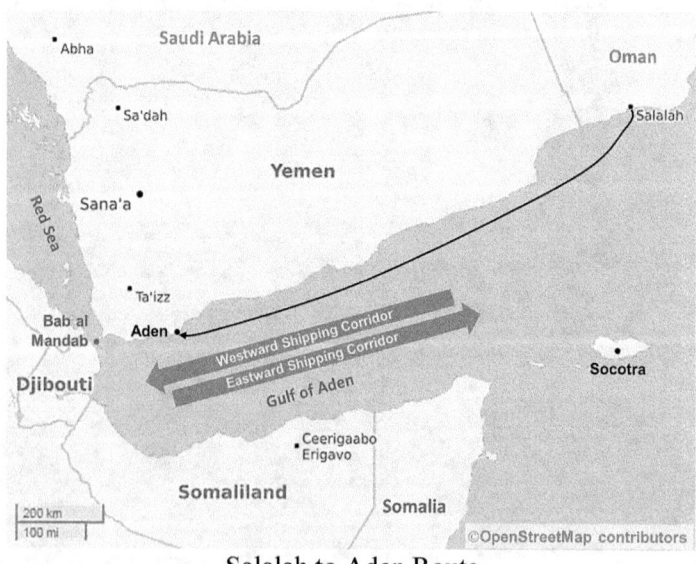

Salalah to Aden Route

A Little Bit of MisChief

10
Yemen: Land of Contrasts

Aden was a ramshackle town, somewhat dingy and dirty and yet noisy and colourful, with friendly locals. We did not need a visa as, having arrived by boat, we were given seven days' seamen's shore passes when we checked in.

In deference to local custom, we had both legs and arms covered, despite the heat. Headwear was not necessary. The first thing we noticed was the striking traditional clothes that many Yemeni men wore, and in particular, the ceremonial dagger up front, tucked into their belt.

On our first foray into the city with Helen and Joe from *Dreamcatcher*, we were working out which bus to take to go to the *Souq* (market) when a man approached to ask where we were going. He practically took over, guiding us into the right bus. But then he also got on board and tagged along to the market. It seemed churlish to tell him that we now could manage on our own, and he stuck to us like glue. He guided us around, showing off various wares in different sections of the *Souq*: spices, fabrics, gold, food, woodwork, metalwork and more. After a couple of hours, we started to wilt. He led us to a kiosk for a refreshing fresh fruit drink, which we paid for of course. We just could not shake him off. When we had had enough, he accompanied us back to the port and wanted to meet with us again, an offer we declined.

Well, the next day, there he was at the entrance to the port. He asked to borrow some money, with some story about needing it urgently. It was not much. We did not believe his sob story, but we did relent - perhaps too eager to rid ourselves of him. And of course, never saw him or the money again.

Joe and Helen (*Dreamcatcher*) and Bjorn and I decided that we would travel up the Red Sea in company: a decision that proved a real bonus both from the safety and the fun perspectives. We got on like a house on fire and looked forward to cruising together. During our short stay in Aden, we would go into town during the evening and select one of the hole-in-the-wall stalls to have our dinner. It was enlightening. At one of our favourite haunts, we were welcomed with open arms and seated at a table with benches; newspaper would be spread all over the table to serve as tablecloths. Then, they placed large, circular flat bread, all inflated straight out of the wood-fired oven. This was accompanied with a number of bowls containing a variety of spicy dips. We would tear off a piece of the bread and watch the bread collapse, then scoop up some of the tangy dips. The main course consisted of a chicken, cut into pieces and placed in the middle of the table on more newspaper. And thus we ate, with fingers, sauce dripping down our chins. Messy, but delicious!

A visit to Yemen would not be complete without a trip to the ancient capital of Sana'a, which is also a UNESCO world heritage site. I had not heard of this place before cruising and Yemen had not yet hit the press with the civil war going on there as I write. Everyone who had visited the old city raved about it. In cruising circles, such news travels down the line, each successive year's cruisers passing on their knowledge to the next generation of cruisers going through.

The four of us decided to travel the 420 kilometres by bus the following day for a three-day visit to the capital. First, however, we needed to visit the local police station to get a visa to be able to travel inland. Our seaman's shore passes for our short stay in Aden restricted us to the coastal town.

After a wild goose chase around town, we finally located the police station. After a short wait, we were informed that we

A Little Bit of MisChief

needed a photocopy of our passports. There were no facilities for photocopying either at the station or anywhere nearby. With the police station due to shut in about an hour we pleaded with the duty sergeant, or whoever he was that looked the most senior, to help us out.

He immediately asked us to follow him, and once outside, pointed to a paddy wagon. "Have we done something wrong?" Joe asked.

The policeman just smiled and pointed to us to get in. He drove us round a few blocks to a shop where he gesticulated we could get our copies done. Then it was back in the paddy wagon and back to the station in time to get our visas for our trip to Sana'a.

We decided to take the local bus to the ancient capital and see more of the country: a big mistake! The bus was ancient: smelly, tatty, dirty and patched up in all colours; it had definitely seen better days. The four of us managed to find enough empty seats towards the back for our seven-hour journey in the most uncomfortable seats possible. As for appreciating the open countryside: well, the desert was covered with low shrubs decorated in blue and pink. The only problem was that these were not flowers, but plastic bags.

The Yemeni are heavy qat users. Qat is the leaf of a bush that they chew. They pile the leaves in their mouths, bulging to one side, the size of a tennis ball. It was a stimulant of course, and we worried that so many of them followed this practice. Half the population seemed to be somewhat drugged most of the time. The qat could be easily obtained at most street corners or markets. It came in blue or pink plastic bags, which were eventually discarded.

The towns and villages the bus travelled through were filthy. We were cautious about using the local 'facilities' when needing to go to relieve ourselves. As in most Arabic countries, the loo was at ground level. Often the floor was wet, so you had to be careful not to let trousers or any other apparel touch the ground as you squatted with one leg on either side of the toilet bowl. Then came the next job of flushing and rinsing one's hands with a dirty bucket of water strategically placed near the loo. That was another challenge. Never had hand disinfectant and baby wipes come in so handy.

We had travelled through south-east Asia and eaten in so many open market places with no adverse effects. However, the shop we stopped at to have a bite on the way to Sana'a really challenged us. To their credit, we survived unscathed and continued on our seriously uncomfortable bus trip to the capital. After that experience, we were determined that we would not repeat the journey south. The fifty-dollar return trip by air was far too enticing.

Sana'a proved to be everything we had heard of, and more. As we made our way through one of the main gates to the old city, we couldn't believe the transformation. Suddenly the streets were clean and orderly.

Sana'a's old town dates back around 1000 years. It had reputedly been the place of residence of the Queen of Sheba. It was a remarkable and greatly enjoyable place to visit with tiny shops of all types peppered throughout. The city walls reminded me of the old fortifications back in Malta, where I hail from originally.

The architecture was unique. We loved the fact that the style of the new buildings complemented the local architectural theme that was attractive. It seemed to be a world apart from the rest of Yemen. Around every street corner, you would find yourself marvelling at the changing and complex design and intricate brickwork of the beautiful old buildings. The locals used brick colour to form all kinds of symmetrical shapes to great effect. A riverbed traversed the city. During the dry season, this became a thoroughfare with cars entering the paved riverbed through ramps as though on a freeway.

The local Yemeni people were friendly and helpful. It is with horror and a sense of despondency that I now think back to these wonderful people caught up in troubles so often beyond their control.

Our hotel was the "Arabia Felix" in the old part. It was a 500-year-old building. We were shown up to our rooms where we took up our overnight bags, climbing an uneven staircase. We had to duck to get in through the small doorways into the

A Little Bit of MisChief

most delightfully decorated bedrooms ever. Each room came with an ensuite bathroom, which of course was a recent addition. The rooms were airy, especially as the window frames and the apertures did not exactly match.

At breakfast the following morning, we struck up a conversation with a lovely Swiss lady whose daughter was an archaeologist in Yemen. She gave us some tips on what to see in the town and encouraged us to visit the outskirts. These were reputed to be as amazing as the old town itself. She provided us with the name of an excellent guide and arrangements were made for the following day.

After breakfast, we made our way to one of the tallest buildings in Sana'a, the famous Burj al Salam Hotel in the centre of the old town. We enjoyed some tea, Yemeni style, sitting cross-legged on cushions in the rooftop restaurant, admiring the surrounding panoramic views.

We were in for more amazing sights the next morning when Mohammed and his driver called for us in a brand new Toyota Land Cruiser. Mohammed was wearing traditional Yemeni clothes, which consisted of the *thoob*, a long-sleeved white robe, and the *Jambiyya*, which was the traditional curved ceremonial dagger worn at the waist. Mohammed spoke excellent English and was a pleasant man in his late twenties.

The ravines and cities surrounding the capital of Sana'a are spectacular: barren land with steep gorges and cliff tops with towns seemingly perched on the edges. In the middle of nowhere, we came across the amazing Rock Palace with intricate brickwork. We visited the ancient city of Thula just in time to witness a local wedding. At the historic town of Shebam, which was the old capital of the Yafurit dynasty in the 10th century, Mohammed had arranged for a traditional lunch. We were ushered to our own cubicle, where we were invited to squat on cushions around a table dressed with all sorts of delicacies.

We had 'oo'ed' and 'ah'hed' all day and were weary on the long return trip back to Sana'a. Suddenly, a Mercedes driven by a young Yemeni did a U-turn in front of us. There was no time to stop and we crashed right into the middle of the car. Luckily for all, no one was badly hurt, though we all suffered from bruises for a few days. The Mercedes was a write-off. Fortunately, our four-wheel drive vehicle had only suffered a bad dent to the left hand front mudguard and was still operable. Our driver was beside himself at the damage to his new Land Cruiser, and the young driver of the Mercedes was most apologetic.

We watched the exchange with interest. Mohammed arranged for a taxi to return us to the hotel. Meanwhile the young Yemeni would accompany him to a local panel beater so that the damage would definitely be paid for.

We flew down to Aden the next morning. The trip to Sana'a had been undoubtedly the highlight of our odyssey so far.

We were now preparing for our next leg: the 1500 miles up the Red Sea. We knew that the east African coast, especially at the southern end, was poverty-stricken. Though Yemen was a much poorer neighbour to Oman, we were able to find good quality provisions. Once again, we filled the boat with fuel, and could not help but compare the dirty diesel with the pristine stuff we had obtained in Oman.

Two days before our departure, I was struck down with a terrible upset stomach. Whilst I self-medicated, referring to our medical kit, we thought it would be prudent to visit a local hospital to ensure it was nothing ominous.

Enlisting the help of one of the taxi drivers outside the port gates, we sped off towards a supposedly international hospital. We ended up at a small and dingy doorway, somewhere down town. Just in case, I had taken our own sterile syringes from our medical kit with us. Upon arrival, nobody spoke much English. I waited half an hour before a young female doctor, from Georgia or thereabouts, wearing the full *hijab* and speaking reasonable English came to my rescue. She laughed at my sterile packs and showed me hers. She assured me that despite the run-down condition of the hospital, hygiene and medical standards were maintained. She saw to my afflictions, taking blood for testing and instructing us to wait until the results were

A Little Bit of MisChief

available in about two hours.

As good as her word, two hours later we were ushered into her consulting room again. The tests had ruled out anything serious such as malaria or typhoid, much to our relief. I had self-diagnosed and self-medicated correctly, thanks to the detailed instructions we had been provided with by the Travel Doctor in Perth. The young lady doctor apologetically asked us to pay for the visit before we could collect the extra medication she recommended. We were amused to find that the cost of the visit - including blood tests and medicine - came to the equivalent of seven dollars fifty, in contrast to our taxi fare, which was nine dollars.

We were now all ready to proceed to our next adventure. We would be out at sea for the next two months. And all four of us decided that haircuts were called for. With that in mind, we headed into Aden down town. There were male barbers all over the place, the same way hairdressing salons abound in western cities. However, we could not spot any place for women and resorted to asking locals for help. The result was that Helen and I ended up with five-dollar haircuts in someone's back yard. Meanwhile Joe and Bjorn were given the full treatment: haircut, an old-fashioned shave with hot towels and head massage. They paid the princely sum of about $25 each. To our amusement, the men turned up with almost totally shaven heads.

"You certainly got your money's worth there," I joked. "You won't need another haircut before we get to Egypt!"

Christina Gillgren

Sana'a: Old Meets New

Aden Knick Knack Shop

11
The Red Sea

By the time we arrived in Aden, after two agreeable crossings and a safe trip along the southern coast of Yemen, we were 'passaged out'. We had not given enough thought to the last part of our journey. We knew that winds in the Red Sea blow from the north most of the year. The best weather window to go north was between mid-February and April, when these winds were at their weakest.

We left Aden on the 9th March on a sunny morning with benign north-easterlies moving us along the coast. Our plan was to coast hop as much as possible, cruising in company with *Dreamcatcher* and *Bluesipp*. We were tired of the long hauls and wanted to see more of the landscape and the countries we were going through. We therefore decided to coast hop up the Red Sea through Eritrea, then Sudan and to Egypt.

This was probably our one major tactical error in this last part of our journey.

On advice from the harbour master at Aden, our first hop was a short four-hour trip to Ras Imran, on the southern coast of Yemen. We had a pleasant sundowner with our cruising friends and retired early. Our alarms were set for 5.00am the following morning for a longer hop to the next anchorage.

At around two in the morning, we suddenly heard footsteps on deck.

"Stay down here and out of sight!" Bjorn ordered. He quickly pulled on a pair of shorts. He opened the cockpit hatch and shouted out loud, as he stepped out into the cockpit.

"What the hell are you doing on our boat?"

A fishing boat lay alongside. There were two men and the third, a very young lad in military gear, was in the process of climbing on board our yacht. Bjorn's yell so surprised him that he almost fell back into the water.

"No stop here. Military. Go! Go!" the young chap ordered.

"This boat is Australian territory!" Bjorn retorted. "You cannot come on board without permission. You must knock first!"

"Go. No stay here."

"The captain in Aden told us we can stop here as long as we do not go ashore." Bjorn replied, using hands and gesticulating to try and convey meaning.

"All go!" The young soldier continued, holding up his gun and pointing to all the other boats.

"The other boats are still asleep. On the blue boat, there is only one man and he must rest as he is sailing alone. We are leaving at sun-up anyway, so leave us in peace until then and we will all go together. A few hours will not make a difference."

This exchange continued for a few more minutes and somehow the message filtered through. We were left in peace to resume our rudely interrupted sleep. But after getting over the scare, it was impossible to lie down again. We resorted to the traditional cup of tea - laced with some brandy - to calm our tattered nerves. It just goes to show that despite being outwardly composed and carrying on with life, deep down we knew we were in waters that were rife with pirates and other troubles. The rule of law was unpredictable and often subject to local whims or interpretations, to say the least.

We left a few hours later and put down anchor at Ras al Arah, in preparation for the long haul through to the entrance to the Red Sea at Bab al Mandeb. This time we took no chances. We decided to leave at two o'clock the following morning. We hoped this would pre-empt any further confrontation with any

A Little Bit of MisChief

military that may have been around. It would also give us more time to get to our next destination, which was 80 nautical miles away, in daylight.

The transition from Indian Ocean to Red Sea could not be more dramatic. We were leaving the wonderfully reliable trade winds of the Indian Ocean. The southern entry to the Red Sea, at Bab al Mandeb, is a notorious blowhole. The local lore holds that if it blows 15 knots in Aden, it would be double at the Bab. We had chosen a day with lighter winds, and had a very fast and pleasant passage through the Bab. However, some 20 miles north, the strong southerlies set in. Suddenly we encountered the full frontal and were flying with 35-40 knots of wind behind us.

Our decision to coast hop meant that we ended up tacking into our first anchorage in the archipelago south of Assab and into these strong winds. The Eritrean coast was a 'moonscape': not much to see, no villages to visit, but relentless windy conditions, often from a northerly direction. This sometimes held us up for days, waiting for gentler winds.

Given the bleak landscape, it would have made more sense to use the southerlies to make as much progress as possible northwards. In fact, most of our friends had wisely chosen to head for Massawa in Eritrea, about a third of the way up the Red Sea.

Mersa Dudo, in Eritrea, was the only stop where we met locals. There was a crater on the tiny peninsula overlooking the bay, which we set out to explore. A small fishermen's enclave was set up along the shore, with nets spread out on the beach for repairs. We spent three days waiting for the northerly 35-knot winds to die down. It was also here that I put our medical kit to good use. One of the local fishermen had a badly swollen foot, the result of an insect bite. The fishermen sought our assistance.

Whilst we had all sorts of medicine on board *Mischief*, Bjorn and I conferred with our other sailing partners. We decided it was too risky to provide any of our medication to the local fisherman. These were poor Eritreans, living in very basic conditions. Instead, we took some vinegar and cotton wool ashore, together with some antihistamine cream. I washed the wound, as all the fishermen gathered around to watch the proceedings. Then I applied the cream. Using the sand as a board, we explained that the foot needed to be elevated for the next couple of days and the cream applied three times daily.

In gratitude, the fishermen gave us an enormous fillet of fresh fish - probably a barracuda. We never felt remotely threatened. These incredibly poor fishermen were shy, but warm and friendly, when approached.

Once past Mersa Dudo, the winds started to abate. The weather windows allowed us to sail further up the coast. As we got closer to Massawa, the waters became less murky. Gradually, coral started to appear. Our anchorage at Shumma Island's Port Smyth, 20 miles east of Massawa, was not a port at all. It was an excellent, beautiful anchorage inside a coral reef: one of the loveliest spots we had visited to date, with clear waters and full of colourful sea life.

We did not stop in Massawa. Word on the cruisers' net was that the authorities were insisting that yachts berth alongside a concrete jetty. As a result, several yachts ended up being badly damaged. The swell/surge rendered the fenders useless in these conditions, and their yachts kept hitting the jetty.

The extensive reef area around Massawa has some fantastic anchorages. We would call into a bay close to midday. With the sun directly overhead, you could see the channels through the reefs more clearly. We would spend a few days waiting for the next weather window. As we waited, up to a dozen yachts would arrive in dribs and drabs. The minute the weather was again favourable, we would all head off. This was going on up and down the Red Sea, with anchorages experiencing a boa constrictor expansion and contraction of the number of yachts.

At this stage we were still travelling with *Dreamcatcher* and *Blue Sipp*. John's crew on *Blue Sipp* had left in Aden and John was now sailing single-handedly. Therefore, where night sailing was required, *Dreamcatcher* and *Mischief* would take it in turns to keep an eye out for *Blue Sipp*. Whilst John slept, the boat sailed on with the automatic pilot. In case of emergency, John had his radio next to his head. We would call him to wake him up.

A Little Bit of MisChief

We were now past the helpful if blustery southerlies, and facing the northerlies. We still had two thirds of the way to go. We had learnt that, in the Red Sea, it is all about patience, and then optimising the small weather windows. Sightseeing stops were limited to the 'must do's. The rest was up to trying to choose the most picturesque anchorages, in order to see as much as possible.

The radio net that I was still running now had about 80 yachts reporting in from time to time. The information relays were extremely helpful. Two occasions in particular demonstrate this. The first concerned our friends on *Sparrow*, and the trouble they had had with their propeller since leaving Phuket. One of the cruisers learnt about their problem over the net. He had a similar 'feathering' propeller and advised that it was no use changing the propeller blades individually. Both the hub and the three blades needed to be changed simultaneously, as these formed an integral unit. Such a small detail, but it made all the difference.

The second incident concerned a Canadian by the name of Peter and his small yacht, whose name escaped me at the time of writing, perhaps for the best. Peter was sailing single-handedly and ran into a little island in the north end of the Bab al Mandeb whilst asleep on one of the legs of the trip. He ended up with a hole to the bow of his fibreglass yacht. The radio was agog with calls for help. Everyone rummaged through their stock on board to see what we could supply Peter with, to help with repairs.

Armed with fibreglass strips, resin and more - all contributions from yachties - Peter called into the harbour at Assab in Eritrea and undertook the repairs himself.

The radio net helped yachts anticipate what was coming next. The trailblazers related their experiences, good and bad, to the rest of the cruisers. Messages travelled up and down the Red Sea. We supported and helped each other as much as possible.

A couple on a catamaran got caught inside a reef for about 10 days as strong winds buffeted them. Many of us noticed that morale on board was getting low. And we were all tired after the exceedingly long trek from Thailand. The twice-daily contact with the rest of the cruising community helped reassure them that they were not 'alone'. They were assured that conditions would improve to allow them to progress further north.

We got to know so many boats at the various anchorages and met wonderful people from all over the world. It established a great sense of camaraderie. It was a joyful experience, when entering a popular anchorage such as Khor Nowarat, to identify who's there. This beautiful spot lay in an inlet behind two long islands. The inlet itself contained a number of sand cays and other islands sitting in the tranquil waters.

We were sitting in the cockpit one morning, reading a book and sipping a cup of tea. Bjorn looked up. "What is that? Camels?" He fetched the binoculars. "There's a train of camels wafting across the shallow waters between islands. It looks like a mirage."

We were held up at Khor Nowarat awaiting favourable winds. We spent the time exploring the area, running around in the dinghy and taking long walks. We had wonderful beach 'pot luck' dinners. Every boat in the anchorage would bring along a pot with whatever they had cooked, and we would all share. This was usually accompanied with an evening of guitar playing and singing late into the nights.

After four days, the winds abated sufficiently to allow us to proceed to our next destination, which was the old slave port of Sawakin. We waved goodbye to two other boats, one of which was *Orca Joss* (New Zealand), and embarked on the hazardous overnight sail that took us through an area strewn with reefs. We checked our route with *Dreamcatcher* and *Bluesipp* to ensure a safe passage. By 9.00am we were outside Sawakin.

"Let's see! Ah, according to the cruisers' net, the local contact is…" I started out as we navigated the narrow channel into the quaint bay inside the reef.

"Don't tell me… Mohammed!" Bjorn laughed. Every boat agent or contact that we had met all the way from Indonesia bore this name. This particular Mohammed, a tall handsome Sudanese, was incredibly organised. No sooner had we put down our anchor in this serene though somewhat eerie

A Little Bit of MisChief

anchorage that Mohammed asked to come on board. He was ferried across by the owner of the last boat he had visited. Within half an hour we had all our needs organised: fuel, gas cylinders refill, Sudanese currency, visas and cruising permits, information on the area and on getting to the capital, and more.

Bjorn ferried Mohammed ashore in our dinghy. Sure enough, the next morning we watched Mohammed's daily ritual during the two-month window when most boats travelled up the Red Sea. He would arrive in his dark green Mercedes 180, kicking up a sandstorm on the unpaved roads to the anchorage. With him would be a pick-up truck with all our needs, including water and fuel.

The waters along the Sudanese coast contain some of the most beautiful coral we have ever seen. The old port of Sawakin itself is what is called a *marsa*, a break in the fringing reef with an inlet and a natural anchorage. A small island in the middle of the anchorage housed the old Sawakin slave fortification, now an eerie mass of crumbled coral walls. This was a significant moment of reflection in our journey. We could not help but think of the horrors, unbelievable terror and suffering that those caught up in the slave trade went through. The islet was linked to the ramshackle village on the mainland by a small land bridge. A basic but bustling market place operated on shore, alongside the anchorage. The vegetables looked good, although the selection was limited. The bread smelt wonderful, as long as you got to it early in the morning. We did not touch the meat, hanging in the open air and covered in flies.

The next day, Jannine and John, on board their boat *Orca Joss*, came in to the anchorage. We had not expected to see them again so soon. Word soon spread of their unpleasant experience and lucky escape.

We caught up with them one evening. And this is their story:

"The next morning after you and *Dreamcatcher* left the anchorage, two young men in their twenties came over the reef in a dugout canoe. They came alongside our stern deck, which is where I stood and is high to climb onto. The 'mother ship' was anchored at the outer island with four to six men watching. One of the men was chewing qat. I also spotted two machetes in the canoe." John told us.

Qat was the local narcotic everyone seems to chew endlessly in this part of the world, similar to what we had experienced in Yemen.

"The feeling we had was entirely different from other visiting fishermen we met. I stood clear from them and Jannine kept talking to me from below. They were looking over the boat gear and studying the layout," John continued. "I had serious misgivings but gave them a food parcel and sent them off, hoping that would be the end of it. But then the master ship picked them up as they crossed the reef. It immediately headed toward the entrance to the anchorage.

"We were ready to leave that night so we immediately took up our anchor. We charged out at full speed. They gained on us in the calms and were edging to our starboard bow. So I edged away to port.

"This was definitely not friendly. If they came within a boat length I had determined to turn and ram them as our only defence."

Orca Joss was a steel boat whereas the fishing boat was made of wood. There is no doubt as to who would have come out the worse off in a ramming match.

"They were less than 50 metres off and closing slowly," Jannine continued. "When we hit the outer swell they slowed and we did not. We were doing eight knots with the engine screaming. Lucky for us, they turned away crossing our stern towards the west shore into calmer waters."

This close encounter with pirates became the talk of the day. John told us that Mohammed had pointed out a number of hulls lying on one side of the port anchorage. They resembled the type of boat construction that had so worried our friends on *Orca Joss*. Mohammed described the culprits as 'very dangerous Yemeni/Somali men', usually renegade fishermen. Their nefarious deeds were well known in Sudan. John and Jannine felt lucky to have outrun them and survived the experience.

One evening, we went to a sundowner on board *Circe*, and noticed that everyone was not their usual merry selves.

A Little Bit of MisChief

"What's up?" I queried.

"We have just received some bad news via email," Birte started out. "Do you remember Malcolm on *Mr Bean* in Langkawi? Well he was murdered. Three young Burmese men tried to rob the boat and it all went very wrong!"

"What? They were the last people we saw before we left Nai Harn. What happened? Do you have any details?" This was devastating. Here we were, in dangerous waters, and this had happened in Thailand, normally a safe cruising ground with hardly any crime to speak about.

Joe and Helen on *Dreamcatcher* heard later that Malcolm had challenged the attackers who turned on him and killed him. His wife ended up being 'trussed up naked like a chicken' for nine hours while they ransacked the couple's boat off the Thai coast. She eventually managed to escape the pirates but not the trauma. It was a sobering moment. We were glad that we had decided to cruise up the Red Sea in company with the ever-sensible Joe, and his lovely wife Helen.

One morning a number of us took the rickety and colourful local bus into Port Sudan. As is often the case in towns such as these, jewellery shops with marble facades stood alongside clapped-out lean-tos in corrugated iron: riches and poverty rubbing shoulders. We walked through the bustling main street strewn with all types of vendors. At one street stall we bought the most delicious pita style bread with fresh filling. We also treated ourselves to ice cream from a newly opened classy ice cream parlour.

A few days later we were on our way again up the Red Sea via the beautiful Tullia Islands, a group of three sandy cays. The area was covered with reefs and the coral was out of this world - probably the best I have ever seen: vibrant colours ranging from white, yellow, bright green, deep pink, orange and the most incredible hues of blue. The Sudanese waters supported an abundant fish supply. Out came our fishing gear. Within minutes, we caught a fish - a 1.2 metre barracuda.

Bjorn and I were so thrilled with our first catch that we

immediately invited our fellow sailors *Dreamcatcher* and *Blue Sipp* to share the fish. Meanwhile Bjorn cleaned the fish and hung it off the side to drain the blood, as we had been instructed by other fisher-yachties.

We were all ready, fish cleaned, cut up, prepared with seasoning, herbs and lemon. A good tranche was happily baking *al cartoccio* on our trusty 'barbie' (Australian for 'barbeque') on the stern of the boat. Joe, Helen and John came on board. We had cut up the rest of the fish into additional tranches so there was a good slice of barracuda for each of our friends. To demonstrate the size, we proudly showed off the obligatory photograph with Bjorn standing alongside the fish.

"Look at that! Our first meal from fish we caught ourselves," I boasted.

"Are you sure that is a barracuda?" Joe asked.

Down I went into the cabin and got out my fishing bible. With book in hand, it seemed the obvious thing to do was to read the accompanying text. Silly me!

"Oh No!" I groaned, really disappointed. "Listen to this. 'Barracuda, being a predator fish, can be full of ciguatera, a nerve poison found in fish feeding off the coral in some parts of the world.' Is the Red Sea one of these areas?"

We all looked at each other, acknowledging the inevitable. We were not sure, and we were too far from civilization to take any risks.

That was it! Out came the 'John West' cans of tuna and salmon, and overboard went the freshly barbecued barracuda, smelling divine. It was a poor alternative, to say the least.

I have never been able to live down our 'first' catch. News of our mishap spread up and down the Red Sea, only to be told later that barracuda in this area was probably quite safe.

It was at this point that we decided that perhaps fishing off the boat whilst under way was not for us. There were plenty of fish available, but we always seemed to end up with very large fish. As ours was a centre cockpit (cockpit in the centre of the boat instead of aft), it made bringing in the fish and cleaning them more difficult and messy. Bjorn - in charge of cleaning and filleting the fish - would often have to work on the narrow

A Little Bit of MisChief

side-decks.

As an alternative we would, where possible, buy fish from local fishermen, thus helping support them.

Another 'must' for us was a stopover at a *khor* along this coast. We had experienced our first *khor* at Khor Nowarat. But other sailors further up the coast were waxing lyrical about the beautiful and different inlets in northern Sudan. A *khor*, another term for *marsa*, is like a fjord. It can sometimes wind inland a couple of kilometres. Khor Shinab certainly lived up to its reputation. The narrow cut through the reef revealed a landscape with beautiful desert colours and undulating hills that led to a secure and pretty anchorage about a mile or two inland.

We set the anchor and Bjorn went into the cabin to log our arrival. He smelt diesel, and did a quick check. "Shit! We've got a very small leak in our fuel tank!"

Some panicked thinking followed. It was a tiny leak, but we still had a way to go before we reached anywhere sensible to have a good look. Over a cup of tea in the cockpit and after conferring with Joe over the radio, Bjorn and I made our decision. Whilst a patch of good weather with little wind prevailed, it made sense to take advantage of the weather window to make headway north before the leak became significant.

We prepared to leave. Joe called us on the radio to let us know that they would keep us company. And so we set off to cross Foul Bay to southern Egypt. From there it was a short hop to Port Ghalib, the first marina since Thailand.

As luck would have it, just as we were motoring out of the *Khor*, our French friends on *Blue Marine* came motoring in. We had last seen them in Phuket and would have loved to get together again. As it was, we made do with a radio exchange and a promise to catch up properly at Hurghada Marina in Egypt.

We had been motor sailing in light winds for about four hours when Bjorn suddenly yelled out to me: "Reef Ahead! Stop the motor!"

"I can't see anything. ...And the chart-plotter does not show anything." But I immediately took the motor out of gear to slow down.

"Back up... turn around! Fast!"

Bjorn ran to the chart-plotter and zoomed in. There it was: a horseshoe shaped, mostly submerged reef. With little wind and no swell, the waves were only gently breaking on the reef.

"*Mischief*! *Mischief*! *Dreamcatcher* calling!" I did not answer immediately as I was busy reversing the boat.

"Glad to see you have turned around! ...What happened? Why were you were sailing so close to the reef?" Joe asked us over the radio.

"*Dreamcatcher*, this is *Mischief*. We had the chart zoomed out. For some reason it stopped showing the reef." It was quite scary to think that we could have run aground here, in the middle of nowhere.

We had heard stories of this occurring. Different charts of the same area sometimes showed up dissimilar data. Usually when we plotted the next leg of a trip, we would prepare the waypoints on the chart-plotter to ensure we navigated clear of all dangers. This was my job. Sometimes, in tricky waters with a lot of obstacles, Bjorn would check me. As we had decided to make a straight run up north across Foul Bay, I had zoomed out of the map. My mistake was that I failed to follow up, which was to then zoom in again on the map and ensure there were no nasties along the way. Sometimes when you zoom in and out of maps, you access different maps that may not reflect the same data. Sailors, be warned!

We were almost caught out but for Bjorn's keen eyesight and lookout.

After almost 40 hours of motoring, with some helpful north-easterlies, we crossed the notorious (for its winds) and appropriately named Foul Bay. As we approached the top of the bay, the north-westerly winds suddenly picked up blowing at 25 knots, right on the nose, kicking up a steep sea. We decided the most prudent action was to seek refuge at Ras Banas, behind a promontory in the south of Egypt.

"My hair feels completely 'salted' through!" I told Bjorn. Even though we were showering in fresh water, it only took a minute out in the cockpit to feel that the sea spray had done its

A Little Bit of MisChief

job again.

After three days stuck amidst the most stunning coral but with intense wind stopping us from going ashore, we were rather cabin sick and longed to stretch our legs. We decided to risk it. Going ashore in a prohibited area, however, was not a good idea. No sooner had we turned the corner to look at the sea conditions outside the bay when a guard challenged us, very agitated, rifle pointed straight at us.

"No tourist here! No!"

We tried to calm him down. Speaking clearly and softly we explained that we were just stretching our legs. This did not help at all. The gun was waved at us more ominously. Then the guard shouted something at us about speaking Arabic.

"Go on, Chris. Speak to him in Maltese," Bjorn suggested.

I did. I explained in Maltese, which is similar to Arabic, that we had just come to look at the sea conditions outside the bay, so we could move on. Again, I spoke slowly and said that we would turn back and go to our boats immediately.

Wonder of wonder, the soldier seemed to understand me. The gun came down and he gaped at us incredulously. It wasn't his type of Arabic, but could tell it was an Arabic based language, close enough to understand.

"*Morru, morru*", he said, waving us with his gun to return to the boats, which we did as fast as we could. With that gun being waved about so ominously, we almost walked on water!

With another two to three day window of calms forecast, and the fuel leak remaining constant and manageable, we set off for Dolphin Reef. We spent a wonderful night in calm waters in this coral heaven. There were a few other cruisers at the anchorage, including our friends Annie and Tony on *Sunburnt*. We were rewarded in the morning by one of the most remarkable experiences so far.

We were anchored behind a two to three kilometre stretch of reef, in ten metres of crystal clear flat sea, our chain meandering along the sand towards the anchor. Sitting in the cockpit with a cup of tea and breakfast, we saw what looked like a reef coming towards us. Binoculars showed dozens of fins, and within a few minutes we were surrounded by close to a hundred dolphins.

I immediately got onto the radio: "*Dreamcatcher*! *Sunburnt*! Quick! Up on deck!"

They swam gracefully towards our boats, cavorting between us, whilst a few provided a stunning display moving backwards above water propelled by their fins.

There was only one thing for it. Fins and masks came out, and before Bjorn realised it, I was in the water. As soon as the air bubbles cleared us, I saw about thirty dolphins swimming up right at me. Oh shit! It only took a split second, but the thought went through my mind: did they know I was there?

I need not have worried.

We were surrounded by these beautiful, majestic mammals. Some young people on board the Danish sailing boat *Njord* got into the water and started frolicking around with the dolphins. The younger fish responded and joined in the fun. Soon the water was all churned up, as the dolphins swam playfully around and between us, jumping out of the water, and joyously splashing about. This experience remains one of the highlights of our odyssey.

We felt elated that, despite our short stay at this fabulous spot, we had been honoured with such a glorious spectacle. With the fuel problem on our mind, we were happy to pull up anchor before lunch. In company with *Dreamcatcher*, we started on the overnight run to Port Ghalib.

After the poverty and basic living of many of the places along the Red Sea, Port Ghalib was amazing - from the sublime to the ridiculous!

Built on the Port Grimaud style of marinas, this modern, sprawling marina complex included colourful luxury apartments and stunning hotels. The hotel next to our quay had an exquisite swimming pool that we could use. We could also walk along to the colourful outer reef and swim in the Red Sea. The boardwalk offered a selection of excellent coffee houses, restaurants, boutiques and shops, including some of the international up-market franchises. We strolled along the quays surrounding the marina in the evenings, debating where to have our evening meal. We couldn't help but be astounded - not least of all because beyond this development was just miles and

A Little Bit of MisChief

miles of sand.

We were overjoyed, tired but elated that most of our Red Sea journey was over. We took the opportunity to wash the desert sand out of the sails and rigging, and everywhere else. It took three rinses to get the worst of the sand off our boat, with Bjorn hoisting me up the mast, hosepipe in hand, to wash the boat down from the very top.

The next job was less fun, but necessary. We emptied the remaining diesel out of our tank into jerry cans and then set about dealing with the leak in the fuel tank. Yet again, the cruiser fraternity came good, donating fibreglass mat and resin for the job. Bjorn used a nut and bolt through the hole and then fibre-glassed all around it. It was a temporary fix. The only real solution was to throw out the old steel diesel tank, which had served its purpose well for 20 years, and install a new one. It went down on our 'to-do' list.

After a week's rest, repairs done successfully and some provisioning, we left for the 113 nautical mile trip to Hurghada Marina. We intended to spend at least a month in Egypt, to be able to do some land travel.

Christina Gillgren

Sundowner at Port Smythe

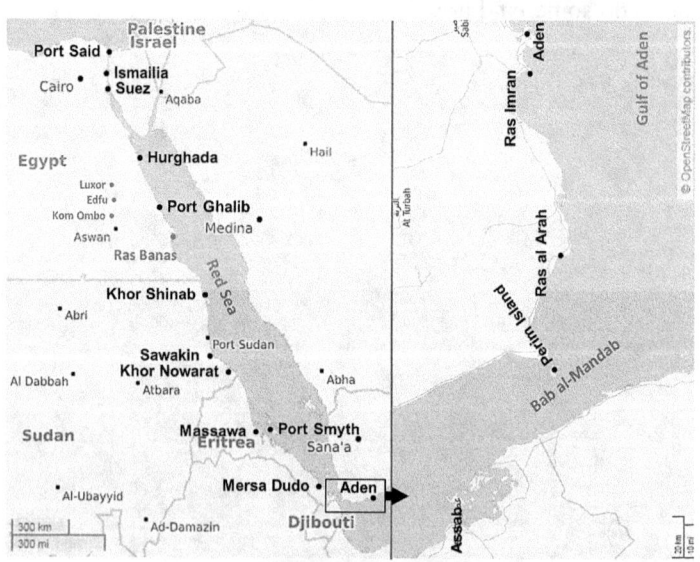

Aden to Port Said Route

12
An Egyptian Escapade

Hurghada was a bustling town, popular with divers. We enjoyed some of the wonderful restaurants both in the marina and in the town. We found a philosopher among one of the taxi drivers at the marina who doubled up as a guide. On one occasion, our cabbie was in a talkative mood. I don't know how the conversation swung around to religions - certainly not a topic we would normally have embarked upon. I let Bjorn engage in the conversation and was only half-listening, when he summed up: "Ahh! ...different journey, same destination!" he told us. If only we all can be as generous with each other.

Hurghada was also a tourist mecca but somehow without the hassling that goes on in other tourist parts of Egypt. In fact, it was usual to walk into a shop and the shopkeeper/assistant would assure us that their place was 'hassle-free'. The diving industry was well established. This was not surprising, given the wonderful pristine waters and coral reefs full of fish of all hues. In fact, we found that this sea is probably one of the only seas left that has not been over-fished.

It would have been silly to come all the way to Egypt and miss out on visiting the world heritage pyramid and temple sites. With this in mind, Helen and Joe (*Dreamcatcher*) and Bjorn and I visited the local friendly travel agent who bent over backward to help us.

Christina Gillgren

Joe had worked out a rough itinerary. At first, our travel agent was aghast that we would even consider taking a *felucca*, a traditional Nile sailing boat with gaff rig, instead of a luxury river cruise ship. We were adamant. For better or for worse, we wanted to sample the local 'flavour' - immerse ourselves fully in the experience.

Our agent organised a 10-day all-inclusive tour, which would start in Cairo. From there we would proceed down the Nile to Luxor and Aswan and other Egyptian sites of interest. Guides were booked to meet us at each destination, escorting us to the sites, back and forth to hotels, and to meals. We had heard many horror stories about Egypt and tipping. So we made sure that all the guides were fully paid for, and that tips were included in the price.

Our new adventure started out with a reasonable bus ride to the capital city of Cairo. The three star hotel where we were accommodated overlooked the pyramids on the outskirts of Giza. The tour commenced with the obligatory visit to the Museum of Antiquities. It was a zoo by any other name. We could hardly hear our guide speak above the cacophony: there were so many tour groups crammed into the historic building, giving their spiel in a variety of languages. And I was glad I had worn my sneakers to keep up with the pace.

After this experience, a cup of coffee seemed in order. Then it was time to tackle Cairo's renowned outdoor *Souq*. Wherever we went there were crowds: noise, hustle and bustle prevailed, as throngs pushed this way and that to get about. Even more annoying was the endless harassment and begging by children. Not even this, though, could detract from the wonderful *Souq* atmosphere, spices and scents wafting out of every nook and cranny.

The second day was saner. It started with the visit to the temple at Sakkara. Excavations were under way, with the guide explaining how the archaeologists went about their business. We visited the obligatory carpet factory to watch carpet weaving in progress. Of course, they sat us down with tea whilst the salesmen tried to get us to commit to purchasing a carpet.

A Little Bit of MisChief

"We're on a boat," Bjorn explained. "Our only home at present."

"Oh! Well ...look ...we have small carpets for your boat!"

We escaped as politely as possible to visit the Great Pyramid. It rose majestically above the surrounding bleak landscape. Two policemen rode on camels, guarding the site.

We were startled when approached by one of the policemen who asked for a 'tip' for posing for a photo for Bjorn. We were not so amused when, whilst taking a photo in a nearby temple, a guy in traditional Arabic garb jumped into the background to appear in the photo. Then he cheekily demanded money for posing for us.

One highlight of this part of the trip was the visit to the church where Joseph and Mary were reputed to have lived with Jesus. They had fled to Egypt, following the slaughtering of young boys up to two years of age (the Slaughter of the Innocents) by King Herod.

Next on our itinerary was an overnight trip on a surprisingly comfortable sleeper-train from Cairo. We were headed up river - and down south - to Aswan. The ride along the Nile Delta was worthwhile, as we watched villagers toil along the narrow delta that then gave way to a moonscape.

After a light lunch in Aswan, we had enough time to visit an obelisk quarry. Huge pillars of rock were carved out of the granite. I am not sure how they succeeded in extracting them in one piece, but there was ample evidence of a number of broken obelisks. A visit to the temple at Philae at the downstream side of the Aswan dam followed. The temple had been moved to higher ground to avoid being flooded, when the dam was built in Upper Egypt (the southernmost part of Egypt).

The highlight of our trip was Abu Simbel, situated several hundred miles further to the south. We left in the early morning for the 3-hour journey that turned out to be a nightmare bus trip. There must have been about forty vehicles - buses, vans and the odd car - stuffed to capacity with eager tourists, like us. Utterly insane Egyptian drivers drove us in convoy at incredibly high speed along desert roads, accompanied by the military to guard against terrorists. At the speed we were going, which we judged to be over 150 kilometres per hour, one false move by one driver and we would all be history. When we complained, we were told that this was for our safety - to make it more difficult for hijackers!

The trip was well worth the journey. The sight of the temple of Ramses II at Abu Simbel was something to be witnessed to be appreciated. The engineering feat to move this temple to its present site from lower ground - again to avoid being submerged - was amazing. I can assure you that Bjorn - ever the engineer - eyed the building carefully, trying to work out how this was achieved.

The temple was chock-full with historic events of the epic, heroic type showing feats such as the conquest of the African slaves. Its' size and the attention to detail were impressive. Next door was the temple to Ramses' wife, Queen Nefertari. It was just as remarkable.

After another breakneck-speed return to Aswan, we were glad we had opted for a relaxed pace as we commenced our return journey northwards. It was time to board the *felucca*, to sail down river towards Luxor. We spent three days and two wonderful nights sleeping under the stars, sailing gently by. Captain Robi and his crew, Mohammed, made us feel very welcome. Cushions were strewn over a flat deck for our comfort; we ate, drank and slept there.

And so we set off! Calls of nature were attended to by a quick stop towards the bank, where a tree or shrub afforded some privacy. All meals were catered for on board - and delicious they were too.

I distinctly recall our first evening when Captain Robi pulled the boat on to the sandy beach and secured it, just after the sun had set. I looked up at the star-studded sky, and then around me, a smile from ear to ear, reflecting how lucky we were to have had these wonderful experiences. It definitely beat the luxury river boats.

During a stopover on the second day, Captain Robi took us to see a Nubian village. We were welcomed with open arms and invited to join one of the families in a hearty meal, sitting around on cushions and drinking *Chay*, the local tea.

A Little Bit of MisChief

Time flew by and soon it was back to terra firma in Kom Ombo, north of Aswan. Here lay one of the sights I most appreciated: an unusual 'double' temple, built during the Ptolemaic dynasty. Our guide explained that the building was unique because its double design meant that it served two sets of gods: the falcon god Horus and the crocodile god Sobek. I was entranced by the depiction of a set of surgical instruments, featuring in particular the ones pertaining to childbirth. These were complete with birthing stool with hole in the middle, and forceps.

Another temple along the way was at Edfu. To be honest, distinct and unique as each temple was, we were beginning to suffer from temple fatigue. We were happy to call it a day after that.

We had been fairly protected from the 'baksheesh' and begging at the marinas. But our tour of the incredibly magnificent historical sites around Egypt had been marred by the constant demand for 'gifts'. It had left us somewhat jaded.

However, a visit to Egypt would not have been complete without a visit to the Valley of the Kings, just outside Luxor. Tutankhamun's tomb was one of the highlights, but we also enjoyed the visit to Hatshepsut's temple in Karnac. Our guide informed us that Hatshepsut was famous for being the only woman to rule in Egypt as a Pharaoh. To this end, she depicted herself as being both male and female. Legend has it that she donned Pharaoh's robes and sported a beard.

The only notable thing about our full day bus ride from Luxor to Hurghada was the agitated Arabic monologue, at full blast, that the driver insisted on sharing with the passengers. Being foreigners, and guests in the country, we suffered in silence. We were very appreciative when, after about four hours of ear bashing, a local approached the driver. He asked that the bus speakers to be turned off. The driver could still listen, but at least we were spared the ghetto blaster.

◇◇◇

Refreshed after a three-week rest at the marina and our tour of the Nile, boat restocked and cleaned, we were ready for the next chapter of our adventures. We left the marina, with all its colour and noise. One thing we were not likely to miss was the calls to prayer from about ten competing mosques surrounding the marina. That was no fun!

We soon realised that our Red Sea challenge was not over yet. As we approached the end of April, the northerlies became more pronounced, and endured much longer.

We headed to Suez, with a mixture of three to four hour calms, some heavy swell as we crossed the busy shipping lanes, occasional strong winds and a few marginal anchorages. We were lucky indeed to get to Port Suez within a couple of days.

Here started our transit saga. We negotiated with one of the advertised Suez Canal agents to look after our transit through the Canal. We were five boats, all of whom were friends by now. We wanted to tackle the Canal on the following day. Towards eleven in the evening, an agent finally appeared. He advised us of our start time the next day. Then he gave each of us the bill for the transit.

"What!" exclaimed Bjorn. "This is extortion! No way does the gross tonnage on our boat amount to 30 tons."

The cost for the transit was worked out on the gross tonnage a vessel could take on board as freight. Our boat, fully laden, weighed about 13 tons. To carry 30 tons would surely sink the boat.

"They've done the same for us," echoed Joe. Everyone was reacting the same way. A quick 'pow-wow' by all the yachties gathered there, and we decided to protest the bills.

"But the pilot? He come at five o'clock tomorrow morning!" moaned the agent.

"You can't come so late in the evening with such a bill and expect us to just pay up!"

Our cruising guides provided tables to work out a yacht's gross tonnage. We had estimated our costs and they had amounted to only about a third of what was being asked of each of us.

So, on strike we went! The agent phoned for backup, but this was to no avail. We decided to stand our ground. We had heard various stories from yachts that had preceded us in crossing the

A Little Bit of MisChief

Canal. We were therefore prepared.

The next morning, Bjorn - elected spokesperson - visited the Suez Canal Authority. He went over the accounts with one of the key people there. It was decided to re-measure the boats. This was done in the afternoon. Before long, new bills were presented to us, much closer to our estimates.

Happy with the fact that we had stood up for our rights and of course, with the outcome, we were now ready for the transit. We immediately informed the cruising net via radio of our victory. Hopefully, the experience would not be repeated.

The journey up the Suez Canal was in two stages, the first taking us to Ismailia where we had to stop over for two days, and the second through to Port Said in the Mediterranean.

The next morning a pilot presented himself bright and early, and came on board. He made himself at home, and commandeered our radio. He then spent the whole day on the radio chatting with everyone else. As we approached our destination in Ismailia, he started to fret and demand his gift. We had been warned that despite being paid as part of the transit fee, the pilots would demand a tip. We had our gifts ready for the pilots, and had decided on 20 dollars and a carton of cigarettes per pilot for each of the two legs up the Canal. Unfortunately, only one of the cartons was a Marlboro. We had decided to keep this for the second pilot.

"This no good! I want Marlboro."

"I'm sorry," Bjorn answered, "But this is what they had when we went to town to purchase the cigarettes. We do not smoke."

We were not prepared to have to hand out cigarettes to everyone who grabbed our ropes - even though we did not want them to. And to whoever even remotely got the chance to come near our boat. In fact, as we approached the quay in Ismailia, a fight broke out as to who would catch the mooring lines. These 'marineros' ended up almost crashing our boat into *Orca Joss*. It was only through some quick thinking by Jannine that we avoided a nasty collision.

The pilot for the next leg was a strange person, with a large black bump in the middle of his forehead. He spoke enough

English to communicate with us, but kept to himself, insisting on steering *Mischief*. As lunchtime approached, and time for a meal which we had prepared for him, he handed me the helm, took off into the cabin. Without so much as a by your leave, he entered the heads (bathrooms on board). We then heard water splashing.

"What on earth is going on? Bjorn, can you go check?"

It was time for midday prayers, and this pilot just put his feet in our basin, splashed water all over, used our towels and then came out to pray.

We would have happily accommodated him and his requirements, had he but asked.

The last farce was when we handed the remaining carton of Marlboro cigarettes (plus the cash) to this pilot at Port Said. He removed all the packing from the carton and tucked the packets into his shirt and all over his body. Then he insisted we hand out cigarettes for the pilot boat that was to collect him (remember we paid for this service already *and* included a 20 dollar tip!) We told him in no uncertain terms that he would have to share some of his cigarettes, as we did not have any packets left. He argued that he must provide gifts.

"You can go on the pilot boat and share the cigarettes; you can jump overboard and swim ashore; or you can continue on the boat. The choice is yours. We are non-smokers and have given you all the cigarettes we have."

Presumably swearing at us (we could not understand his language), he jumped on to the pilot boat that came alongside to collect him. We were careful to ensure we had enough fenders, mindful of payback.

We can now report that the moniker of 'Marlboro Channel' for the Suez Canal is no exaggeration.

We waved him - and Egypt - goodbye, and sadly, good riddance. Undoubtedly ancient Egypt provided some of our most memorable and impressive sights, certainly a must once in a lifetime. It was a pity that you can take no act as a goodwill gesture in Egypt. It is all about money, even the piece of cardboard proffered to fan myself in the sultry, oppressive heat in the Valley of the Kings.

A Little Bit of **MisChief**

For *Mischief* and her crew, the Mediterranean beckoned. Our dream had become a reality, and we sailed peacefully out of Port Said towards Larnaca in Cyprus.

Christina Gillgren

Down the Nile on a Felucca

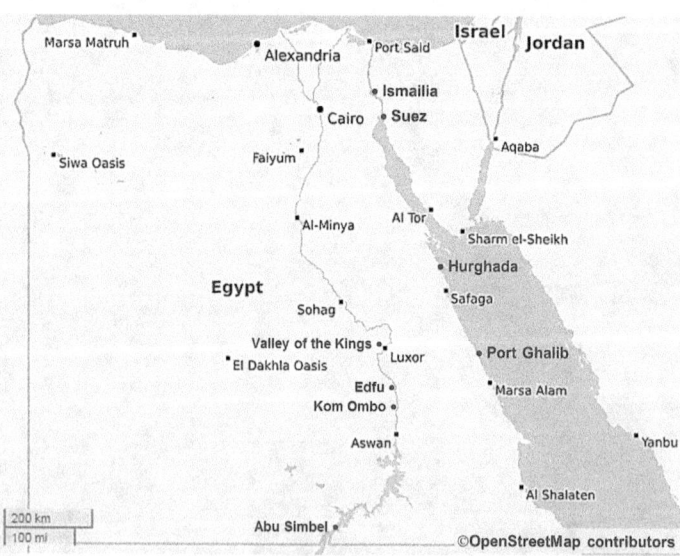

Egypt Travel

13
Finally the Med

Fifteen months after leaving Perth, Western Australia, and having completed our first ocean crossing across the Indian Ocean and up the Red Sea, the sight of the Mediterranean and its promise of 'civilization' were like manna from heaven.

The Red Sea challenge was over, as was the longest crossing Bjorn and I have ever undertaken. It had taken us five days to cross from Dampier in Western Australia to Bali, Indonesia, then 10 days from Phuket to the Maldives. The trip to Oman had taken another nine days and the final long leg, between Oman and Aden in Yemen had turned into one long motoring stretch of five to six days.

All legs had to be timed to fit in with weather conditions and trade winds. We started out from Fremantle in April, as the cyclone season was coming to an end. You cannot leave Phuket before end of December, as the trade winds will not have set in yet for the Indian Ocean crossing. Then you have to be in Aden by the end of February and ready to go up the Red Sea in March, or April at the latest. If you leave it too late, you will run into strong head winds that make the going tough. Even with clement weather, it will take at least six weeks to sail up through the Red Sea.

With these short weather windows, we could only stay for a week or so at any of the destinations on the way.

We had entered the Red Sea tired after the long passages and with some trepidation. Chatting with fellow sailors, it became obvious that others adopted a more leisurely pace. We should have spent a couple of seasons in south-east Asia before venturing across the Indian Ocean. As it had worked out, we had been on the move all the time since we left Australia. No wonder we had been feeling somewhat jaded in Aden. We quickly got to enjoy the change of pace of stopping almost at the end of each day for a sundowner and a good natter, even though we should have sailed past Eritrea to maximise the southerlies. We had also discovered and explored some beautiful *Marsas* and *Khors* along the Sudanese and anchored at some wonderful islands and coral reefs. It is not surprising that the Red Sea is world renowned for its diving and snorkelling.

For us, the endless tacking to make headway north had not eventuated. In waiting for the appropriate weather windows, we had been much slower than many other boats going through the Red Sea that year. The benefit was that we had enjoyed our experience. An assumed trauma had turned into a pleasurable cruise indeed.

The Red Sea had taught us to take it easy. This style of easygoing travel was to become our hallmark of cruising from here on.

As always, we had picked our weather window carefully. We had a good run to Suez. From there, we made our way first to Ismailia and then to Port Said through the 'ditch'…or the 'Marlboro Channel', as the Suez Canal is often referred to by sailors. Once out of the Canal, we were finally in the Mediterranean.

The first stopover for *Mischief* and her weary crew was Cyprus, 200 miles to the northeast. The wind was a convenient north-westerly blowing gently at 10-15 knots. Bjorn and I settled into the one and a half day's sail, hoping to make it to Larnaca before nightfall.

We were still sailing in company with our dear friends on *Dreamcatcher*. We made it into the small port of Larnaca just as dusk settled. We radioed the harbour master, tied up, and were ready for a good night's rest - after a glass or two of vino of course.

"We're here Joe," Bjorn radioed. "There is an outer harbour at Larnaca. We have tied up along the breakwater."

"We're still about one to two hours away," Joe replied. "We may have to hove to and spend the night out here." 'Hove to' is essentially backing the fore sail so that it counterbalances the main sail, so the boat practically stands still. As a rule, Joe never entered harbours, especially ones he had never visited before, at night.

"It is quite straightforward, Joe. Head towards this waypoint I am going to give you. When we have a visual of you we will put on our spotlight on low power and just follow the light in." Bjorn advised. "There are no reefs or other obstructions in the way, and the line of sight comes in cleanly between the two breakwaters."

"Ok, we'll give it a go. See you soon, hopefully."

Dreamcatcher made it to the waypoint and into the outer harbour without hiccups. We helped them secure the lines, and notified the authorities who were happy for us to go through the formalities in the morning. It was time to settle in for our first Mediterranean sundowner.

Cyprus was a pleasant surprise. Finally, western civilization, farewell to pirates, and hello to fresh produce galore. The southern coastline of Cyprus had some touristy parts with many English people taking up residence along the coast. Overall, Cyprus was understated in a way, but it had everything.

I vividly remember going to the supermarket in the morning with Helen and Joe, and Bjorn of course. We "oo'ed" and "ahh'ed" at the variety of produce, after the paucity we had encountered since leaving Phuket. The cheese counter, about seven to eight metres long, took our breath away. The shop assistants gave us curious looks, amused by our antics as we viewed the fresh produce, the incredible range cheeses and the endless display of small goods. For the non-Aussies, 'small-goods' is how we refer to cooked, dried, cured and otherwise processed meat products, such as salami and manufactured meats.

Sauntering through the streets of Larnaca, Joe would sometimes take the lead, as he had in other locations we had visited. "We've been up this road; so we'll take a different road back." Of course, we often got lost. That was part of the fun.

"We'll call this the 'Joe Principle'," I said. "From now on, wherever we are, we will tackle a different route and avoid going back the same way."

Cyprus seemed to have it all. Lovely mild climate, warm clear waters, lovely beaches ...and mountains, where you could actually ski in winter. If not for the fact that the marina was small, full and could not squeeze any more boats in, it would have been a winter stop for us. We were feeling rather cruised out after the long relentless haul from Thailand. Many of our sailing friends had just reached Turkey and a good marina. They were not even going to bother to cruise this summer as they were so tired.

As it happened, we managed to get two temporary berths for *Dreamcatcher* and *Mischief* for about eight days. Just enough time to explore the island. We rented a car between us for three days. After the magnificent temples in Egypt, however, the ruins in Cyprus seemed to be just that - ruins.

We visited beaches and the towns of Lemesos (Limassol) and the pretty port of Paphos on the west coast. In the capital of Lefkosia (Nicosia), we managed to cross the border into the Turkish side of the island. The mountainous region through Trodos to Mount Olympus was very scenic with a few wineries along the way to entice us. It was a welcome break to be back in the west if only for a short time. One of the things we noticed, that first evening, was the absence of the call to prayers five times a day.

Turkey loomed ahead for us. We had some misgivings about our plans to spend a full year there. Yet whomever we had spoken to had been so enthusiastic about their stay in Turkey and full of praise, assuring us that we would love it. That had made us curious. We were happy to wait and see what it turned out like.

The other attraction of Turkey was catching up with our

A Little Bit of MisChief

daughter Annika and her partner in mid- summer. They were participating in an international windsurfing meet in Alicati, south of Izmir.

After a few stops along the southern shores of Cyprus, the sail from Pissouri Bay in the western end of Cyprus to Finike, in south-west Turkey, took us about 30 hours. We entered the harbour in mid-afternoon and cleared customs. Ashore, to greet us like long lost friends were many of the cruisers we had met along the way.

We were on the lookout for the marina facilities to select where we would spend our first Mediterranean winter. Everyone assured us that this three-year-old marina was a great, safe harbour. It was well planned for yachties like us who wanted to spend the winter on board their yachts. In fact, many yachties had made it a permanent home. The weather was also more benign, or so we were told: up to ten degrees warmer than further up the coast. This suited us, as it was to be our first winter in four years.

Finike was a small quaint town, off the tourist beat: a bonus, as this meant that the prices were significantly cheaper than the better-known places of Bodrum and Marmaris further north.

Bjorn and I had no hesitation in signing up to spend our first marina winter at Finike. The added attraction was undoubtedly the fact that we would be surrounded by many of our fellow trans-Indian Ocean cruisers. The marina management team was welcoming. In addition, a customs and immigration office was conveniently located on site. We obtained our cruising visa for the year - with a little surprise. We were using our Maltese-European Union passports, and Malta had a special arrangement with Turkey. As a result, the visa fees were waived.

It promised to be a fun winter, with so many of our friends opting to spend the winter together. However, we still had a whole summer's cruising to get through. The rest of the west coast of Turkey beckoned.

Christina Gillgren

Coffee Time after Morning Mass

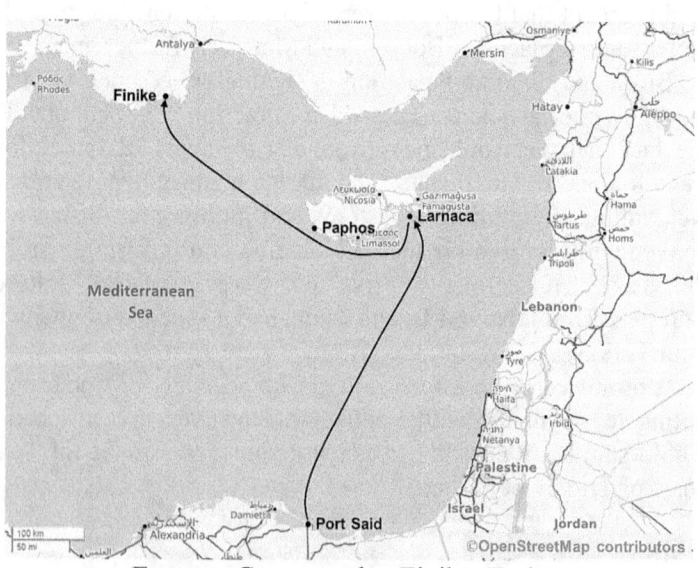

Egypt to Cyprus and to Finike, Turkey

14
Turkish Delight

Our first impression of Turkey was the town of Finike at the south-western tip. At first sight, it seemed like a return to third world countries, especially after our brief stay in Cyprus. After fifteen months of African and Asian experiences, we had looked forward to being back in the 'west'. This left us feeling more unsure than ever about this country.

Finike is no tourist town, which was good, but it also appeared basic. How wrong we were. By the first weekend, and a visit to the sensational farmers' market, our conversion was under way.

"Look at the incredible display of fruit and veg!" I cried in delight. "The market seems to go on forever."

This was an aspect of Turkish towns we grew to relish. We were unprepared for the gradual seduction. It would leave us with a heavy heart when it was time to say goodbye, some twelve months later.

We met friendly people everywhere, some more so than others. After our Egyptian experience where every act of 'kindness' so often turned out to be simply a claim for 'baksheesh', we were wary of friendliness.

The Turks, especially those away from the tourist areas, were something else. Nowhere in our trip so far had we met their generosity of spirit. People will go so much out of their way to help - including phoning an English-speaking friend or relative to help. The lengths to which they go to help are almost embarrassing at times. There was also that genuine enjoyment of simply talking to you: someone from somewhere else with different experiences; and a merchant would invite you to have some *cay* (pronounced 'chai'; tea) and a chat. Even when you explained that you were not in the market for a carpet or whatever wares were for sale, they would still invite you in.

Our memories of Turkey are potted with us drinking *cay* whether at the hairdressers or at the chandlers. Or even at the local souvenir shop in Finike.

After five days at the superb marina at Finike, it was time to head off for the summer cruising.

Sailing in Turkey was essentially exploring deep bays separated by headlands. These forked out like fingers into the Aegean. They all seemed to have a Greek island at the end of them, forming a wind tunnel between the two. The main wind in this region was the *Meltemi*, the Greek Etesian wind that sometimes came howling down from the north across the Aegean Sea. We knew it would be a case of finding the appropriate weather windows to make our way north, especially as we rounded the 'fingers'. The added wisdom of sailing veterans was that the wind tended to increase around the middle of summer. We had to make our way north before the *Meltemi* established itself. This challenged our sailing itinerary even more.

Our first stop was just around the corner from the marina, at an inlet called Kekova Roads. We caught up with Birte and Jorgen on *Circe*. They were veteran sailors, celebrating completing their circumnavigation. They had set out on their odyssey from Turkey, many years previously.

Over the next couple of days - and a few sundowners - Birte and Jorgen supplied us with wonderful information: where to visit, safe and interesting anchorages, and what to see along the Turkish coast. I had my Turkish coast cruising guide with me and furiously took notes. We discussed everything from dress codes to Mediterranean mooring (more on this later). I distinctly remember Birte telling me one morning, over a cup of tea, "It is

A Little Bit of MisChief

OK to wear a bikini. But the bra must be padded. The nipples must not show through."

So much for my desire to skinny dip whenever I could. I usually made sure that we were either far enough from the coast or else in an isolated anchorage. There was nothing better than a swim without any encumbrances. Besides, why waste precious sweet water on rinsing bathers?

"Be careful about the *gulets*," warned Jorgen. "When you go into a bay, even if there is no one, it is best to put down your anchor so that you can easily tie up to the shore. If other boats come in and the bay fills up, you will have no choice. And never argue with a *gulet*." A *gulet* is a traditional Turkish two-masted or three-masted wooden sailing vessel that used to ply up and down the coast with cargo. Nowadays they are converted or purposely built to ferry tourists around. They tended to barge their way through into an anchorage. They tied up wherever convenient, even if the anchorage was a small one, or full of boats. This was to prove invaluable advice.

The other useful recommendation that *Circe* gave us was to start out early. The secret was to get to the next anchorage or harbour in time to secure a good place. Then sit back and enjoy the sunset rush. This stood us in good stead throughout the years of cruising in the Mediterranean.

Kekova Roads has some delightful anchorages all strewn with sarcophagi and ruins. There was an underwater city where the land sank after an earthquake some 1500 years ago. It was a rare treat to take the dinghy for a slow drift over the old ruins, the occasional amphora and other sunken relics. We enjoyed a few wonderful, leisurely days and savoured some of the best Turkish delight I have ever tasted. My favourites were made from kiwi fruit and strawberries. Of course, there was the obligatory carpet seller, found in every village or town. This one was kindly. We would often finish the daily walk ashore with a chat over a cup of *cay* with the owner.

We waved goodbye to *Circe* then sailed to the superb enclosed harbour and town of Fethiye via stopovers at Kas and Kalkan. Fethiye Bay was the first indication of how popular cruising - and the charter industry - had become in Turkey. The boat charter capital of Turkey was located at Gocek in the north-western end of the bay.

After our long trek across the Indian Ocean and up the Red Sea we had become used to having anchorages almost entirely to ourselves. This was our first glimpse of sailing boats in all directions, and anchorages filled with numerous boats. We also had our first practice run at Med (Mediterranean) mooring. This is when you put down your anchor and then reverse onto the shore or quay. The trick is to ensure that the anchor is in line with your boat so that it does not get snagged with other boats' anchors. You also have to have enough chain out so that the anchor holds. The general rule is to let out a minimum of three times the depth of the water.

Bjorn hated this type of anchoring. It gave him visions of damaged rudders and propellers. You can't be sure of the sea bottom conditions, such as a rock sticking up, when reversing. Besides, *Mischief* (a relatively long-keeled design with a skeg-hung rudder) reverses about as well as an airplane. Many were the times that we watched with envy the modern short-keeled yachts with spade rudders 'parking' their boats with relative ease. Mind you, being traditionalists when it came to boats, we wouldn't be caught in one of those crossing open seas.

"Damn, the boat keeps on reversing to the left" I complained to Bjorn. This was a common feature on many sailing boats. It was the result of the water flow from the propeller along the hull, and was commonly referred to among sailors as prop walk. Once the boat got under way, it would continue to reverse in a straight line. I was familiar with prop walk. It had turned out to be convenient when backing out of our marina pen back in Fremantle. But trying to reverse between two boats, with only just enough space between them to squeeze in, was another matter.

"I'll try going in again. This time I'll start out at an angle so that when the boat veers to the left, we can slide straight in." Of course, you also need to allow enough room to drop the anchor in line with the boat.

This worked - when there was little wind! Med mooring was to be the bane of our Mediterranean cruising. I had no choice

A Little Bit of MisChief

but to figure out the angle in relation to wind and current every time we entered a busy anchorage.

We were delighted therefore to find that the anchorage in the town of Fethiye was a lovely large bay. The fully enclosed, wonderfully sheltered harbour was set against the stunning backdrop of tombs carved into the surrounding cliff face.

There were about 30 boats lying at anchor. This was so much easier! We dropped our anchor at a waypoint given to us by *Circe*. This placed us outside a hotel with a tiny marina, which catered for sailors. The owners were very friendly. They ran a superb restaurant as well as providing showers and other facilities to visiting yachts. We recognised several boats. And of course, the evenings would see the dinghies whizzing around from one boat to another. Sundowner time was a social time. The custom was that we often arrived carrying our vino or whatever grog was current, some dips, snacks and the like.

Sometimes it was a 'pot luck' dinner to share:

"*Dreamcatcher*! *Dreamcatcher*! This is *Mischief*!"

"Go ahead *Mischief*!"

"Come over to our boat, we have a lovely salad going!"

"We've got some meatballs. We'll bring them along!"

You could hear echoes of this type of conversation in busy anchorages.

Modern Fethiye is located on the site of the ancient city of Telmessos. This was our first taste of a Turkish city, and we were impressed with what was on offer. The town was well worth exploring. It offered an excellent range of facilities and services, including a marina, good chandlers, an extensive outdoor market, a fish market, shops and restaurants galore. Then there was the history, and we knew we would have to return for a tour of the area.

The larger Fethiye-Gocek bay hosted numerous coves and inlets which we decided to explore on our return journey. Our primary concern was to make as much headway north before the dreaded *Meltemi* started blowing. We wanted to get as far as Izmir in time for the arrival of our daughter and her partner.

We had just left Fethiye and were making our way up the coast when suddenly the radio came to life: "Moody sailing boat! Moody sailing boat! This is *Blue Gardenia*."

"*Blue Gardenia*, this is *Mischief*. We are a Moody 425 like you!" It was not unusual for boats of similar types to greet each other and compare notes.

"*Mischief*, this is *Blue Gardenia*," came the response. "We have a problem with our fuel system. The fuel pump is not sucking fuel out of the tank. There seems to be a problem with the tank." We were all too familiar with this problem.

"How can we help?"

"Can you spare a jerry can of diesel? We will hook this up straight to the fuel pump and return to Fethiye to fix the problem."

"Sure! No trouble! We will come around the stern of your boat and throw you a rope. Then you can haul in a jerry can with fuel. We have to be careful not to come too close as there is quite a swell!" In fact, there were two-metre waves and the sea was churned up, bouncing off against the cliff face some 50 metres away. The transfer went without a hitch and the jerry can returned to us in the same way, with some money for the fuel. We stood by to ensure that *Blue Gardenia* and their French crew got the engine going.

"Thank you so much. I hope we meet up somewhere and get to know each other."

"Before you leave, we should tell you we had a similar problem! It plagued us for months. We fixed it by installing a small fuel pump on the tank. We have had no problems since!"

It is always a good feeling to help. Yet we were only too happy to start motoring again to get away from the cliff face.

Marmaris was another chaotic sailing mecca. The port town's name derives from the Turkish word *mermer* because of the rich deposits of marble in the area. It lies at the bottom of a quasi-enclosed bay surrounded by mountains. It also sports two excellent marinas. They offer a range of services, including repairs and maintenance, for the yachting world.

We were staggered at the sight of hundreds of *gulets* lining the foreshore. Every day many would set out, full of day-tripping tourists, to every nook and cranny along the coastline. So, it was not surprising that this was also a start of the

A Little Bit of MisChief

anchorages where you had to compete with the local *gulet*s. Though it is customary for the first boat to have choice of mooring location, we were mindful that they were bigger than we were. They could do us more damage, if we did not accommodate their needs. Also, we were guests in their country.

Bjorn and I caught up once more with *Dreamcatcher*. We enjoyed a meal together ashore at one of the many restaurants that line the shore.

The evening was a nightmare! Ashore, a hectic nightlife ensured we had to endure deafening music from the open-air clubs and music venues. Afloat, we watched in horror as the tourist *gulets* criss-crossed the bay with gay abandon, sometimes motoring only a metre or two from us. *Mischief* swayed violently in response to the wake the passing boats created. Our first reaction was to re-anchor in the hope that we would find a quieter place. No such luck!

The next morning, we decided it was time to move on and continue on our northerly trek. After so much time together and the adventures we had shared, we sadly waved Joe and Helen farewell. They also left to cruise the Greek islands.

We headed along the coast to a small fjord-like anchorage called Bozuk Buku. To our delight, there was a beautiful, tiny bay just inside the entrance. A small restaurant with a little jetty attached was the sole dwelling. This was perfect! We tied up for an overnight stay. After a light lunch on board, we went ashore. We walked uphill to what was left of the ancient ruins of Loryma, which overlooked the bay. Then we followed this up with a swim in the lovely, warm and clear water.

Bjorn and I celebrated thirty years of wedded bliss at the little restaurant. The very fresh local fish prepared by the fisher family was more than sumptuous and suitable for the occasion. The restaurant owners rose to the occasion and prepared a special fruit dessert for us. Then we had to enjoy a few rounds of Raki, a popular alcoholic drink in Turkey made from grapes and flavoured with aniseed similar to the Italian Sambuca. In many ways, it was an evening to remember.

We skipped the whole Bodrum area with its numerous inlets

and bays to save for the return trip south at the end of the season. At this stage, weather permitting of course, we would hop between two or three anchorages and then spend a few days at the next bay so that we would not be moving every day. Wherever we went, we sailed within a couple of miles of a Greek island. They were dotted all along the Turkish coast.

Our journey took us past the island of Simi (Greece) to the quaint town of Datca. After an overnight at this not-so-good location, we moved on to the ancient harbours of Knidos at the tip of the Marmaris peninsula. There were two harbours. The northerly port was silted and unusable. We had called into the southerly harbour. The problem was that the 'holding' was not the best. This meant that if the wind really blew, the anchor could drag and we could end up on another boat - or the rocks.

With a relatively good weather forecast, we decided it was safe enough to go ashore and explore this otherwise wonderful old port.

The remains of the ancient city were strewn all over the hillside. The ruins revealed a large, well-organised city, with two theatres, a number of temples, and an agora. The setting and site were impressive, but our enjoyment was suddenly interrupted by yelling across the water.

"Oh no! Look! That large boat's stern rope to the shore has broken. It is swinging out."

"Quick! To the dinghy!" Bjorn shouted out as he ran down the slope to the slipway.

The wind had come up enough to disturb the anchorage. A large black-hulled boat was tied stern-to to the shore. It presented a wide target for the wind, straining the ropes that finally let go.

Our boat was not in immediate danger. Jumping into the dinghy, we drove straight to the boat moored next to us. It was about to be hit. We drove the dinghy between the boats to keep them apart. Then we helped them with fenders whilst they got the engine going.

We were not impressed with the owner of the black yacht. Although he had seen the problem, he took his time, and turned up eventually. Then he blamed his wife for not tying up the

A Little Bit of MisChief

stern ropes ashore properly.

We would have totally forgotten about this incident if it were not for the fact that we would run into this boat again, with some not very pleasant memories.

We spent another overnight stop at Akyarlar, a bay just west of Bodrum. Then we headed to Gumusluk, on the Aegean side of the Bodrum peninsula. We had made good progress and covered more than half the distance to Izmir. With time on our hands, we decided to sail at a more leisurely pace.

Gumusluk was a lovely inlet, popular with sailors. With good holding for the anchor, many boats could be accommodated into the bay. Here we encountered some crazy boat handling techniques. As more yachts arrived looking for a clear space to drop their anchor, we kept watch on deck. It was important to inform incoming boats as to where our anchor lay. This was to avoid getting it fouled.

Not everyone listens, unfortunately. A charter boat came and moored his boat next to us, catching the anchor of two nearby boats. It took hours to untangle the mess. In fairness, the yacht skipper who caused all the trouble was very apologetic. He listened attentively as those around him explained how to tackle a busy anchorage, and how to judge where you can put your anchor down.

We spent a wonderful week in Gumusluk. We took the *dolmus*, the local bus or van, into Turgutreis, the nearest town and to the surrounding areas. The rock that towers over the entry to the little inlet presented a challenging climb. We were rewarded with a commanding view over the surrounding landscape and islands. Dinner ashore was different. The dinner table at the restaurant was set on the sand, with water lapping at our feet: handy for cruisers, whose summer footwear usually consists of bare feet or thongs (the ones you wear on your feet and not the clothing variety).

With the right weather window for going north, we headed to Gulluk Korfezi to explore all the coves and bays over the next ten days or so. The area is attractive but slightly marred by the numerous fish farms. This made the water in some of the bays murky, and we gave these a miss.

On the plus side, we were also getting away from the charter fleets and the *gulet*s. To our surprise, we found ourselves blissfully alone in delightful coves and inlets with deeply wooded steep slopes coming right down to the water's edge. Asin Limani (*limani* is the Turkish term for harbour/port) was one such spot. The ruins of a breakwater of an ancient port were barely visible until close. They guarded the narrow entrance into the bay, overlooked by the watchtower that stood amidst the tall pines.

One of the stops in this area was at a place called Paradise Bay. It was a cosy quaint place, and soon more boats joined us. We had settled down to a peaceful sundowner when a large barge came in - towing an even larger fish pen.

"What on earth is he doing?" Putting down my wine glass and book, I joined Bjorn on deck.

"That fish pen is enormous. And there's not much room to manoeuvre here."

However, the reckless captain of this craft just pushed ahead between the moored yachts. Of course, the inevitable happened. The fish pen crashed into a nearby yacht, and they were headed on to us.

"Quick, Chris! Engine on!" Bjorn called out. He rushed to the bow to take up the anchor. All around, everyone scrambled to get their boats out of harm's way.

"Oh shit! Bjorn! The engine won't start. It's not even turning over!"

This was a bad time to have engine problems - or problems of any sort. Bjorn went down to check the batteries and the terminals. "All OK here," he called out. "Dammit! It must be the starter motor!"

We were now engineless. Bjorn and I called out that we could not move as we helplessly ran around the deck with fenders. Luckily, the barge and its tow, and the neighbouring yacht managed to evade us - only just. The barge succeeded in wending its way into the bay, and we sighed with relief.

"What do we do now?" I wondered aloud.

"I'll go to the big American flagged yacht. Perhaps they can give us a tow out of the bay in the morning." Bjorn did just that,

A Little Bit of MisChief

but they only very reluctantly agreed. The problem seemed to be that the captain on the yacht was not the owner.

The Turkish flagged yacht that had been crushed by the fish pen had not suffered any major damage. The owners had overheard the exchange between Bjorn and the American yacht. They came over to us in the dinghy.

"What is the problem?"

"The starter motor is not working. We need to get out of here tomorrow morning and past the fish pens. Then we can sail. There is a marina at the northern end of the bay. We'll see if we can get help there," Bjorn explained.

"That is the new marina at Didim. We are going in that direction. We will give you a tow until the morning breeze comes in."

We were chuffed! Here was a yacht, slightly smaller than ours, offering assistance, whereas the larger yacht had been so reluctant. Who knows? It is unusual for yachties not to bend over backwards to help each other out. We knew there was a difference between long-term cruisers and what we called 'summer swallows' - yachties that fly in for the season and then fly out again. And charter yachts were a different ball game altogether.

At around 8.00am the next morning, in dead calm, we were towed out of our anchorage. Once past the fish pens, the wind came in slowly blowing at around five knots. Bjorn got on the radio.

"We should be fine now. We can make our way slowly to the marina at Didim. It is not far from here, about 10 miles."

"It is OK," the kind Turkish sailors told us. "We can tow you a bit further until the wind reaches at least 10 knots."

An hour later, the wind obliged. We threw off the line with a fifty Euro note for the fuel, and a bottle of wine in thanks. Then we were on our way. The wind continued to increase to a pleasant 15 knots. It was not long before we were outside Didim Marina. A call on the radio to explain our plight was all it took, and a dinghy came out to tow us in.

We discovered that the marina was about to be opened in the next few weeks. Fortunately, some trades had already set up shop. Bjorn went for a stroll and found two incredibly helpful young Turkish mechanics. They came on board, removed the starter motor, and took it into town for fixing. Before we knew it, they were back on the boat. Hardly two hours had passed.

We had anticipated that it would take a few days to have the problem resolved, so were over the moon with the progress. The moderate cost was another pleasant surprise.

"We're paid up for three days, so let's stay and visit the nearby sights," I told Bjorn.

Our first stop was at Altinkum. The town was overrun with British tourists: fish and chips shops abounded as did all tourist traps. It was crowded and not much to our taste. When we got to the beaches, we could appreciate why this resort town was so popular: a sheltered bay, pretty landscape with golden sands and aquamarine waters, and all the beach services and water sports on offer. Instead, we made our way to the nearby ruins at the Temple of Apollo at Didyma.

Once back at the marina, Bjorn got chatting to our new friends, the engineers. Discussing engines, Bjorn explained how difficult it was to source some spare parts such as the oil filters for our British Thornycroft engine. It was a 'marinized' Ford small car diesel engine. Parts were hard to come by, especially in countries that did not import Ford motor cars. Nothing was a problem for these great guys. They phoned their head office in Istanbul, and tracked down the oil filters. It would take two to three days to receive them.

With some strong northerlies forecast, we left the marina and decided to wait for the filters at an enclosed bay called Talianaki, east of Altinkum. This was just round the corner from the marina. We were disappointed to find that the holiday village along the beach was deserted. But we were not left alone for long. A stream of tourist-engorged *gulet*s interrupted our peace during the day.

On the second day, we spotted a small beach concession to one side of the entrance. "Bjorn, there are people on the beach. Let's go explore."

The wind was blowing at around 30 knots. With a sandy bottom, our anchor had dug in well; so we were happy to leave

A Little Bit of MisChief

the boat to go ashore. To our delight, we found that this was a swimming beach for a number of holiday homes tucked away in a heavily wooded area, totally out of sight. Walking through the village in search of a mini market for some fresh bread, we met a young Turkish couple (Mine and Gokhan) who startled us by their perfect English. In response to our queries, they explained that they lived in America. They were 'home' visiting family. Through them we met, and were adopted by, the whole family. Every afternoon, we would go ashore to get away from the strong winds. There was much to keep us entertained on the wonderful beach concession: a few tables were set up with games of scrabble and dominoes. In addition, the locals had great fun teaching us to play OKEY (a form of gin rummy played with 'tiles', not unlike those used for Dominoes). To Bjorn's disgust, I often ended up discussing politics with Mine's elderly uncle as her cousin Ayjin tackled the task of translating. We had a ball.

We loved the set up. A well-equipped bar and friendly staff, delicious and inexpensive food Turkish fare, lounge chairs and umbrellas on the cement quay, clean showers and toilet facilities, and even a washing machine which the owners graciously offered for our use.

We could easily have spent the rest of the summer here, but we had an appointment up north with our daughter.

On the third day, we received a phone call from our engineer friends at Didim Marina.

"Your parts have arrived. Where are you now?"

"We are at Talianaki," Bjorn replied, giving details of the beach concession.

"OK, we will drive round this afternoon." Which they did. To our amazement, these lovely young Turkish men only charged us for the filters, glad to be of help. We offered them refreshments. They accepted a coffee and a chat. Bjorn was introduced to the Turkish version of espresso, sweet strong *kahvesi* with lots of sugar in small glasses. Not being a coffee drinker, I abstained.

Whilst at Talianaki, our friends on *Interlude* contacted us via the radio network. We had crossed the Indian Ocean at the same time and we both intended to leave the boats over the winter months at Finike marina.

Katie and Kurt called into the bay and we had some wonderful shared evenings. This included being treated to a guitar session by Katie and Kurt on their magnificent boat - a 74ft Deerfoot. Now that's cruising in style!

"This is quite a windy anchorage," Kate said to me. "We stopped at the bay outside here on our way up north. It was nothing like this."

"Maybe that is why the shore in lined with wind generators. The land seems to be lower here. It must form a wind tunnel," Bjorn surmised.

"Ah, that must be why the cruising guide gives more prominence to the anchorage outside. And I thought I was so clever, discovering this almost fully enclosed bay."

I had learnt something new. The coast was on occasions decorated with these giants. From now on, they would become a semaphore for 'it can be really windy here'. Keep away from anchorages with wind generators ashore. Kate and Kurt gave us some useful tips regarding where to stop over on our way up north.

One afternoon we returned to our boat to discover the back deck splattered with blood and feathers. The reason was obvious. A pigeon had committed 'kamikaze'! It had flown into the wind generator, whirling away at high speed, and charging our batteries. Our trusty wind generator that had survived near storm conditions was now at a standstill, the blades ruined. Bjorn suspected that the alternator might also have suffered some damage. We had a spare set of blades on board. Bjorn, ever the efficient engineer, set to replacing the blades, glass of whiskey in hand. I am not sure what he did with the alternator, but I was happy to see the wind generator back in business once again.

◇◇◇

We resumed our northbound trek, saying 'au revoir' to *Interlude*. One of the stops was at a small inlet called St Paul, about a mile across from the Greek island of Samos. It was a

A Little Bit of MisChief

quiet night with little wind. The boat kept swinging around in the very narrow inlet, getting close to the rocks on shore at times. Whilst enviously eyeing the lovely bay across the water at Samos, I had no choice but to sleep in the cockpit and keep a lookout.

The reason for sticking to the Turkish side was that we had been warned about the vigilant Turkish Coast Guard. They whizzed around in superfast patrol boats, and took a dim view of boats leaving and re-entering Turkey without proper procedures: not that we had ever caught sight of one.

Once north of Samos, and having time on our hands, we stopped at some lovely, quiet inlets on the way to Alacati. We had booked a berth at the marina, intending to spend three weeks with our daughter during the windsurfing meet.

We arrived in the marina just in time, with winds clocking 40 knots in the bay.

"Ha! Another blowhole!" Bjorn started out. "No wonder this place was chosen for the windsurfing championships. There's even a whole cluster of wind generators, and now we know why."

The marina facilities were excellent. In addition, the marina lay conveniently next door to where the championships were to be held. This suited Annika and her partner as hotel rooms were at a premium and further away from the action. It also allowed mum to address some daughter withdrawal symptoms, as I hugged my 'little girl', who incidentally is much taller than I am.

Most mornings we watched Annika and her partner prepare, test and tune their sails. Clad in rashies (rash vests to protect from the sun, a sort of Lycra for surfers), they sped up and down the bay, wind-swept and with a look of both utter concentration and sheer exhilaration. We watched in fascination as they teased the sails and manoeuvred the boards to gain that extra advantage.

When the Windsurfing World Cup races got under way, the beach was transformed into a windsurfing mecca. Stalls sprouted everywhere. They stocked all types and makes of sailboards, sails, accessories and equipment, and clothing. Food stalls, bars and beer gardens were set up to cater for the hundreds of competitors from many different parts of the world who had come together for this spectacular event.

During the day, we hired lounge chairs and umbrellas on shore and watched the races, glued to our binoculars. Our home town of Perth hosts many keen windsurfers and kite fliers, especially on the Swan River. We were used to watching the spectacle of boards flying past in all directions. However, the explosion of colour of the sheer number of sails in Alacati Bay astounded us. The bay became a mass of speeding colour and spray as about a thousand windsurfers took to the water. We watched in amazement many a near miss - and also an accident or two.

After the races, the waters cleared of windsurfers. We finally felt safe to enter the water to cool off. Then it was time to join the international windsurfing community on shore for a drink and much chatter about the day's contests, results and near misses.

Both Annika and her partner, who are not professionals, placed well. Having seen our daughter in action confirmed our nickname for her: zoom, zoom Annika.

The town of Alacati, about five kilometres away from the beach, was charming and obviously catered to the well-heeled. It came alive in the evenings. We often went into town for a stroll and tried out some of the highly recommended restaurants.

After the world meet, the wind relented, just on cue! We took the opportunity to go cruising for a few days. We were sailing away gently, when Annika piped up: "Gosh, this boat goes slow."

I couldn't help but smile, as I recalled how she would whizz around our boat on the river in Perth, with a grin that said: "Catch me if you can!"

"Well, it is not a windsurfer."

After the hectic and lively atmosphere at the windsurfing event, Bjorn and I welcomed the beautiful, serene bays at Sarpdere and Kirklidim, southeast of Alacati. These bays had been highly recommended by our friends on *Interlude*. They

A Little Bit of MisChief

certainly merited the praise. They offered excellent shelter. Incredibly, we had the bays to ourselves - not a boat or soul in sight. It is hard to believe that in the very busy Mediterranean, you could find such jewels.

It was a different matter for our daughter. She would jump into the dinghy, and take off at high speed to explore the nearby coves.

Exploring the main inlet in Sarpdere Bay with binoculars, we spotted a small resort at the bottom of the bay. We hoped to find bins to leave our rubbish. Bjorn and I took the dinghy ashore. On the way, we noticed a discreet, screened enclosure to one side of the bay. We caught sight of a woman and her child.

"Bjorn, this must be a segregated bathing beach for women! Quick, let's get away from here. We certainly do not want to offend!"

We went to the main beach, and pulled the dinghy up on the sandy beach. Bjorn spotted two young men whom he approached. He apologised for any inadvertent intrusion, explaining that we were looking for an appropriate place to leave the rubbish. The men appreciated our approach and directed us to the bins.

Once back at Alacati Marina, we made plans to go sightseeing. It would have been unforgivable for us not to explore the area with so many world-famous sites. We hired a car and travelled inland to Cesme, Izmir and down to Kusadasi. On our way, we stopped to visit Ephesus, which was a 'must-see'. Just inside the entrance were the ruins of the Library of Celsus, dating back to around 550BC, which reflected the maturity of the civilization that had existed. We were impressed by how much of the facade and building remained intact, although the guide explained that some parts were reconstructed. What attracted us most was that instead of the glorification of Pharaohs that we encountered in Egypt, we were here experiencing how city life was organised and how the community lived. Other excavated ruins included the Temple of Artemis, which was one of the Seven Wonders of the Ancient World.

From Kusadasi, we took a ferry across to the lovely Greek

island of Samos for two days. This was our first visit to a Greek island.

Crossing back and forth from the Turkish mainland to the Greek islands - usually only a couple of miles apart - seemed to be a common occurrence. We were sorely tempted to do likewise. Being newcomers to these countries, we had opted to follow the rules. In theory, one should not cross over on a yacht from Turkey to Greece and back without checking in and out in both ends. Imagine our surprise when, as we stepped off the ferry at Samos, our Turkish marina neighbours greeted us cheerfully.

"We could have given you a lift here if we knew you were headed this way!" Even the Turks traversed back and forth with impunity, it seemed.

We enjoyed a few pleasant days exploring the island.

"I like it!" Annika said. "In Turkey, it is old men with dogs that you see. But here it seems to be old ladies and their cats." Our daughter is a dog-lover - and they love her too. She had managed to have a dog follow her around faithfully whilst in Alacati.

Our other neighbours at Alacati Marina were a German couple, Birgit and Wolfram, living in Istanbul. Birgit invited us to visit the capital, and we readily made plans to do so in the autumn. Whilst we were at Alacati, we also got an invitation to attend the official opening of Didim Marina, where we had sought shelter to repair our starter motor. The date of the opening coincided well with plans for our return trip to Finike.

It was time to say goodbye. We saw Annika and her partner off to the airport, and returned to a boat that suddenly felt so empty.

◇◇◇

As the *Meltemi* established itself, it was easier to sail south. Our trip was marked with meeting more wonderful people: cruisers and locals. We revisited some of the attractive bays south of Alacati. After our experience at the anchorage of St Paul, however, we decided to risk stopping over at Samos. We anchored at the little bay I had admired so longingly from

A Little Bit of MisChief

across the water in Turkey on our way north. To our amusement, we were greeted by a couple, naked, swimming away merrily. We had heard that once we started westwards in the Mediterranean, nudity was the order of the day on many yachts. Not always a positive experience as our Croatian experience would show later.

"Come on, Bjorn. In we go!" We loved the freedom we had so much enjoyed on our passage from Australia. Away from any land, we had indulged ourselves, gained an even suntan, and saved on the washing.

Didim Marina contained about 30-50 yachts, most of them summer cruisers. We took the opportunity to give *Mischief* a good fresh-water clean, polished the stainless steel and dressed up the boat for the occasion of the official opening. The marina was launched by none other than the President of Turkey. We enjoyed a spectacular evening with a sumptuous meal, varied entertainment including acrobatics and fireworks, and great company.

A week passed quickly, with sundowners galore. Wherever we went we practiced our 'beer o'clock' and 'four, five and six thirsty'. I was sleeping ever so soundly: all due to sun, fresh sea air and just maybe the occasional glass of wine that we imbibed.

As soon as we reached Bodrum (formerly the ancient Greek city of Halicarnassus) and September, the wind tap was turned off. We dropped our anchor just below the 15th century Castle of St Peter that dominated the peninsula.

"Look Bjorn, there is the jetty with the orange canopy. That's where we were told we can leave our dinghy."

The cruisers' network had come good again and we were welcomed and offered unimpeded access ashore. We set off to explore.

Bodrum's extensive history goes back to ancient times. One of the most famous ruins is the Mausoleum of Mausolus, another of the Seven Wonders of the Ancient World. We loved Bodrum town, but the anchorage was noisy. With a whole month up our sleeve, we moved on to explore the Bodrum - Datca - Marmaris area at leisure, visiting numerous bays, and discovering some spectacular sites and villages such as "Old"

Datca.

Our friends on *Circe* had recommended the bay at Orhaniye, which was the last inlet south of the Bodrum peninsula. Unsurprisingly, there they were. This was an ideal place to spend some quiet time after the hectic summer months. An added bonus was its location. It was a *dolmus* ride away from Marmaris, where we could check out boat services for the coming winter months. The bay hosted a marina and supermarket. There were also a few restaurants dotted around the bay with small jetties that would accommodate four to six boats.

"Hello!" we heard someone call out, the next morning. We came out to the wonderful smell of freshly baked bread, brought to our boat by an enterprising boatman.

"That looks very appetising," Bjorn said, handing over a Turkish Lira. It was twice the price of what one would have paid ashore. Yet who would argue with the service of having it delivered to you fresh each morning in time for breakfast?

Orhaniye was a popular resting spot for cruisers. Throughout the day, other boats would come up to us selling a small variety of fruit and vegetables, or fish, or even ice cream. It was one of the little quirks of cruising in Turkey that would be repeated in popular anchorages around the Mediterranean.

After a few days in the bay, we took the opportunity to tie up at The Ersoy Restaurant jetty for a few days. This delightful little restaurant offered water and electricity and a laundry service - and the freshest array of seafood.

The next set of bays to explore was just round the peninsula in the Yesilova/Bozburun area, a few miles across the water from the Greek island of Simi. We stopped at one of the tiny islands on the way into the Bozburun inlet. At sundown, over a glass of wine, we watched a man motor up in a little boat and call out to the goats grazing on the islands. Immediately they all swarmed down to greet him. He climbed onto the rocks and spread food and water for them. Such a little everyday thing, and yet somehow so delightful!

Our next stop was a few miles away in Bozburun. We tied up, stern to, to the town jetty. One of the local restaurant owners

A Little Bit of MisChief

arranged for a motorbike for us to explore the surrounding highlands. At the village of Kizyler, we stopped for lunch. The locals went about their business: women with stacks of sticks balanced on their heads, and men with their donkeys, laden with goods. As word of our presence spread, the local Imam came to greet us. Proudly, he showed us their lovely mosque, explaining that the men worshipped on the ground floor. The first floor balcony was reserved for the women.

On one of our evening walks around Bozburun, we came across several boat yards where *gulets* were under construction. Bjorn had a lovely time discussing boat building. One of the yard owners gave a good show-and-tell, bringing out old tools that had been retired in favour of modern powered ones. He bemoaned the passing of the old days, complaining that the wood that had previously been used for construction was so much better.

The Greek island of Simi lay a few miles across the water. Unable to resist the temptation, we cautiously sailed across and anchored in a bay, east of the main town. A bus ride over the mountains to the bay of Panormitis, on the southern edge of the island, was on our must-do list. As the bus rounded the corner and the panoramic view came into sight, an audible sigh of appreciation reverberated through the bus. The driver pulled over so that we could all scramble down and take photos. The picturesque bay, shimmering with its turquoise waters in the sunlight, was almost fully enclosed. The narrow entrance lay to the west, whilst a monastery graced the eastern shore. We knew that we would somehow return to this anchorage before we left the area for good.

Before we departed from Simi we stocked up on bacon, salami and pork products which were difficult to come by in Turkey. We then called into a small bay in Rhodes. Our goal was the Lidl store. Paired up with other cruisers, we went ashore and walked the short distance to the store. We returned to *Mischief* laden with around 50 litres of wine for the winter months in Finike Marina. The Turkish local wine was variable and sometimes not up to our delicate palate, trained on Australian 'plonk'. So, Italian Lidl plonk it was! The Turkish beer *Efes* was quite good however, and popular.

We spent another wonderful fortnight in the Fethiye area, visiting Gocek and many of the inland sites: incredibly beautiful ruins, gorges, caves, beaches, and of course, the scenic bays in the protected large Fethiye/Gocek area. It was almost the end of the season, and much quieter. In one of the bays, at Boynuz Buku, we thought we could get away with just putting our anchor down. We spent a leisurely day swimming around, having the place all to ourselves. Five o'clock struck and suddenly two yachts came in and tied up to the shore with their anchors up front. We still hoped we would not have to do anything. Suddenly, this medium sized *gulet* came in and threw his anchor not far from us.

"We will have to tie up the stern." Bjorn told me as he prepared the lines. Just as he was about to dive into the water the captain from the *gulet* called out to us. "Hey! Don't worry! We will take your line ashore." - Which they did.

The skipper was most accommodating. This experience left us with a very good feeling that civility exists everywhere, proving that 'what goes around comes around' works in all countries.

We drank to them that evening.

In Fethiye we caught up with Joe and Helen on *Dreamcatcher*. They were returning from a summer in the Greek islands. We rented a car together, eager to explore the numerous historical sites in the mountains east of Fethiye. These included the ancient city of Tlos, with its amazing Lycian ruins and tombs carved into the rockface. The whole west coast of Turkey hummed with history, reflecting the strategic importance and resultant turbulent past of this part of the world.

Once away from the coast and the main tourist areas, you could appreciate the very fertile countryside, but this was thirsty work. We stopped for a cup of tea at a roadside shack, lying on raised flat beds propped up with cushions. The host presented us with the obligatory and refreshing pomegranate juice, a Turkish staple. On our way back, we passed by the remains of

A Little Bit of MisChief

the Greek village made famous in Louis de Bernier's book, *Birds Without Wings*. This tells the tragic story of the expulsion of Greeks from Turkey, and vice versa, in the early 1920s. In fact, following the population exchange between Greece and Turkey, Fethiye was resettled with Turks from Greece in 1923.

I loved Fethiye and the market on Tuesdays was truly great. We loaded up with Turkish delight (the edible type) and could not help reflecting how ill-founded our initial concerns about Turkey were. The whole experience has become one huge Turkish delight, and our love affair with this country was cemented.

Our slower passage seemed to coincide with that of many boats heading towards their designated winter marinas. At the same time, the number of *gulets* and charter boats had decreased dramatically. We now understood why so many Europeans who keep their boats in Turkey/Greece choose to cruise in May-June and then again in September-October. It is great sailing weather without the blustery *Meltemi*. This year it had seemed to be permanently in gale force mode throughout August.

It was now almost the middle of October. The signs for seasonal change were becoming more obvious with more cloud and occasional rain. We watched the weather more carefully. We made our way south, still swimming every day and enjoying balmy weather.

We left Fethiye, sailing in company with *Dreamcatcher* on our last part of the trip south to Finike. Our friends sailed into the tiny bay of Karacaoren just ahead of us. They were immediately shooed away by a yachtsman on a big black yacht. We had come across this boat in Knidos earlier in the season, when they had lost their stern line.

"I have 75 metres of chain out," the owner called out, essentially blocking the whole bay. In small bays, it is normal practice to tie up to the shore. This creates more room, so that other boats also have the opportunity to tie up.

Not this sailor!

Joe turned his boat around in disgust and headed out of the bay into a nearby bay. We did not give up so easily and motored in past the black yacht, eyeing some moorings ahead.

"Well, we can't use these," Bjorn began. "The restaurant ashore will expect us to go and eat there tonight. I want an early start for our long leg tomorrow."

A boatman who had come up in a dinghy from the restaurant overheard us. He had watched the exchange between our friends and the black boat. "Don't worry! You can tie up here for free. And you don't have to come ashore tonight!" He even took our line and tied it to the mooring buoy for us. We gratefully handed over a well-deserved tip. This was another tick on the credit column for Turkey.

Next morning, at first light, Bjorn took up the anchor and we started sailing south accompanied by *Dreamcatcher*. Immediately we saw the black yacht pull up their anchor and follow us. It soon became obvious that this was a race to get to the next anchorage first, which they did. Again, as we entered the bay, the arrogant owner of the black yacht came on deck. He shouted that he had 75 metres of chain out. When anchoring, it is normal practice to put down chain equivalent to three times the depth, especially in benign weather conditions. This meant that they need not have put out more than 45 metres. To make matters worse, this captain had the habit of not reversing on his anchor to ensure it had gripped the bottom well. This made it harder for other yachts to gauge where he would end up.

Joe anchored *Dreamcatcher* ahead of the black yacht, and I took *Mischief* to her stern, leaving a good distance in between. There were no other choices.

It soon became apparent that the black yacht was either dragging her anchor or just stretching the chain out. They were nearly upon us. I lost my temper. I called the offender a selfish so-and-so who did not observe sailing etiquette. Bjorn tried to calm the waters by calling them on radio. We finally agreed to a watch-and-see situation with only a boat length between us. This was way under what feels comfortable, as we settled down for the night.

Of course, the next morning it was another frenzy to get to the next anchorage first. Luckily, this happened to be Kekova Roads, where there was ample space as the bay was a fair size.

A Little Bit of MisChief

To our delight, the black yacht motored right up into the bay. We were overjoyed to see that they were a good distance from us.

The area on the south shore of Kekova was strewn with sarcophagi, obviously a necropolis. We decided to climb up to the hilltop where an old castle was perched, flags flying. Knowing the terrain was rocky and very uneven, Bjorn and I pulled out our sneakers, which had not seen the light of day since leaving Australia. Imagine our surprise when, half way up the hill, Bjorn's soles started to come apart.

"It's the glue." Joe started out. "When you spend time in the tropical conditions of south-east Asia, many of the glues stop working. It must be the excessive heat and high humidity." Joe explained. "In fact, our dinghy had suffered this fate when we were in Malaysia. We couldn't find the right glue that would do the job, and then, we practically had to rebuild the dinghy."

Ever the practical person, Bjorn used the shoelaces to keep the shoes and soles together. He looked like the proverbial cartoon vagabond with his shoes and generally dishevelled look.

We spent the last evenings on anchor saying 'au revoir' to those heading even further east to other marinas in the area. It had been an amazing year: crossing the Indian Ocean, then up the Red Sea; and then straight into a summer of cruising along the Turkish west coast. Another first awaited us: a winter in a marina. We looked forward to a break from all the travel. It would be a time for reflection, making plans. In calm waters, we motored out of Kekova Roads and made our way round the southernmost headland of Turkey. We arrived in Finike in the last few days of October - just in time before the first good winter storm.

Cay (Turkish Tea) in Style

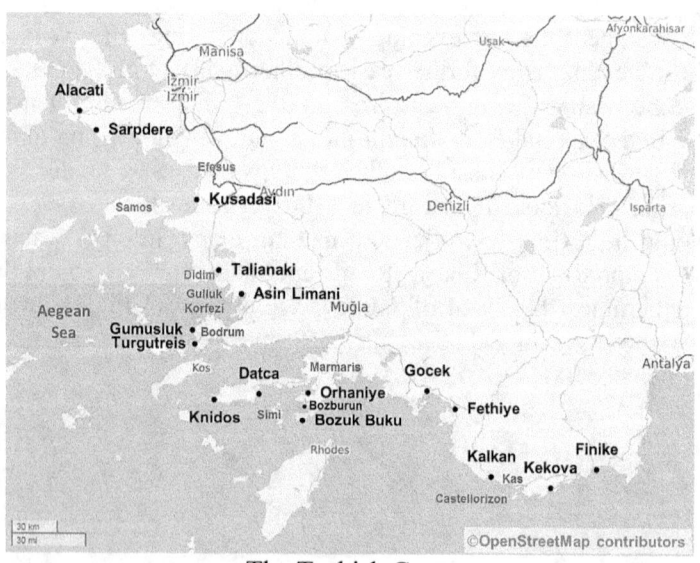

The Turkish Coast

15
Winter in Finike

We motored into Finike Marina for our six-month winter stay at the end of October. It was a balmy morning. The 'marineros' were there to greet us, direct us to a pen and help us tie up. The marina was set up with four pontoons forking out from the quay. Large boats/yachts over 20 metres were accommodated on the breakwater. We were lucky to be given a pen in one of the middle pontoons close to the quay. This meant that it was closer to walk to the facilities. Our friends on *Dreamcatcher* were tied up opposite us, and *Circe* and others were on the neighbouring pontoon.

Finike Marina was a well- planned marina. It was equipped with a fully-fledged hardstand boat yard, boatlift and engineering shops to tackle all sorts of work required. The marina area was set up to accommodate the number of yachting folk that would spend at least part of the winter there. On the quay straddling the pontoons was a large building. This housed a generous number of toilet and shower facilities: women to the left, and men to the right. They were separated by a well-equipped laundry in between. The laundry ladies were ever present during the day, taking in laundry and keeping the facilities clean and tidy. There was also another laundry room at one end of the long building, for those who preferred to do their own washing. And washing lines were conveniently placed on the rear of the building, out of sight.

'What's this?" Bjorn queried, coming across a very large, outdoor, shallow basin. "It looks like a low, empty swimming pool."

We turned round to see a sailor wheel his sails on a small marina cart. We were even more impressed when we realised that this was a sail bath. The sailor spread out one of his sails, got out the broom and detergent, wet the sail and started scrubbing.

Next, we set out to walk around the marina to see who was around. The live-aboards over the winter had come from everywhere: the UK, France, Germany, Holland, the Scandinavian countries including Finland. There were several US and Canadian boats. And this year there was a strong Aussie and New Zealand contingent. Besides those sheltering for the winter, many cruisers had made Finike their semi-permanent home.

The pontoons came alive during the day with a babble of chatter as everyone greeted each other, going from language to language, exchanging information and generally enjoying getting to know each other. This was complemented by the usual marina sounds of ropes clanging away on masts in the breeze. After a few days, the novelty wore off. We had to ask one of our neighbours to secure the ropes in such a way that we could sleep without the din on windy nights.

We caught up with many of our fellow travellers that had crossed the Indian Ocean with us. Our friends on *Dreamcatcher* and *Circe* were there. *Interlude* was moored next to the large yachts on the breakwater. In addition, there were Tony and Annie on *Sunburnt*, Clive and Jane on *Jane G* (Wales), Paddy and Carolyn on *Kristiane* (Australia) and Jannine and John on *Orca Joss* among so many others too numerous to mention.

Our first month was taken up with packing up the boat for winter. We took the sails down and washed them. When dry, we handed them over to the highly recommended local sailmaker. He would check them out, carry out any repairs and then fold and store them for us until spring. We took down any ropes or lines that could be stowed away. These were washed and rinsed

A Little Bit of MisChief

with conditioner to soften them and ended up smelling unusually of lavender. We cleared the decks of anything removable, except for the fenders of course.

The next task was getting to know the town and the facilities. It was not long before a walk into town would include a *cay* with the carpet seller who wanted to practice his English. We looked forward to the Saturday market: one very long street with side roads full of the freshest produce, some of which were new to us. For example, nowhere else have we come across the stoneless small oval avocado, not much larger than a plum.

"Try this," the young female vendor said, handing us one each. "They are even better than the large ones."

"You welcome! You very welcome!" another vendor called out to us, showing off his produce.

A utility truck with a large bullet tank stood at one end of the market. Here we could purchase fresh trout. The vendor would clean them for us, all for the princely sum of a couple of Turkish Lira (one dollar). After the morning spent at the market, we usually visited a local kebab house for lunch. Typical fare included a soup and some meze, selecting from the *beyaz peynir* (feta-like cheese), *haydari* (yogurt with herbs), *patlıcan salatası* (cold eggplant salad), and sometimes *kalamar tava* (fried calamari). We avoided the hot pepper paste.

The well-stocked supermarkets on the main street were reasonably priced. Close by a number of butchers had set up shop in a small square. We found a butcher who sold pork and some pork small goods, but they came at a price.

It was not long before we experienced the first winter storm. The marina breakwaters were strategically located to protect the boats from waves. Yet in certain conditions, the swell still found its way in. We checked our mooring lines, ensuring that fenders were in the right place to avoid any damage. As soon as the storm was announced, the 'marineros' came around to check boat moorings, especially for unattended boats. A roster was organised and they patrolled the pontoons throughout the night. We were impressed! This was reassuring given our impending departure to Australia for two months. *Mischief* was in safe hands, with friends and neighbours also keeping a lookout for us.

◇◇◇

We had a great welcome in Perth. Family and friends greeted us with hugs. We seemed to be whizzing from one set of friends to the next. It was a good feeling to be back in our hometown after almost two years at sea. At our yacht club in Fremantle, we celebrated having completed an Ocean crossing. The time flew by, which was in contrast to the leisurely pace of cruising life.

Whilst we were away, a bad storm hit the marina in Turkey with severe hail. Our friends reassured us that *Mischief* was fine. On our return from Australia, the marina manager came to greet us. He showed us photos of the whole marina covered in timber and weed that had washed down from the mouth of the river nearby.

We were anxious to examine our boat. Sure enough, we found that we had suffered the fate of many others. The masthead wind instrument sensor was broken. In addition, the ice that had gathered on the dodger, the shield against rain or spray, had caused the clear plastic to get brittle with the cold. This had made it crack and some of the stitching had come loose. All in all, these small items could be attended to locally.

Now that we were back for at least another three months in the marina, we settled down to enjoying the world of live-aboard life. In many ways, the marina enclave was like a village of our own. Next to the shore facilities was a clubhouse, with a library, bar and barbecue facilities, including chairs and tables for our Sunday barbecues.

The marina regulars were well organised. All sorts of activities were planned. These included endless varieties of keep-fit and yoga classes in the mornings, a weekly movie, quiz and games nights, and a pub night on Fridays. Any skill that a cruiser had was shared. Musicians such as our friend Clive on *Jane G* were running music classes. Frances on *Tulameen II*, whom we had last seen in Malaysia, was giving art lessons. Her picture of our boat lying at anchor in Fethiye takes pride of place in our living room.

There was nothing planned for the Thursday nights so I

A Little Bit of MisChief

offered to run a topics night. I put up a notice asking for volunteers. Before long, we had a list of interesting themes. These included information of different cruising areas like Greece, the Red Sea and Croatia - very useful for those planning to visit these areas. In our case, Greece was our next destination. We gratefully sat down with our cruising guides to plan for our next summer. Of course, we reciprocated. We gave as much detail as possible to Alain and Marie-Joelle (*Kowekara*, France), sailing on a Moody similar to ours, for their planned trip through the Suez and into the Red Sea.

The Sunday barbecue (BBQ) was the highlight of the week. Before lunch, tables for the food were placed outside the clubroom, and tables and chairs were set out on the paved area. The marina kindly supplied two barbecues, with firelighters and charcoal. The cruisers supplied salads and desserts, each of us bringing a dish of our choice. This was in addition to whatever we were barbecuing on the day.

On our first BBQ, Bjorn and I prepared our version of ratatouille. I cooked it in a small pressure cooker I had found at the market in Finike. I liked these utensils as they reduced cooking time and gas use. Also being sealed, they were practical at sea. The dish was so successful that it became our regular contribution. Bjorn and I loved the fresh trout from the market wrapped in foil. Occasionally we had a break to have some grilled steak instead.

The BBQ was special in that it would last the whole day. After lunch and clearing up, guitars and other musical instruments would appear. Fully wined and dined, we would sing lustily to popular tunes with lyrics supplied by the well-organised musicians. This was also a good time for budding musicians to practice their craft. We were surprised at how many sailors played a musical instrument, and how many had a wonderful voice. Mine was not so good, but my dear friend Dominique on *Lobea* (France), whose voice was outstanding, would grab my arm and sing alongside, swaying to the rhythm.

Dominique and Claude (*Lobea*) were moored further along the same jetty from us. We came to an agreement that she would speak to me only in English and I would answer only in

French. After three decades in Australia, my knowledge of the foreign languages I had learnt needed some practice. It worked very well, and soon others joined in, as they strolled back and forth past our boat each day. This included Andi and Georges with their delightful daughter Lea on *Te Ara* (Monaco). They would become lifelong friends.

Apart from the musical entertainment, a Finnish couple staying at the marina produced some wooden throwing pins. This was for a Finnish throwing game called *Mölkky*. It soon became a custom for many of us to have a go. Though I have to admit, I was an abject failure at judging how to throw these pins: I blamed the wine at lunchtime, of course.

Marina life was pleasant and varied. We learnt that there was an excellent *hammam* in town. One Tuesday morning, usually women's day at the baths, a small group of us took off to experience the Turkish baths. We were greeted by an attendant. She guided us to a personal dressing cubicle, and gave each one of us a pair of sandals and a colourful towel to be tied around the waist for modesty. From here, we proceeded to the *hararet*, or hot room, where we shed our wrap. Naked, we chatted away, giggling naughtily and relaxing, allowing the important sweating process to begin in earnest. We were seated in a large side alcove. It was part of an impressive room, completely covered in marble. It featured a big dome, several basins with a central, raised platform above the heating source. After washing up and a massage, it was time for the scrubbing. As my turn came up, the attendant ushered me from the central platform to the place of action. I was unprepared for the torture that was to follow. She started scrubbing vigorously - or should I say sandpapering - my body. Oh, was I relieved when this was over. And very glad, when she massaged some oil into my sore back.

One of the topics to emerge from the Topics Night was a fascinating local history talk. Sheila, a cruiser who had spent a couple of years in Finike, was a key marina organiser. She was also a historian. She gave us an overview of the Lycians. They were an ancient people who inhabited the surrounding area. The land between Fethiye and Antalya is a compact, mountainous territory, and most of the Lycian sites were to be found atop

A Little Bit of MisChief

steep mountains. Sheila explained that what was particularly distinctive about these people was their sense of community. As a result, they enjoyed peace amongst themselves whereas other Greek city/states were constantly at war with each other.

Sheila's historical presentation was complemented by a talk from an archaeologist. He spoke to us about 'reading' ruins. To put our newfound knowledge to practice, Sheila organised an outing. We visited the ruins of one of the Lycian cities perched atop a mountain north of Antalya. The uphill walk was well worth it. The talks had made all the difference. Making our way gingerly over this rugged terrain, we proudly identified 'holes' that were grain silos, several buildings shared by the community, and thoroughfares almost completely obscured by the undergrowth.

On the steep slopes east of Finike, we visited a 'Chimera'. It was about half an hour's walk up the rocky path to reach the flames sprouting out of the sheer rock face. The flames shot out of the rock at several crevices. At one stage, we were admiring a bank of flames when all of a sudden another flame lit up just behind us. These natural gas flames dotted the hillside.

"We should have brought some sausages for a barbecue," I mused. To which Bjorn and our friends retorted, "Not really! Can you imagine the taste with that horrid sulphurous smell?"

The Chimera has been burning for many, many years. Apparently, the original Olympic flame is thought to have come from this location. At the bottom of the hill, a sign explained the local myth about the origins of the phenomenon: A king had inadvertently killed his brother during a hunting expedition. He was exiled to Lycia. The King of Lycia sent the exiled king to fight the Chimera: a half-man, half-animal beast. The exiled king hit the Chimera with a lance and spread the flames around the area.

On our way back to Finike, our coach got a punctured tyre. This occurred on the crest of one of the mountains, just as the sun was setting. We all got off the bus, and huddled together in the very cool evening air. Being the shortest, I opted for the middle, and was surrounded sportingly by everyone else - all a head taller.

"What amazing views!" I remarked, poking my head out. You could see all the way down into Finike. Greenhouses stretched before us down the slopes and through the surrounding fertile valleys reaching to the sea, presenting an eerie white shimmer. Did I mention that Turkey is one of the few countries in the world that is self-sufficient in produce?

On another occasion, we took the local bus with our friends Joe and Helen (*Dreamcatcher*) to visit an amphitheatre outside Myra. The amphitheatre was in excellent condition, with much of the surrounding building intact. We were sitting at the back of the theatre, admiring the view when some other cruisers walked into the arena. Among them was our Finnish friend, a tenor.

"Come on, sing for us," our friend Helen called out. We were treated to a solo performance in the wonderful open-air theatre, nearly bringing some of us to tears.

'The acoustics work so well!" Joe observed.

As we walked around Myra, we came across impressive rock-hewn tombs that were carved all the way up the face of the cliff. We walked past numerous greenhouses. Wild tomato and bean plants lined the streets, and we helped ourselves to the ripe broad beans.

Our next stop was the 11th century church in nearby Demre, which once housed St. Nicholas' remains. This is now the *Noel Baba* or Santa Claus Museum. Saint Nicholas was born in this area in the 4th century, became a priest and rose to the rank of bishop. He was much loved and brought joy to the area. According to lore, he came from a wealthy family and used this to aid the locals in need in a number of ways, whilst trying to remain anonymous. One story is that he would drop small bags of gold coins down the chimneys of houses where poor families needed to provide a dowry for their daughters (One can't help but wonder as to how he got up to the chimneys). This earned him the moniker of *Noel Baba* (literally: Christmas Father).

Over time, Saint Nicholas was depicted as the jolly Christmas figure called *Sinterklaas* or similar in Holland and neighbouring European countries. One theory has it that this evolved to become the Santa Claus we know today.

A Little Bit of MisChief

Cruisers know St Nicholas well. Apart from being the patron saint of reformed thieves, pawnbrokers, children and prostitutes among others, he is also the patron saint for sailors.

"That's quite a mix!" I remarked. "Prostitutes and sailors? What does it say for us?" I should mention that St Nicholas is also the patron saint of Russia.

Some of the local entertainment was not so exciting. I recall once visiting the camel wrestling in one of the surrounding mountain top towns: two male camels wrestle, typically in response to a female camel in heat being led before them.

"The dust is unbelievable!" I muttered, trying to find something to shield my nostrils and mouth. "And all that drooling just doesn't do it for me."

"Same for me! Let's go find a cool place for a drink. A pomegranate juice is called for, I think."

The *piece de resistance* of our Finike winter stay was probably the regular trips to Antalya for shopping followed by a concert, ballet or opera. One of the more permanent marina live-aboard cruisers, a Dutchman, was also a musician. He got to know the members of the orchestra at the concert hall in Antalya. Every couple of weeks he would organise a mini bus. This would take us on the hour's trip to Antalya, leaving in the afternoon. Our first stop was at a shopping centre, where we all scrambled to the supermarket or to the hardware store foraging for some exotic product or tool. At six thirty, we had our appointment with a local restaurant that served traditional fare. I loved the way they would bring out the bread, straight out of the oven and all puffed up. This would be placed on wooden boards along the table.

At eight o'clock, the concert hall beckoned. We were treated to some wonderful performances. The standard of the musicians and artists never failed to amaze. Often guest musicians from Europe and elsewhere were invited to join the repertoire for the evening. On one occasion, we were treated to a Russian opera. Our Dutch friend had organised a handout in English setting out the operatic story for us to be able to follow. The incredible part of it all is that the cost of the afternoon and evening's entertainment including meal and transport was always 20

Turkish Lira per head - that's about ten dollars.

◇◇◇

Finike offered a varied choice of restaurants. A favourite among the cruisers was a place called the *Mavi Sofra* (Blue Table). Whilst deciding on what to eat, guests were presented with a lovely salad with fresh lemons on the side, and warm Turkish bread. This was a healthy way to start the evening meal.

The restaurant was one of several situated on the riverbank walkway. One morning, as we sauntered past, we noticed the staff eating a dish different to the traditional Turkish fare offered at the premises.

"Good morning!" The owner greeted us.

"A lovely morning. Not so cold today. That looks delicious." It looked very much like a traditional Maltese dish I grew up with: a meat and vegetable casserole in a tomato sauce. "I do not think we have seen that on your menu."

'Ah, it is only for the staff."

A group of eight of us had become Wednesday regulars. As this was the designated day, I asked, "Can we have this tonight? We would love to taste what people around here eat."

"Yes of course! We will cook a special one for you."

Another eatery we frequented was a fish restaurant. One of the specialities was *hamsi* (Black Sea Anchovies). I love whitebait. The way it was cooked was just right, quick deep fried, crunchy but not 'spiky'.

We also got to know the two dogs that had adopted the marina and its residents, creatively named Big and Little. They were friendly creatures who followed us around the marina with their lop-sided grin. Everyone stopped to give them a pat, and often dog snacks. The news spread like wildfire when Big was hit by a car. The response was terrific. Before you could blink, enough money was collected to have him tended to by the local vet who valiantly tried to save one of Big's front legs.

It was touching to watch Tony from *Sunburnt* don his wetsuit every afternoon to jump into the water and exercise the dog in an effort to save its leg. This went on for a week or so. Unfortunately, this did not work out and the leg had to come

A Little Bit of MisChief

off. It didn't stop Big, always a happy-go-lucky dog, from running up and down the pontoons.

◇◇◇

The winter sojourn was an excellent time to carry out some necessary boat repairs and maintenance. Our list had grown long by this stage. There was an excellent chandler at the marina, where we could get most of the stuff we needed. We ordered a new mast-top wind speed sensor to replace the one damaged by the storm. I hauled Bjorn to the top of the mast, using the anchor winch, to replace it. The hail damage to the bimini was addressed by the sailmaker across the road from the marina, who was storing our sails. We still had to deal with the fuel tank leak that Bjorn had provisionally repaired in Egypt. Apart from that, our two 20-year-old aluminium water tanks also needed replacing. According to the people in the know they had been corroded by the chlorine in the water.

Armed with a map of Marmaris, Bjorn and I took the bus north to this cruising hub. We tracked down the person recommended to replace the water and fuel tanks. A long chat followed. Bjorn had a good look at the materials (for yachties: a new type of polyethylene from Germany that was recommended for fresh water tanks). Then a discussion of the construction process ensued. Once built, a tank was subject to pressure testing. The standard of work was impressive and we were in business.

We also ordered a new black water tank (for non-yachties, this is so that the toilet waste - hence the name - does not go out into the sea, especially in bays when we are at anchorage). We were not so sure about the type of material recommended for the diesel tank; the manufacturer's website did not guarantee the material for use with this type of fuel. The temporary fix for the leak that Bjorn had carried out in Egypt still did the job. So, we decided to leave this tank for changing in Malta over the next winter.

'Here is a drawing with full measurements," Bjorn started out.

"Yes, this is good. But I must come down and measure

myself to make sure it will fit."

Three weeks later, Bjorn and I installed our new water tanks and black water tank. They fitted perfectly. Soon, we had a trail of cruisers wanting to see the final product, before proceeding to order tanks for their boats. We should have charged a commission.

Mischief needed to be hauled out and the bottom prepared for the next sailing season. The many layers of antifouling needed removing, the hull resealed and antifouling applied. After talking to the boat yard manager, we were convinced to try a new type of antifouling paint. Being an epoxy based copper laden paint, this would seal the hull preventing water intrusion and osmosis problems (where water seeps in between the hull layers and cause 'bubbling' and potential weakening of the hull). This new product was reputed to last up to ten years. It only required a mild sanding between sailing seasons to re-expose the copper and prevent the hull from fouling up.

"It seems that we will need to have the boat on the hard for about three weeks. The yard manager said it will take about a week to sand down the bottom. I do not fancy being on board whilst this work is carried out."

'I definitely want to be here when the sanding is finished, before they start applying the paint." Bjorn replied.

"Why don't we use the first week to visit Istanbul?"

That is what we did. A bus ride to Antalya and a flight to Istanbul and there we were. Birgit, our marina neighbour during our stay at Alacati Marina, greeted us at the airport.

Istanbul, with its magnificent history spanning centuries, was on our bucket list, and well worth the visit. We were lucky in that Birgit, having lived in Istanbul for a few years, knew her way around the city. She took us to our first stop, the Galata Tower, where we could see the city and the Bosphorus Straits sprawled beneath us. Over dinner that evening, she helped plan our sightseeing trips. Armed with a map, we set out to explore the city the next morning.

"After hearing so much about the Hagia Sofia and the iconic Blue Mosque with its six minarets, it is almost unbelievable to be finally here in person." I told Bjorn. "Istanbul is incredible:

A Little Bit of MisChief

truly a meeting point of east and west; a real melting pot."

"Yes, somehow it seems more authentically Turkish. Cruising along the west coast, you don't get that strong sense of the traditional side. Certainly, more women here wear the traditional *hijab*."

We had great fun going through the Grand Bazaar. It is one of the largest and oldest covered markets in the world, with thousands of colourful shops. We visited the spice bazaar, exuding all sorts of pleasant smells. Bjorn and I spent a full and delightful week, well looked after by our friends Birgit and Wolfram. Apart from the 'must see' places such as the Ottoman era Topkapi Palace, we also managed to fit in some shopping for the boat. Another must was catching up with our Turkish friends whom we had met at the beach concession at Talyanaki, on our way up the west coast.

We returned to the marina just in time for the antifouling paint to be applied to the hull. With workers milling around everywhere, living on the boat was not a pleasant option. Instead, we checked into a small hotel on the hill behind the marina that was known for its varied Turkish breakfast buffet.

Over the winter, Turkish immigration laws had changed. We had to renew our Turkish visa. Accordingly, we set off on the Visa and Bacon run. This involved a bus trip to the town of Kas. There we took a ferry across the two miles to the island of Castellorizon, a tiny Greek island. We took the opportunity to purchase a number of pork products, including bacon. Then it was back to Kas and on to Finike with a fresh visa stamped in our passports.

◇◇◇

As spring approached, we noticed that the snow on the mountaintops surrounding Finike was starting to thaw. Everyone was now busy getting their boats ready, and planning their cruising season.

The more clement weather also meant that more and more people were taking the opportunity to go exploring. One of the places people were raving about was Cappadocia, in central Turkey. This semi-desert region was renowned for its unusual landscape, rock dwellings and the famous 'fairy chimneys'.

Our friends on *Dreamcatcher* had been there. "We stayed at this wonderful little hotel in Goreme," they told us. "The rooms were carved into the rock face."

"We have to check this out!" Bjorn told me.

"There is so much to see, and do not forget the early morning balloon rides."

So began our planning for a four-day visit. We were having a sundowner with our friends on *Interlude* and, hearing of our plans, asked if they could join us.

"We'd be delighted!" we both chorused and decided on the travel dates together.

Our journey started at the Finike bus terminal. The first stage was a bus to Antalya. As there were no direct flights from Antalya, the only option was an 11-hour bus drive to Cappadocia.

The bus journey was long and tedious to start with. As we passed Konya and approached Kayseri, we started to see more of the traditional buildings, including the *Caravanserai* between Konya and Kayseri. A *Caravanserai* was an enclosed building used as a safe way station or resting stop for travelling caravans and traders.

As we approached Goreme, we were fascinated by the changes in the landscape. Tall, cone-shaped rock formations dotted the area. Our destination was the same rock-face hotel where our friends had stayed.

"We are taking a hot air balloon ride early tomorrow morning," I told Katie and Kurt and they soon confirmed they would join us.

The hot air balloon rides were very well organised - impressive, in fact. We were picked up at the hotel by coach early in the morning and taken to the launch site. We were then guided to our balloon basket, which held 10 people. We gently rose into the skies. The next breathtaking half hour was one of those magical moments as the balloon pilot skilfully navigated the balloon and basket over the fairy chimneys, unusual rock formations, valleys and local villages, sometimes steering deftly between pinnacles. As the ride came to a close, the pilot guided

A Little Bit of MisChief

the balloon down and landed the basket on the back of a truck with unbelievable precision. Our heartfelt applause was greeted with a glass of champagne for all.

Walking around the outskirts of Goreme was fascinating.

"Those walls and fairy chimneys look unreal - as though they were part of a film set." I told Bjorn. I went up to see if they were genuine, which of course they were. Our intrepid friends opted for a beach buggy. It was not long before they tore past us up the road, hair blowing in the wind, waving merrily.

The highlight was undoubtedly the Goreme Open Air Museum. It contained numerous churches and chapels, carved into the rock. Entering what had seemed to us to be primitive edifices we were surprised to find superb frescoes dating back to the 9th century.

We took a tour to where many homes dating back to the Bronze Age had been carved into cliff faces. Over time, these were used as refuges, including by early Christians. Our tour concluded with a visit to the underground city at Derinkuyu, which could accommodate as many as 20,000 people. The number of levels and complex tunnels that were constructed without the help of today's mining knowledge fascinated us. Walking through the sometimes narrow passages, we came across all manner of cells or rooms used for a variety of purposes. Amenities included various storage rooms, sleeping quarters, meeting rooms, refectories and chapels. These cities also catered for livestock, and included stables and wine cellars. Fresh air was supplied via a complex system of vents, another engineering feat.

If Sana'a, the capital of Yemen, had been one of the highlights of our odyssey so far, then Cappadocia, in central Turkey, ranked as another equally magnificent discovery: a natural fairyland.

Back in Finike once again, we were now on a countdown to leaving the marina in the first week of May. Everything came out of storage: sails, ropes, canvas. We prepared the boat for going back out to sea, checking everything including rigging for wear and tear, and ensuring all split pins and rings were in place to stop rigging or anything else coming apart. We checked our route and plans for the summer, making sure we had enough safe havens along the way in case of a storm. Finally, we provisioned the boat, eager to get going.

This was our first winter stop at a marina, and it had been terrific. We had completed an impressive list of and managed a full and varied social life, forging new friendships that we would never forget.

A Little Bit of MisChief

Cappadocia Fairy Chimneys

Getting Together in the Marina

Christina Gillgren

16
Idyllic Greece!

Cruising the idyllic Greek islands has been a dream for so long! Yet when the time came to make this dream come true it was not without some hesitation. Two issues were uppermost: the first was the mood of Greeks given the economic crisis that had hit them. The second point was how to deal with the dreaded *Meltemi*, the north-westerly winds that can blow down the Aegean with real gusto, sometimes reaching Beaufort Force eight or nine.

The vast Greek Archipelago can be divided into groups of islands. On the Aegean side between Greece and Turkey, there are the Dodecanese Islands, which are the easternmost islands and include the well-known island of Rhodes. They stretch up along the Turkish coast and are often only a few miles away across from the Turkish mainland. West of these are the Cyclades, which include Paros, Mykonos, and Santorini to name a few. To the north of the Aegean are the Sporades Islands, and then on the western side, between Greece and Italy, are the famous Ionian Islands, which include Corfu. Of course, there are other smaller island groups, apart from the island of Crete.

Our plan was to cruise the Aegean for a season, and return to cruise the Ionian Islands the following year. With a four-month cruising window for our first Greek season, we planned to start out from Rhodes. We had agreed to pick up our son and his wife in early June and spend two lovely summer months cruising together. The journey from Rhodes northbound would take us through many of the Dodecanese Islands that lie along the west coast of Turkey to Patmos. This route was meant to dovetail with the *Meltemi* season, going as far north as possible before the northerly winds started blowing in earnest from mid-July. From there we would then head south and east through the Cyclades to Thira (Santorini) and then north-west to Poros, in the Saronic Gulf. We would then proceed through the Corinth Canal and cruise gently through the Gulf of Corinth, with stopovers to do some land travel, including seeing Delphi. After such a full itinerary, we hoped to be able to spend August gently bobbing somewhere at one of the Ionian Islands.

In the first week of May, we waved goodbye to Finike Marina with some sadness. It was hard saying goodbye to so many cruisers after a really enjoyable and varied winter - our first winter marina stay. Our experience of Turkey, and of the wonderful sites and places we had visited such as the inland trip to the stunning fairy-tale land of Cappadocia, was something we would carry with us in our hearts as our journey progressed.

It was good to be out and about again and enjoying balmy spring weather. We cruised up into the wonderful anchorages at Kekova Roads with its Lycian ruins spread both above ground and under water, and spent a week readjusting to life out of marinas. In one of the picturesque bays, we caught up with about eight yachts from other marinas, most of whom we had met cruising along the Turkish coast in the previous summer. Cruising tradition held true. We got together to enjoy a barbecue on shore, trading stories of our experiences of the different marinas, our winter adventures and plans for the summer season.

We made our first Greek stop at the islet of Castellorizon, some two miles off the Turkish town of Kas. We anchored in a gorgeous little bay surrounded by boats all making their way north. Castellorizon, though not officially part of the Dodecanese, is typical of the Dodecanese architecture with a strong Venetian influence. We loved this small island, perhaps

A Little Bit of MisChief

because so many of the islanders had made their home in Perth, Western Australia, some of whom we counted as close friends.

With very little wind, we returned to the Turkish coast making our way to Fethiye. We spent two weeks here. This was an opportunity to say goodbye to the country and to the gentle, friendly Turks we had grown so fond of.

As the date for the arrival of our son Mark and his wife Bridget drew close, we formally checked out of Turkey. With gentle winds blowing, we motor-sailed about 40 miles across to a bay on the north-east coast of Rhodes. First thing the next morning we called the marina on our VHF radio. We were told to try our luck in Mandraki Harbour. As it was early in the season and mid-week, the chances of finding a berth in this small port were better. As advised by friends, we contacted one of the yacht agents who operated at the harbour. We were quoted a price and told to proceed and tie up to the northern breakwater wall. No sooner had we done so that this agent came along asking for 80 Euros.

"You told us we could tie up for 30 Euros!"

"Ah, the economy in Greece is not too good. I have to make money for the winter too. You must pay me. This is how I make my living! I give you water and power, but you must pay me 80 Euros."

Bjorn and I looked at each other. This was not a good start to our cruising in Greece. We knew that the harbour charged seven Euros for the night, but we decided to go with the flow. Through bartering, we reached a compromise of 50 Euros. It seemed bizarre that anyone could just commandeer harbour berths and charge whatever they wanted, well above the charge due to the harbour master.

Next on our list was to check into the country. We had to walk all the way around the harbour to the harbour master's office only to be greeted by officials watching the European soccer, and totally indifferent to us. We finally got their attention long enough to be told we had to go across to cruise ship quay first, where the Greek immigration and customs office was situated. Off we trotted to the other end of the harbour. After paying the dues and obtaining our cruising permit, we trekked back to the harbour master for the final stamps. We found that this arrangement, criss-crossing the town to get to the 'right' authorities, was a Greek feature at many islands. This perhaps explained why so many cruisers just did not bother with formalities once they checked into the country.

We decided to walk off our 'steam' and the antidote was just along the harbour quay. On our way back to *Mischief*, we spotted the French flag on the stern of a boat we knew so well, and the owners just emerging from the main cabin.

"*Bonjour* Marie-Christine! *Bonjour* Yves!" We were delighted to have come across our friends on *Blue Marine*, whom we had first met in Malaysia, and in a few places along the way to Hurghada, Egypt where they had spent the winter.

"We must go and have dinner in town together tonight," Yves said. "I know a good Greek restaurant where they serve delicious traditionally baked lamb."

"We are off to the airport to pick up our son and his wife." I replied. "But I am sure they will be only too happy to do so." Well, this was a better start to our Greek adventure.

We spent a week on the island of Rhodes, catching up with our friends, sightseeing and shopping, the latter part involving going to the local Lidl store and purchasing about 80 litres of wine in readiness for the summer. This was an adventure in itself as Bjorn and Mark took off on the bus, equipped with Mark's enormous rucksack and our grannie trolley.

"You should have seen the face of the check-out girl! Dad placed a wine cask on the check-out counter, and told her we have 80 of these."

"Yes," Bjorn added. "So then Mark took a Mars bar from the display, saying that we should have something to eat as well."

"And then there was the challenge of getting back on the bus. The rucksack was so heavy I couldn't lean forward to get up the step, so dad had to push me up."

The sightseeing highlight was undoubtedly the castle and the old city, where we spent many an evening, strolling along the town streets and looking for restaurants and *tavernas*. We also immensely enjoyed taking a bus to visit Lindos, on the east coast, known for its clifftop acropolis, and its quaint

A Little Bit of MisChief

whitewashed buildings meandering down narrow lanes to the enclosed white sandy beach.

The Mediterranean is often called the 'Motorannean' among cruisers. This is because the wind is either blowing at gale force when it makes sense to remain in harbour or at anchorage, or totally absent, in which case the trusty motor has to play its part. With guests on board getting their 'sea legs', we were glad of the gentle winds that we encountered as we started out through the southern Aegean islands, heading north to Patmos.

Our first stop was at the pretty island of Simi, going into the aptly named enclosed bay of Panormitis, which we had so admired on our visit the previous summer. On our next stop, we anchored at Pethi to avoid the main town of Simi. We were aware of the nightmare of berthing along the quay in Simi harbour with fouled anchors and irate sailors. It was easy enough to take the local bus to the mountains above the main town, enjoying the beautiful view of the busy harbour below, bustling with life both on land and on the water.

With the Dodecanese Islands being tucked in between the peninsulas that jutted out from the Turkish coast, it made sense to make an overnight stop at the old Lycian port of Knidos (Turkey). From there we headed to Kos and berthed along the jetty in the pretty, circular harbour with the Castle of the Knights dominating the port. Kos was replete with ruins and our son, an enthusiastic and tireless trekker and researcher of sites to visit, was full bottle on the Hellenistic and Roman ruins all around us. With Mark relating the history, we paused to enjoy the shade under Hippocrates' Plane Tree. Hippocrates reputedly taught his pupils the art of medicine under this very tree, which would have made the tree old indeed, seeing how the sage had lived here around 400 BC.

I decided it was time to 'best' my son. "Bet you haven't heard about the Philosopher's Song." I started out.

"Oh, yes, I have," he grinned, and immediately got his iPhone out to play it for us, to our delight. As for you, dear readers, you will have to look it up: Monty Python's Philosopher's Song!

After an overnight stop at a lovely anchorage at the very tiny island of Pserimos, we called into Kalymnos, a traditional Greek town away from the tourist mainstream.

We liked the island of Leros, almost completely overlooked by tourists and despite its not promising description by other cruisers. It was customary when going into a harbour or anchorage to glance around to see what flags other yachts were flying. If it was an Australian or New Zealand flag, the day would usually end with a get together and a sundowner. We were also able to distinguish long-term cruisers from the charter boat fleets, usually by the amount of equipment on board the yacht. The greatest giveaways were the solar panels, the wind generator and the wind steer automatic pilot. Charter boats did not usually include these items. Also, we tended to be more wary of them as sometimes the skippers were not so well qualified and did some silly manoeuvres such as putting down an anchor too close to another yacht.

As we approached Ormos Lakki, we spotted Bob and Liz on *Birvidik* (UK) whom we had first met over the winter months at Finike. Bob advised us that the holding was not too good, and this proved to be true as we tried anchoring three times, with no luck, before giving up and taking a mooring buoy. We enjoyed a couple of sundowners together. Following their advice, we took the local bus around the island, coming across a stunning medieval castle and some pretty villages and bays on the east coast. From here, we moved to the small island of Lipsi and a lovely anchorage to wait out some northerly winds. Luckily there were some moorings that we could use as the holding for the anchor again was not the best, and *Mischief* had started dragging onto the rocks. Ashore, the only *taverna* in the turquoise bay provided us with one of the best Greek meals ever.

Our itinerary had us moving north at a reasonable pace, only stopping at islands for two to three days. We wanted to get to Patmos in time to meet up with cruisers from the Fremantle Sailing Club in Western Australia, our home base. Patmos is composed of three barren volcanic lumps, with the stunning monastery of St John the Divine and the winding streets with whitewashed houses of the Patmos *Hora*. We were to discover

A Little Bit of MisChief

that *Hora/Chora* was the name of the main town on almost every island. It was usually perched on a hilltop, as was the case with the Lycian and other cities in antiquities we had come across. This was so pirates could be spotted in advance and defence positions adopted. Curious as to why the name was so prevalent across the islands, we asked locals. No one seemed to have an answer.

"Well, it seems that each *Hora* is what we make of it," I chirped up. "So let's go and leave our own brand of mischief: make our own memories of each place!"

We moored stern-to the quayside in the port of Skala at Patmos. As usual, our first stop was the harbour master, where we paid the princely sum of a few Euros for tying up to the quay. The next morning heralded our scheduled meeting with a group of cruisers from the Fremantle Sailing Club, and we waved them in enthusiastically. Among them were our cruising mates from *Jacqui Mac*, *Jandanooka* and *Pegasus II* who had seen us off at Fremantle and then again at the Abrolhos Islands in Western Australia. The group had chartered three boats between them and had sailed from Athens, travelling together as a small flotilla. As they were headed in a south-easterly direction to Rhodes, the opposite to our sailing plan, we were able to give them heaps of information as to where to stop and what to see on the way.

"This cruising life is great. It seems to be one big party interrupted by pleasant sailing. And swimming in the most exotic places," Mark reflected. "In a way, it is not unlike our three year, round the world trek. We met some great people along the way, and then kept bumping into them down the road: happy reunions as everyone traded information and news."

It was a full and 'wet' two days and we had a memorable catch-up meal to celebrate our reunion with our home club sailing friends. This added to the appeal of Patmos, where John the Divine is reputed to have written the *Apocalypse*. Given its content, we could only surmise that some of it was a result of sitting in an uncomfortable cave on the hillside, probably either sweltering in the summer heat or feeling rather cold, wet and miserable in the winter months.

A major part of cruising is undoubtedly saying hello, and then farewell. Wishing each other fair winds, we waved goodbye to the Fremantle cruisers and to the Dodecanese islands, and set out to sail south to the Cyclades on the back of a good north-westerly wind blowing at a reasonable 15-18 knots. Unfortunately, the sea was not on our side, and we had the only uncomfortable trip in the Aegean. The swell was confused, leading to 'lumpy' conditions. We were pleased to see that both Mark and his wife took to the water well, despite the state of the sea.

The very small island of Levitha offered a wonderfully safe overnight anchorage in a narrow inlet. The sole inhabitants were two brothers who ran a small restaurant and offered mooring buoys and an evening meal, both of which we took up. The next day pleasant northerlies gently pushed us south to the long, narrow island of Amorgos with its steep-sided eastern flank. We tied up at the south-westerly harbour of Katápola (Vathy). Many of the harbours in the Greek Islands were called Vathy, which could cause some confusion. So, as with *Hora*, when using the term Vathy/Vathi, you also had to add the name of the island.

"The Monastery of Hozoviotissa is a must!" Mark informed us.

We rented a car and had a great day driving around Amorgos, which boasts some lovely, picturesque hilltop villages at the northern end. As we drove along the cliffs, and just before we took the turning to visit the monastery, Mark shouted for us to stop.

"Look at that bus stop!" he said, taking out his camera. There stood a quaint, whitewashed, little bus stop, very much like a church pew with a cross on top. I should mention that apart from being an encyclopaedia on what to visit, our son is also a keen photographer.

The whitewashed monastery, clinging to the cliff side some 300 metres above the Aegean Sea, stood out against the stark cliff-face. After making our way up the enormously long entrance stairway hewn through the rock, we were greeted by one of the three monks who now call it home.

A Little Bit of MisChief

"These pants are wide enough to fit both Mark and I," Bjorn started out. "And you get away scot free!"

We were amused by the fact that the men were given trousers - size extra, extra large - to put on over their shorts, in order to visit the monastery. Ladies, on the other hand, were allowed in, regardless of wearing pants (in my case, three quarter length trousers). We did not require a shawl as we had thought ahead and worn tops with sleeves.

"The same happened to us in Bali. I remember one of the monks giving Bjorn a wrap to cover his legs, as he was wearing shorts. But there was no problem for me!" I guess his legs must be sexier than mine, for monks anyway.

We toured the monastery, which was in very good condition. Imagine our delight when, after our tour, the Abbot handed out *loukoumi* (Greek equivalent of Turkish Delight) and a shot of Ouzo (the anise-flavoured aperitif that is widely consumed in Greece, very similar to the Turkish Raki) heated with honey and spices.

Amorgos and its whitewashed *Hora* with winding, narrow streets lined with bougainvillea and geranium was delightful. This was not an obvious tourist destination. Its main inhabitants seemed to be the endless number of goats roaming the hillsides.

Next stop was Santorini - classically Thera, and officially Thira - with its magnificent volcanic crater and whitewashed towns. We decided to try the small harbour on the southern end of the island. A friendly yachtie waved us over and helped us tie up alongside, explaining that this was the norm in this tiny harbour. Going ashore meant going over his boat. There were boats everywhere, cruisers mixed in with fishing boats and other workboats. Everyone was ready to lend a hand.

"The marina fees are very reasonable!" I said. "I expected we would have to pay through the nose on this island."

"We have just handed in our car." Our friendly yachtie told us. "It is the red one there. If you want it, just phone the owner. The key is under the carpet!" The car was yet another pleasant surprise, at 20 Euros per day.

We had gone from one of the quieter islands to Santorini which is probably the most renowned and visited Greek island.

This welcome was unexpected. We drove up to visit the fantastic hilltop towns perched on the edge of the cliffs. They overlooked the semi-circular caldera with its spectacular multi-coloured cliffs. The main town of Fira is the picture postcard of the Cyclades with its immaculate whitewashed houses, lanes and walls and contrasting blue roofs.

"I think it was a way to defy the German occupation during the war," Bjorn mused. "Greeks were forbidden to fly their blue and white flag; I can see that as an act of defiance they painted their houses blue and white."

"Well, that's one theory." Mark countered. "On this island the majority of the buildings were originally built using volcanic rock. Dark colours absorb heat, making dwellings unbearable especially in the height of summer. Painting the buildings white to reflect the sunlight was a practical way to stay cool."

"Why blue?" I wondered aloud.

"Blue became the most common colour because it was cheap. I think it was used for laundry, and so was easily available."

'Laundry?" I queried. A distant memory - almost a picture - came to mind. "Ahh …when growing up in Malta, my mum used to add something called the *bluena* (my spelling: apologies to the Maltese language) to the laundry to make white clothes whiter."

Much as we loved Fira, we all agreed that the even older town of Oia at the northern tip, with its cave homes, was more striking. The sunset at Oia was not to be missed. With a bottle of champers and some snacks, we made our way there, despite the hordes that had the same idea. Every square inch of wall or roof top seemed to be taken, but we managed to find a rooftop alongside a church for our sunset picnic. With two iconic windmills to one side, the view was breath taking and the moment of sunset almost spiritual as we disturbed the peace with the popping of the cork.

Mark was convinced that no visit to this island would be complete without walking up to the crater. The next morning, we left the small marina early and motored into the caldera, just

A Little Bit of MisChief

below Fira. We anchored in one of the tiny bays on Nea Kameni, the crater core which is still active. One look at the jagged rocks and we let Mark go ashore on his own, whilst we sipped a cup of tea in the cockpit.

Santorini was the southernmost island on our agenda. After a light tuna salad lunch, we started on our north-westerly route to a quiet anchorage on the south side of the island of Ios. The next morning we headed around to the main harbour to pick up my nephew, Ben and his partner Nadine. We won't say much about Ben turning up with his leg in plaster and on crutches. Ben had stepped off a bus in Athens and badly twisted his ankle. Plaster and all, Ben, a character larger than life, was determined that this was not going to impact on swimming, partying and having fun. The good thing is that even with six of us on *Mischief*, we all spread around and had a great five days of partying and cruising. Actually, we let the 'kids' do the all-night parties, and watched the late morning hangovers with bemusement. Being older, wiser and having more practice in these things we have learnt how to pace ourselves. Though I suspect many of our cruising friends will be falling out of their chairs, laughing at this assertion.

Ios is definitely a 'fun' island for the young. The main *Hora* is not only an attractive Cycladic village with the usual labyrinth of narrow winding lanes with thatch roofs straddling the lanes. It is also filled with lively nightspots, which are relatively inexpensive by Greek standards. This island grew on us. We left a few days later to explore more islands and anchorages.

The island of Sikinos, only seven miles away to the west sported the most delightful small harbour we had seen so far. We anchored just outside the harbour in crystal clear waters, but realised that this would not do as an overnight stop if the wind blew up. Reluctantly we left in the afternoon and headed 20 miles north to a safer anchorage at Antiparos for the night. The next morning it was a short but interesting trip to Ioannis Cove in the northern end of Paros.

After relentlessly moving from island to island for the last six weeks, we were delighted that we had now crossed the main waters of the Aegean without too many adverse winds. We were all - well, except Mark, that is - feeling somewhat jaded from visiting so many islands, monasteries, and Hora. The lure of spending some time standing still, swimming and relaxing was enticing. What luck then that the large and almost fully enclosed bay at Ioannis Cove was turquoise heaven. Lovely, tiny secluded sandy beaches dotted the northern shore. The added bonus was that this was a safe all weather anchorage.

There were about half a dozen boats in the Cove. As we manoeuvred to find the right spot - usually a sandy patch - to put down our anchor, we immediately recognised *Cormorant* (USA). This lovely double-ender (sailing boat with a round stern) belonged to Harry and Jane who were on their world circumnavigation. Going past them and waving, we then put down our anchor further along the northern shore, tucked more into the bay. By this stage, and to my delight, Bridget had taken over as the main boat food planner and shopper. Bridget has always enjoyed cooking. She makes the most creative and wonderful salads, and we looked forward with relish to her creations. She also became our anchor alarm setter. This was an important function as it meant that the alarm was set as soon as the anchor was put down, and not after we finished anchoring. Bjorn had pre-set the alarm to go off if the boat dragged beyond a radius of fifteen metres, so that meant that we could have a good night's rest, even on the windiest nights.

Bridget was also the water maker and fresh water usage controller, another important function with six people on board. Bjorn and I had worked out a system of showering. We would jump off the stern of the boat into the water - usually in our birthday suits - to wet ourselves. Then it was back on board for a scrub, using the biodegradable soap and shampoo, which we had bought for the purpose before setting out sailing. We would jump back in to rinse, and finally use the fresh water shower to rinse all the salt off. With so many of us on board, we thought swimwear was the way to go. But for the more intrepid among us, the important rule was that the one showering would shout: "Shower!" so all heads would face away from the stern. This saved on awkward moments.

A Little Bit of MisChief

As soon as we were settled in, we all got into the dinghy to go ashore and explore, heading for a small jetty jutting out of one of the main beaches. There was a fully-fledged beach concession with a bar and restaurant, sunbeds and umbrellas, all attractively laid out on a number of terraces going down to the beach. We discovered that there was also a regular ferry service from the jetty into the charming town of Naousa about two miles across the bay.

We had been let into the secret that Ben, our nephew, was to propose to Nadine on this trip, when they got to their next stop at Santorini. Imagine our grins therefore when these lovebirds went off to find their own little secluded beach for the afternoon. You do not get much privacy when there are six people on board. We were amused when, walking along the beachfront, we came across a chapel with a notice that read: 'These grounds are holly - plese do not swim in the nude' (sic).

"Don't worry," Bjorn sniggered. "With their even suntan they won't be distinguishable from the sand!"

That evening we all took the ferry into Naousa, a typical Greek village built around the water's edge. Ben treated us to a lovely *meze* meal which included dips, spinach and feta pastries, dolmades, meatballs and fritters, all washed down with wine and *ouzo*.

The next morning we bid Ben and Nadine farewell. We would miss their infectious laughter. A few days later, we welcomed Clare and her brother Lucas, friends of Mark and Bridget, for a short visit. We spent some lovely, balmy days jumping on and off the local buses as we explored the island. Then strong winds blew up and we had a first taste of a full-blown *Meltemi*. Our guests left us, and there was no alternative but to stay put until the weather improved. The next morning, as the wind meter clocked forty knots and more in gusts, Bjorn decided that he would stay on board, just in case. Ever eager to explore, Mark suggested that the rest of us take the ferry to visit Delos, one of the most important archaeological sites in Greece, and to the island of Mykonos. It promised to be a lively, bumpy ferry ride and Bridget decided to keep Bjorn company.

"This is a very ancient site. The scale of the ruins is

impressive. I like the Terrace of the Lions." Mark told me, as we explored the ruins of Delos. The *Meltemi* was blowing so hard that the sea between Delos and Mykonos was covered in spray. Mark and I fought the wind to remain upright. To be honest, there was so much sea spray that I kept my head lowered and shielded. I probably missed half of the sights our son was waxing lyrical about.

"I'm glad we did not try to get here with *Mischief*. We would not have been able to leave the boat in these conditions."

Mykonos Harbour was just as wind swept. We enjoyed a light lunch and a beer on the waterfront, and later a stroll through the town. On our return to our boat, Bjorn and Bridget regaled the day's exciting events.

"The wind was so strong that it simply lifted *Cormorant*'s dinghy with outboard motor attached clear out of the water and then flipped it over."

"Yes, then Bjorn just jumped into the dinghy to go round and give them a hand. But Harry was calm about the whole affair. He wanted to wait for the weather to settle." Bridget added. "Meanwhile *Mischief* was really straining against the anchor, but luckily it held!"

The blow lasted two days, and then just as suddenly the calm returned. We all went over for a sundowner on *Cormorant*, and we were amused to hear Harry relate how the engine had not only survived its dunking in the *Meltemi*. For the first time since purchasing the motor, it was working perfectly.

We ended up spending 11 days in Paros. As the winds and seas settled, we resumed our easterly crossing and sailed off to Serifos to see what was, Mark assured us, the most stunning *Hora* of the Cyclades. At anchor in the bay of Livadi, Bjorn, Bridget and I settled down to a cup of tea in *Mischief*'s cockpit. Meanwhile Mark went ashore, camera at the ready, to climb up to the whitewashed houses atop two steep peaks, one higher than the other, and crowned with the ruins of a Venetian *Kastro* or castle. He returned hours later to regale us with photos and more history of the island and its *Hora*.

A Little Bit of MisChief

From here we moved on to Kithnos. Just before we reached the island, we had one of the biggest scares ever when a ferry came racing down on us, cut a corner and almost ran us over. I had tried calling on the radio to see which direction the ferry was headed so we could stay out of the way, but was ignored. Then the low-life at the other end started speaking foul language: "I will f*** you!" and more in this vein and laughing - this on the emergency channel. We all were very unimpressed!

We had an otherwise quiet night at one of the lovely cosy anchorages on the eastern coast of Kithnos, the last Aegean island on our itinerary. We had visited a total of nineteen islands. Our route had been chosen with the *Meltemi* season in mind. Whilst I would love to put it down to my exquisite planning, the wind gods had been on our side, and we had enjoyed good winds and a great passage from Turkey.

We had a pleasant sail crossing over to the east coast of the Peloponnese. We went around the top of the island of Poros to a channel on the western end that led to the large safe bay between Poros and the Peloponnese mainland. Our destination was the picturesque anchorage called Russian Bay. This anchorage was another great tip we had been given. We planned to stay put for a week or so, celebrating our Aegean crossing.

No stay to Greece, however, would have been complete without a visit to Athens. We did this in two lots, with Mark and Bridget taking off to catch up with some friends there. On their return, we left *Mischief* in their capable hands and went to Athens ourselves, taking the bus to the town of Poros and a ferry across to the Greek capital. We had not chosen the right day to climb up to the Acropolis, crowned by the Parthenon overlooking the centre of Athens, It was a sweltering day, and hundreds of tourists milled about the site. The view was well worth the effort, though. We strolled along the charming Plaka district, but the heat got to us. It seemed that a return visit to Athens at a cooler time of the year was called for. But a good outcome of this trip was that we managed to have a new hard drive installed on our computer (the old one 'crashed').

It was refreshing to get back to the cooler conditions on the boat for a few more days of rest and relaxation. The quayside on the lovely quaint town of Poros allowed for gentle strolls where we could stop for a meal and a refreshing drink or two. This was apart from the sundowners in the wonderful wooded anchorage at Russian Bay. Or so we thought!

There were two other cruisers with us in this bay that we had kept coming across, namely *Cormorant* and *Feijao* (Australia). We had spent a week at this haven, and our anchor was well settled having worked its way through the weed into the mud. One afternoon, with the wind forecast to increase later in the day and overnight, we were sitting in *Cormorant*'s cockpit enjoying a sundowner, when a Greek flagged charter yacht pulled into the bay. On board were about half a dozen decoratively dressed women, obviously having a good time. The skipper pulled up in front of *Feijao* and dropped his anchor - right on top of *Feijao*'s.

"You just put your anchor on top of mine! You will end up bumping into my boat!" Lenny called out. The arrogant male captain just strutted across the deck, shouting what we took to be obscenities back at us. More words were exchanged but the skipper, with all the females looking on, did not want to look like the fool he was. He insisted he knew what he was doing. It didn't take long before the charter yacht started to fall back onto *Feijao*. Immediately Bjorn, Harry and Lenny jumped into our dinghy, that being the more accessible, and went over to *Mischief*. Bjorn fetched the wire cutters, and then they made their way to the charter yacht.

"If you don't take up your anchor and move away, we will cut your anchor chain." Bjorn threatened. It was an empty threat, as there was no way that the cutters would do anything at all to the chain. A seasoned sailor would have laughed them off. Luckily, Bjorn had sized up the skipper as a beginner who was trying to impress the female passengers on board.

Meanwhile, Harry took out his camera and snapped the skipper and the boat, with the boat's name showing. "Smile for the lawyers sucker," he shouted. Whilst this was going on, the girls preened and posed for the camera, not having a clue as to what was going on. The combination must have done the trick but the worst was yet to come. Fuming with rage, the skipper

A Little Bit of MisChief

stormed to the cockpit and started the engine. He threw the switch to haul out the anchor. Then he started motoring off without even looking back, his chest puffed out and white captain's hat at a jaunt trying to look the part.

Well, as he motored off in a huff, *Feijao* followed suit! The idiot did not even realise what was happening. Bjorn immediately took off with the dinghy to overtake the charter boat and point out the disaster he had caused. The skipper sheepishly stopped the boat. As Bjorn drove up to the front of the boat, the mess became obvious. The anchor chains of the two boats were well and truly tangled. It took the three men a good half hour, getting drenched and dirty as they tried to work the heavy chains - weighed down with the anchors - loose. Meanwhile the Greek charter boat so-called skipper just looked on. Once free, the charter yacht skipper, totally embarrassed, took off at top speed. Lenny was left to retrieve his anchor and motor back into the bay. He drove around a few times as the anchorage had now filled up with yachts. It did not help that the wind was picking up. He finally managed to find a spot close by and put down his anchor. He was lucky that the anchor held fast immediately.

We had seen a number of incidents in harbours with anchors getting fowled, but nothing had prepared us for this. We were yet to see worse as we approached August and the summer shutdown in many parts of Europe. We had been warned about the hordes making their way to the waters, often totally unaware of the basics of seamanship, and a danger both to themselves and to others. But that is for another chapter.

Christina Gillgren

Amorgos Bus Stop

The Aegean

17
The Corinth and the Ionian

We left Poros with gentle winds and a good forecast for the coming week and cruised up along the Peloponnese coast towards the Corinth Canal. Our first stop was at the historic town of Epidhavros. We proceeded between two beacons into the sheltered bay at the base of steep wooded slopes.

"The Greek theatre outside the town is worth visiting," Mark informed us. "It is one of the best preserved of all Greek theatres."

We spent a pleasant afternoon at the ancient theatre. It was all that was promised, including the fact that the acoustics were so good that you could drop a coin in the arena, and it would be heard clearly from any one of the 14,000 seats.

Then, in company with *Feijao* and *Cormorant*, we made our way to Kalamaki, just to the east of the entrance to the Corinth Canal. The Canal connects the Ionian Sea via the Gulf of Corinth with the Aegean. On the way there, we suddenly saw a large motor yacht - the proverbial gin palace - approach at a reasonably fast pace. It was heading straight for us.

Bjorn, who was at the helm, shouted: "Watch out!" He quickly disengaged the autopilot, put the engine on full power and steered the boat away at a right angle. The boat missed us by what felt like only metres, the gleaming polished stainless steel looming large. Even more amazing was the fact that there was nobody in sight - the fly bridge was empty! The boat was on autopilot with nobody on the lookout.

We watched in shock, cursing the stupidity of whoever was in charge when this person, the owner or skipper, just walked out of the cabin, drink in hand. He suddenly noticed us, and his mouth fell open - totally surprised to see us so close.

I'm sure he heard my not so polite language as we held on. Our boat rocked violently from side to side thanks to the enormous wake of the powerboat.

We love adventure and excitement, but certainly not of this stupid type! As we anchored at Kalamaki, we decided on the vino before we thought of dinner. We needed to calm down.

Early the next the morning we checked in with the Corinth Canal authorities, paid our dues to go through and then had to wait until given the go-ahead to proceed. The wind started to pick up. After a harrowing two-hour wait, during which time we had struggled to keep the fenders in place as the boat rolled up and down against the quay, the authorities instructed us to follow a small freighter. We were told we had to keep the speed up with the freighter, which was quite a challenge for a sailing boat. The canal, about four miles in length, is narrow and dramatic with steep sides that were heavily eroded in places.

"It feels like we are at the bottom of a deep ditch. The state of the walls is not reassuring. They look like they could collapse onto us any moment," I wondered aloud. "It does not seem as though much effort is being made to maintain it, despite the hefty fee to go through."

Fortunately, there was only a small counter current. With engine on full throttle, we motored behind *Cormorant*, with *Feijao* following, all trying to keep up the speed. On the way, we had to go under a bridge. As we got close I watched *Cormorant* go through with what looked like very little space between mast and bridge. I looked up in horror. "I think our mast is too high. I don't think we'll make it!" I realised I had not checked the height on the sea chart.

We all held our breath as we motored along, and were relieved when no mishap occurred. It took us about an hour and a half to get through, and then we were in the Gulf of Corinth.

A Little Bit of MisChief

Up went the sails as the wind started to pick up. Before long we had 20 knots plus head winds and a short sea that was becoming very choppy and wet. We gave up on our original plan to go through to Galaxidi and decided to go to one of the closer bays at Antikiras. With steep slopes split by spectacular ravines, we were protected from the swell, but had to endure some strong gusts blowing down the slopes until sunset, when it finally all died down. In the morning, we made an early start before the wind picked up again and motored round the corner into Galaxidi, which turned out to be one of the prettiest little harbours we had visited to date - but also with an ominous clunking sound in the gearbox.

"Look, there's a spot left between those two boats," Bjorn pointed out. Soon enough Peter and Dorothy on the catamaran *Purr* (Australia) helped us reverse into the tight mooring, Peter jumping on shore to take our ropes and help tie up.

Peter and Dorothy also came from Perth and from the same yacht club of Fremantle, but this was the first time we had come across them. *Feijao* was tied up two boats away, and *Cormorant* had decided to stay at anchor just outside the tiny harbour, unaware of our engine problem. Presently, Peter and Bjorn were deep in conversation.

"We've got a problem," Bjorn started out, describing the ominous sound, and where it came from.

A check of the engine, some fiddling with the gearshift, and Peter opined, "I think your problem seems to be the drive plate."

For the technically minded, the drive plate sits between the engine and the gearbox and its sole purpose is to soften the connection between the two. Peter pointed out a mechanical shop along the harbour, and soon the mechanic was on board, confirming the diagnosis.

"The drive plate needs replacing." He said. "I will order one from Athens. It will be here in two days."

Meanwhile Bjorn, ever cautious about repairs in exotic places, looked up the engine manual and found out which part was required. Sure enough, when the mechanic returned with the drive plate, it was the wrong size (the metric versus imperial measurement standard, namely centimetres and not inches). After an afternoon of chasing around with phone calls all over Greece, Bjorn ordered the part from the UK with express delivery from our trusted source we had called upon in Phuket. Much to our delight and surprise, this ended up being only half the price quoted in Greece.

Whilst waiting for the part to arrive, we had great fun exploring the local restaurants. The *Mischief* team, Mark and Bridget, and Bjorn and I, took this opportunity to visit Delphi. We went by bus to the town of Itea, further along in the bay we were in, and there connected with another bus to take us up the mountain. This renowned historical site, which also includes the famed Oracle, was considered by the Greeks to be the centre of influence of the ancient world. It was by far the most stunning site we had been to in Greece with a commanding view of the Gulf of Corinth. The museum is modern, well set out and definitely worth the visit. Thank goodness, there was a modern town with the same name nearby, where we could have lunch and rest our weary feet after following the ever-enthusiastic Mark through the terraced ruins spread over the mountainside, and then again following in his footsteps in the museum.

Our return to Galaxidi was met with the terrific news that the engine spare part had arrived. It was the right size and match for our somewhat exotic and proudly imperial Thornycroft engine. Now came the hairy bit of replacing the drive plate. By this stage, Bjorn was wary of the local trades.

"We can do it," Peter offered. We were lucky to have the assistance of such a helpful cruiser who knew a thing or two about engines. I could not bear to watch while Bjorn and Peter, with Mark helping, pushed the shaft back whilst the boat was still in the water.

"Come on Bridget. Let's wait ashore." I could see the boat going glug ..glug ..glug … down to the bottom of the harbour, but knew better than to voice my thoughts aloud.

'Success," Mark yelled out, a couple of hours later. Bjorn, buoyed by Peter's expertise and confidence and with his help, had successfully replaced the plate. Mark had played his part, diving under the hull to convince the shaft to go back in again.

A Little Bit of Mischief

And *Mischief* was still afloat, bobbing happily in this quaint little harbour. Once again, my darling chief engineer (definitely in the captain's good books, so that meant bonus points ...but that's between the two of us!) had risen to the occasion, doing a tremendous job.

That evening, the four boats got together and we went out to one of the local restaurants that Peter and Dorothy had discovered. We had a wonderful evening, a great meal, washed down with a lot of good vino. We followed this up with more of the same on *Purr* that, being a spacious catamaran could accommodate us all.

Whilst in Galaxidi, we had another of Mark and Bridget's friends join us, bringing more boat spares from the UK. We invited Harry and Jane (*Cormorant*) over for a sundowner cum light dinner and Bridget made the most delicious pizza on thinly sliced eggplant and zucchini on the grill - another success for our head chef.

A few days later, we motored out of Galaxidi to continue our trek eastwards towards the Ionian Sea. We were delighted with the return of a smooth running engine, happily putt putting away in the light conditions. We were headed to a pretty, enclosed bay on the small island of Trizionia, some 15 miles to the west along the Corinth, for an overnight stopover. Many other cruisers had warned us to keep clear of Patras, known unflatteringly among sailors as "Putras" because of the stench and grubby appearance of this busy port town. Our destination was the island of Ithaca, some seventy nautical miles away. Mark and Bridget were competent sailors but, as it was approaching the end of their stay, we decided it was time for them to experience an overnight sail before they left. So we left at 5.00pm, had a light dinner together and then split up. Bridget and Bjorn took the first watch from 8.00pm to midnight, with Mark and I scheduled to take the midnight to 4.00am watch before Bridget and Bjorn returned to the post.

The bridge at Patras, with a span of over two miles, is the longest suspended bridge in the world. As we approached, things got quite hectic: ferries crossing in all directions and a lot of boat traffic around. Though it was time to go for our nap, it was too exciting in the cockpit. Five miles before the bridge, I called the water traffic authorities to seek permission to transit the bridge. It was divided into zones, with the central zone with the highest distance above water reserved for commercial traffic. Westbound yachts, like ours, went through the northern zone, and eastbound traffic used the southern part of the span. The advantage to transiting at night is that the whole bridge is lit up and each zone is individually lit and more easily identifiable.

"Rion Traffic! Rion Traffic! This is sailing yacht *Mischief*!"

On the third attempt, I got an answer. After supplying the authorities with the boat dimensions including mast height, the response came through. We were told to traverse the bridge on the northern shore at a certain number of pillars from the right.

"I hope that is high enough for our mast," I muttered. I would have preferred to be closer to the middle of the bridge. No matter how much you are told of the distance between water and bridge or whatever is overhead, it always seems there is not enough height when you are approaching with a fifteen-metre mast on top of the deck.

Nor was that the only excitement for the night.

"Look, that ferry looks like it is coming straight at us," Bridget cautioned.

"No, they probably know what they are doing." Mark added.

"Mmm, I think it is headed in a more southerly direction towards Patras. See, now we are beginning to see its port light." That was Bjorn, but I was not so convinced.

"You have to really watch out for these ferries, Mark. They drive like maniacs, and enjoy giving us yachties a good scare! Remember the ferry off Kitnos? And that power boat before the entrance to the Corinth?"

Luckily the rest of the night proved to be uneventful. We had become progressively aware of the significant increase in boats and traffic, probably due to the fact that we were closer to mainland Greece and to the time of the year. And with greater activity on the water, there was a parallel increase in near misses and poor seamanship. It was vital that you keep one eye on what others in the vicinity were doing.

A Little Bit of MisChief

After slowing down for the last few hours of early morning, we motored into the harbour at Vathi on the island of Ithaca at around 7.00am. Ithaca was the island home of Odysseus accordingly to Homer. The harbour town is built amphitheatrically around a deep, sheltered bay with a narrow entrance and overlooked by mountains with steep, wooded sides reaching down to the water. What a stunning place this was, seemingly a very safe harbour and beguiled by the tranquil waters. We decided to rest up after the overnight sail, and then go ashore in the afternoon.

"Hey, the wind meter is showing gusts of up to 25 knots!" I called out.

I had just awoken and, hearing the wind blowing over the deck, went up into the cockpit to check it out. The cruising guide warned about fierce gusts blowing down the steep cliff face straight into the harbour in the afternoons, even if the forecast for the area was only light winds. They were not wrong! Bjorn checked the chart-plotter and saw that we had not moved, meaning that the anchor had dug in and was holding well.

We had a wet ride going ashore in the dinghy and the wind seemed to be increasing. We had a light lunch at a harbour-side *tavern*. And then sought out the ferry terminal where we made enquiries as to how Mark, Bridget and their friend Lucy were going to get to Corfu, their next destination. The direct ferry service had been cancelled and it seemed they either had to take a ferry back to Patras (a whole day) and then another one back out to Corfu, or else try and make it to the next island of Levkas from where a ferry service operated to their destination. Yet to get to Levkas, it seemed they had to get a taxi to the north of the island.

"You won't make it," I told them. "The time is too tight and there are too many uncertainties! Bjorn and I can come back and explore Ithaca later, so I suggest we enjoy the afternoon, have a meal ashore, and then head back to the boat. We'll get up early tomorrow and head for Levkas."

We had a lovely last dinner together, washed down with wine and Ouzo. Luckily, the wind eased off at dusk and we had a drier return trip to *Mischief*.

With favourable weather forecast, we upped anchor the next morning and motor sailed north to Nidri Harbour in Levkas.

"We are not allowed to tie up at the jetty, so make sure you have all your stuff ready to go. I will go alongside so you can disembark," I said, giving them all a big hug. It was sad to wave farewell. They had been with us for a good two months, and we had had such a great time together: not a cross word, but rather plenty of good times.

◇◇◇

With a bit of a heavy heart, we motored to Tranquil Bay, the little bay across the water from the quay at Nidri. "Ahoy, *Mischief*!" came the welcome as we spotted Harry and Jane on *Cormorant*. This helped cheer us up.

We stopped in Nidri for about a week, adjusting to being on our own again. Bjorn and I tried to work up some enthusiasm for cruising the Ionian. In truth, after visiting so many islands, more *Chora/Horas* than we could remember, numerous churches, ruins and other sites we were somewhat exhausted from sightseeing and needed a breather. The cruisers around us were full of suggestions. They gave us good tips for anchorages in the area, where we could swim, relax and enjoy the beautiful bays. What we had not factored in was the August holidays and the invasion of yachts by Italians and northern Europeans. This heralded the crazy - and sometimes downright dangerous - manoeuvrings of some of the yacht skippers and charterers.

We cruised around the island of Meganisi, which had a number of picturesque inlets on its north-eastern shore. These gave excellent protection from the prevalent winds of the area. As usual, we made sure to get in around midday to find a good spot before the hordes arrived. At Abelike Bay, from where we could walk over the hilltop to the capital of (yet another) Vathi, ended up having to tie up stern-to to the shore as there were many boats in this idyllic popular bay. The cruising guide warned against aggressive rats ashore. So Bjorn put the rat protection wheels (these were made from a rope reel, cut in half, so that you had a tube to pass the rope through which

A Little Bit of MisChief

would make it spin around and thus disable any unwanted 'visitors' from climbing on board) on the stern ropes which were tied up to the shore. I guess it had to happen sooner or later but, a week after our arrival in this bay, to our horror we got a stowaway.

We had just fallen asleep when Bjorn heard a crackling sound. "What's that!" He jumped out of bed and, after looking around in the galley, noticed that the plastic bag that was wrapped around the bread was chewed up. A check of the bread inside confirmed our worst fears. We had a 'visitor' on board.

The next morning, we got up early, went ashore and walked over to the general store in Vathi. We were not surprised to find an impressive array of rat catching devices, given the island's reputation. The storekeeper recommended a rattrap and some glue strips as being the most effective. Armed with an array of these products, we returned to the boat. A few yachts had left the anchorage, so we took advantage of the added space and untied our stern lines, to swing freely at anchor.

Well, that somewhat turned me off the idyllic Ionian; but in truth, these pests exist everywhere. We left Meganisi in disgust and tried to find another anchorage where we would not have to tie up to shore. Following up on a tip from *Cormorant*, we visited the lovely bay at Port Leone and here we succeeded in catching the culprit on the second night. Unfortunately, this was not after the dammed rat had started to chew on our new VHF coax cable which went right to the top of the mast, and which we had only just installed with great difficulty a year before! Following the trail of droppings and bits of rubber, we worked out that the rat must have tried to come aboard on the rope tied to shore and fallen into the water because of the rat protection wheel. Then it must have somehow swum to the front of the boat, climbed our anchor chain and made its way to the hatch where it chewed our fly screen to get in. Once inside the boat, the galley was its goal. The trap we had placed here had gone off, but had not succeeded in trapping the wily pest. However, the gluey strips worked well for they trapped the very unwelcome guest as soon as we put them out in the evening - and before it did more damage.

A few days later, we decided to put this incident behind us and visit the southern Ionian, starting with Ithaca, where we had cut our visit short. Following up on another tip, we left Port Leone at first light and called into the tiny harbour at Kioni, on the east coast of north Ithaca, before noon. Our luck held, and we found just about the last spot on the harbour quay - and right alongside Georges, Andi and daughter Lea on *Te Ara* whom we knew from our winter at Finike Marina. This called for a celebration. Out came the bottle of vino, even though it was not yet four 'thirsty'.

Georges and Andi had been in the harbour for a day or two. "You will get a show this afternoon! At around four, we will all gather on the fore deck and watch! You will be amazed."

At the appointed time, a glass of wine in hand, and lots of nibbles to keep us going, lying on some cushions propped up against the mast and with great anticipation, we watched as the boats started to trickle into the harbour.

Now picture this: a small harbour at the head of a small bay, which could accommodate perhaps 15-20 yachts along the quay, all of which are usually taken up by midday. Then, come the afternoon, the trickle turned into a stream, and soon that transformed into a melee as suddenly a flotilla of charter boats appeared and the whole harbour came alive with boats jostling about and dinghies flying by all over the place trying to secure a spot before the next guy. We counted about 70 boats one evening, looking to tie up for the night. As there was deep water throughout the bay, boats would have to anchor close to shore and put a stern line out to tie up. The yelling, shouting, trying to get a place first, dangerous tactics, swearing and colourful language in Italian, German and other tongues certainly kept us entertained every evening, as we kept watch to ensure our anchors did not get snagged and we came unstuck. 11,000 nautical miles from Fremantle to the Mediterranean, and this was definitely the scariest bit of boating we encountered!

"Look at that mad man! He is reversing full speed to get in ahead of that other boat! Hell, they are going to collide... Oh! No! There's a dinghy in the way!"

"Now you see why we have decided to stay here for now,"

A Little Bit of MisChief

our friends on *Te Ara* told us. "This is the "Ferragosto" season when many companies and factories in Europe close down for the summer break and everyone goes on holiday." Having watched these antics, we decided that we did not want to run the gauntlet at this time of the year. The word was that everywhere was just as crowded and crazy, and so we stayed put. We rented a car with our friends on *Te Ara* and took off to explore Ithaca, spending a wonderful day and many pleasant afternoons together.

Then suddenly one afternoon we were in the middle of the fray.

"What are you doing? There's no place here!" Bjorn shouted as a Dutch boat started to reverse between the next boat and us. The Dutchman continued reversing relentlessly. There literally was perhaps half a metre between our neighbours and us.

"Quick, more fenders," Bjorn continued, as he grabbed one and went to the prow to try and stop the Dutch boat from crashing into our hull.

By now, all the skippers close to us collected on the quay or on the nearby boats, shouting for the guy to go away. Our neighbour emerged from the cabin, enraged that his boat was being knocked about, but this Dutchman was a stubborn one. The fenders between *Te Ara* and us started squeaking away in protest. The Dutchman continued reversing, revving up to push his way through. As he squeezed in, all the boats started moving to give way, and up to five boats away in every direction had to re-adjust their shorelines, as we were now packed in like sardines, the language around us suddenly very colourful and angry.

"We are going to have to wait for him to leave first," said Bjorn, as he stomped angrily to the stern to get yet more fenders as he watched *Mischief* and this newcomer almost rub against each other, expecting the quasi-flattened fenders to explode with the pressure. "If we go first, we are likely to pick up his anchor and that will be a real mess!"

That evening's sundowner was to calm us down. It was obviously time to move to new pastures. The next morning our unwelcome neighbour squeezed out again, waved off by more than one universal sign by angry cruisers.

"Good riddance! Hope there are not more of the likes of him around!" our neighbour hissed at the Dutchman who was now pulling up his anchor.

We left later that morning, and headed to Tranquil Bay in Nidri where we could swing freely at anchor. We spent our last week in the Ionian in this bay, getting ready for our crossing to Sicily and then to Malta for the winter.

Towards the end of the first week in September, we left Nidri, Levkas heading straight to Malta. We had a lovely sail for the first 36 hours with northerly winds of around a comfortable 10-15 knots. Some 50 miles from Syracuse, we ran into an unpleasant swell that was slowing us down dramatically and making it uncomfortable on the boat with little wind to counter this. Therefore, it made more sense to revert to our original plan and change direction for Syracuse. We got there early morning to see once again our friends on *Cormorant* at the northern end of anchorage, just underneath the old city of Ortygia, which is the historical centre of Syracuse.

We had made it to Syracuse in time to avoid a big blow between Sicily and Malta. Unfortunately, the swell worked its way into the north of the bay and made it uncomfortable. Therefore, *Cormorant* and *Mischief* moved to the south of the large bay that was more in the lee. It was here that we celebrated Harry's birthday in style.

We spent close to a week waiting for favourable winds to sail the last 80 miles to Malta. In the meantime, I rediscovered Ortygia, which has been transformed from the dirty, grotty city I remembered from some 40 years ago, to this incredibly pleasant, scrubbed up and restored old town - charming, warm and friendly. We literally drooled at the lovely fresh produce, the array of fish and the range of cheeses and salamis at the excellent market just outside the old city. We fell in love with the place, and would have stayed on but for the need to get to Malta and secure a winter berth. With a little bit of sadness we had to say farewell once more to good friends.

A Little Bit of MisChief

The Corinth Canal

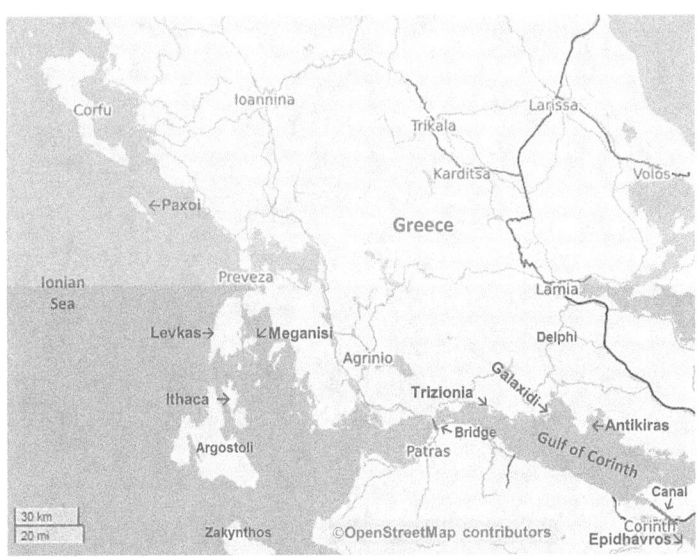

The Corinth and the Ionian

Christina Gillgren

18
Finally, Malta

We had a pleasant crossing to Malta, sailing for the first part and then motoring as the wind died down overnight. If you draw a line across the Mediterranean from Gibraltar to Syria and then north to south from the middle of Sicily to North Africa, roughly at the intersection will be the beautiful and historic island of Malta - my country of birth. Its location in the middle of the Mediterranean has meant that every shift in power in the region has left its mark on the island. Temple ruins that date back to prehistoric times, a succession of invaders and occupiers that included the Phoenicians, Romans, Arabs, the Knights of St. John and the French have contributed to the island's rich heritage. After about 170 years of British rule, Malta became a Republic in 1974.

"Land Ahoy!" I began.

As the sun rose, different landmarks came into view. We had been living in Australia for about 35 years. Though we had visited the island often enough, it had been a long time since I had had the pleasure of approaching the island from the sea, as had been the case in my sailing days of old.

"It looks so different. The coastline had been transformed. Look Bjorn! That must be the Portomaso Tower to the right. The sea front buildings in Sliema dominate the skyline." It wasn't until we were closer that we could see the majestic bastions that surround Valletta, pointing the way for us.

I cannot describe the emotions of finally sailing into Marsamxett Harbour in Malta in our beloved *Mischief*. We put down our anchor close to the point of the Ta' Xbiex peninsula. We were a bit tired after our overnight sail and eager to make contact with family and friends on land. After breakfast and a strong cup of coffee, we launched the dinghy and headed ashore. Car hire was top of our list, and we got an excellent three-month deal. Then it was off to Customs, Immigration to check in, and the Marina offices to try and find a berth.

A few calls to family followed and our next stop was a short visit to my elderly parents who lived roughly in the middle of the island.

That evening we decided to dine at one of the restaurants on the shore nearby but not without having a celebratory drink beforehand. After so many countries, bays, ports, harbours and anchorages, it was truly amazing to have our first sundowner on *Mischief*, overlooked by the 600-year-old imposing bastions that surround the capital of Valletta and the neighbouring city of Floriana.

As the sunset, Bjorn proposed a toast: "Here we are, in the heart of the Med, after an epic trip of over 13,000 nautical miles to get here." This is just a bit more than halfway around the world - 21,600 nautical miles.

"Yes, we made it! And what an adventure it has been."

"And with more to follow we hope." We hugged and shed tears of joy. It had been a terrific and sometimes somewhat terrifying journey. And on the personal level, we had transitioned from independent, successful and powerful high-flying careers to living together in close proximity in the small space a boat provided, however comfortable our beloved *Mischief* was. It was amazing that, despite the distance covered, we had not encountered one bad storm whilst actually out sailing at sea. The strongest winds we had experienced were those at the Tantabiddy anchorage when going up the coast of Western Australia and then again in the Aegean Sea with the *Meltemi*. Yes, we had had some fun with strong currents outside Bali, and thunderstorms and waterspouts around the Equator in

A Little Bit of MisChief

Indonesia - and maybe the odd brush with suspicious looking vessels. *Mischief*, with our mythical Swedish houseguest on board, had looked after us well.

We had worked fantastically as a team, Bjorn ever supportive of my role as Captain. This had caused enough 'mischief' in certain countries not used to dealing with women in charge. And Bjorn had delivered much peace of mind as my trustworthy and dependable chief engineer, always with a solution at hand. Together we had made it a voyage to remember, both the richer for it.

I had been warned by other cruisers that getting a berth in Malta could be difficult. I had contacted the various marinas on the island via email, only to learn that many of them were almost full. So it was a good thing that we had followed advice and arrived on the island early in the autumn season. Banking on the fact that many local yacht owners choose to take their boats out of the water during the winter months, I approached the marina manager to try and coax a berth at the very safe Msida Creek Marina. It took a few days and we had to move around a bit to begin with, but we finally managed to secure one of the guest berths on the marina breakwater quay.

We were lucky to have a friend, Daniel, with an empty house in Malta that we could move into. Everything came off *Mischief*, and she got a thorough scrubbing and airing.

It was wonderful to be able to spend time in Malta again. The leisurely months ahead meant this was a great opportunity to reconnect with the extended family and all the young newcomers, and familiarising ourselves with the island and its quirks once again. Before long, our anticipated quiet time turned into a full social life. A television interview on our journey brought out old friends, sailing and land-based, and we enjoyed many a reunion, exchanging life stories. Lifelong friend Johanna was there ever ready to lend a helping hand or join us in a sundowner or a movie evening. In fact, I distinctly remember watching *Mamma Mia* the movie, sprawled in the cabin after a cosy dinner, wine in hand and cabin heater going.

We also made sure to catch up with Yves and Marie-Christine on *Blue Marine*, and Andi and Georges on *Te Ara*, both of whom were in Malta, and share our knowledge of the island with them.

"You have to try some traditional Maltese food." I started out. "We will take you to my brother-in-law's restaurant *Ta' Marija,* which is named after my eldest sister. It is situated roughly in the middle of the island at Mosta. And their son Ben will provide us with a taste of a variety of Maltese specialities." Yes, this was the same Ben who had cruised briefly with us in Greece that summer.

Amidst all this, we prepared *Mischief* for the winter months, washing her down from top to bottom, stowing away cleaned ropes and sails. On our 'to do' or maintenance list was a new fuel tank, to complement the new water tanks we had replaced in Turkey, and a new engine for the next legs of our voyage. We were now considering continuing cruising around the world after exploring the Mediterranean further.

With Bjorn's mum's birthday coming up in mid-November, we took a 10-day trip to Stockholm, his place of birth. The snow had not yet arrived. It was an eerie late autumn visit with short but sunny crisp days, the temperature fluctuating between five and ten degrees. It was just long enough to catch up with all the family and help celebrate another milestone for his mum.

Back in Malta, we now concentrated on the most significant job ahead. Bjorn had to decide on whether to change the engine or overhaul the old one. He immersed himself in the task, exchanging views with other cruisers, doing his homework on the internet, and generally getting to know what was available on the market. He negotiated with a number of marine engine repairers and dealers. In the end, we settled for a new Yanmar engine to replace the Thornycroft.

"…and you are going to remove the engine whilst the boat is in the water?" I asked Bjorn.

"Yes. It's fine. It's done all the time." Peter, a Dutchman who had his own boat and had lived on the island for many years, and whose son was a diver would be there to lend a hand. And so began the saga.

A Little Bit of MisChief

The date for taking out the old engine was set for late November. Our location on the breakwater quay made it easier for a small crane to drive down to be able to lift out the engine. The first job was for Peter's son to dive under the boat and pull the shaft out gently, just enough to disengage it from the engine and then to secure it. Then it was all hands on deck with Peter on the quay directing the crane. We moved the boom to the side, and Bjorn and the Yanmar chief engineer coaxed the old engine, now disconnected from all appendices, forward and upwards through the hatch - but not before I had ascertained that the boat would not sink when the shaft was pushed back.

"No water leaking in." Bjorn reported.

"Phew! That was smooth! And she's still afloat," I sighed with relief. "She's come out without a glitch."

We had to wait a week before the new engine would be replaced during which time the new mountings would be prepared. Bjorn and I used this window of opportunity to clean up the engine compartment, coat it with soundproofing foam and finished it off by lining the compartment with industrial strength aluminium foil.

"It looks great." I started out, feeling somewhat high, probably due to the inadvertent glue sniffing! "You almost need 'sunnies' now with the glare from the new alfoil-lined insulation."

"The sound proofing will make a big difference. You won't hear the engine so much up in the cockpit," said Bjorn, justifiably proud of his handiwork.

Of course, we complemented the glue 'high' with another high as we always celebrated little or big jobs with a glass of vino. Well actually, when there wasn't a job, we just celebrated - being there, alive and healthy.

A week later, the crane was called back again and the performance was repeated in reverse, with the new engine being lowered into the engine room. Now began the task of getting the engine and shaft properly aligned, and it turned out to be quite a dance.

"The shaft is not straight. It will have to be changed." The chief engineer informed Bjorn.

"Oh, no! Are you sure?"

"Well, there is only one way to find out. We have to remove it and take it down to a mechanical workshop to get it checked."

Peter and his son were called upon once more.

"What about the boat? How will you make sure it won't sink?" I was always uncomfortable with any underwater aperture not being properly sealed.

"We'll put a wooden bung and some plastic bags," Peter explained. "That should do the trick." That night I could not sleep and kept on waking up to check that I was not stepping out into water. That would have taken a bed afloat a step too far! I checked the bilge under the engine and could see no water had leaked into the boat.

"You look a bit bleary-eyed," Bjorn chuckled the next morning.

"Yes, I know. I should know better. But I'm sure you checked it out as well!"

The verdict on the shaft was delivered the next day. It did indeed have a very slight bend to it, not apparent to the naked eye. Bjorn was not entirely convinced. After all, the shaft had worked perfectly all the way from Australia, and before that from New Zealand where we had purchased the boat. However, he could not dispute the tests.

"The previous owner must have got some heave ropes tangled in the prop," was all he could say. "We had better measure it then, length and diameter. Being an English boat, everything tends to be in inches. I hope we can find one on the island."

We were now looking for a solid stainless steel rod with imperial dimensions. Bjorn got on the phone to every dealer of shafts on the island, but Peter put him on to the right person, and we struck gold. A shaft of the correct dimensions was delivered to us by Peter and soon it was back on the boat.

I watched anxiously from ashore, and was relieved when the deed was done.

"Come and look," Bjorn called out from the cabin. "The bung was pulled out and the shaft inserted with very little water coming in."

A Little Bit of MisChief

Once the shaft was in place, Bjorn's favourite new 'toy', a state of the art new propeller, was attached to the shaft. For the technically minded, this was a *Bruntons Autoprop*, a unique propeller design for sailing and displacement yachts. This propeller had self-adjusting blades, which would optimise pitch angle for any given operating condition whether under power or sail, reducing fuel consumption and increasing range under power.

The saga did not end here. The alignment of shaft and engine was proving hard to achieve.

"Near enough is not good enough." I heard Bjorn muttering to the Yanmar engineer.

It took a few heated discussions before Bjorn finally got the engine bed to be raised with specially manufactured skims. This made it easier to align with the shaft. It did the trick.

Replacing the diesel tank had luckily proved a more straightforward task. Bjorn had found a local fibreglass tank manufacturer who specialised in building fuel tanks, using a special chemical resistant resin. Thus, we finally replaced the old steel tank that had survived on a 'temporary' repair since the Red Sea. The manufacturer had assured us that it was especially suited for diesel, and used by many Maltese fishing boats. Once the tank was built, it was an easy job to replace the old with the new and connect it all up.

"That should be all the major jobs now." I said to Bjorn. Reflecting on this as I write this up, I am sure many of you cruisers are having a quiet giggle. There is no such thing as 'no more jobs' on a boat!

In early December, I took *Mischief* out for her sea trials with the new engine. Under instructions from the Yanmar engineer, we took the boat through her paces. She performed immaculately. The soundproofing was doing its job, and the engine purred away quietly as I revved up and down the harbour. Meanwhile Bjorn monitored the shaft: "All's well down here," he cooed happily.

During the autumn months, we had noticed that when the north-easterly winds blew in Malta, the swell would enter into Marsamxett. As the waves bounced off the surrounding stone walls this could be nasty, putting severe stress on the ropes and cleats. Though we were in the innermost creek at Msida, we noticed that the swell just made it to where we were tied up. We had ropes with special rubber mooring snubbers, very much like shock absorbers, to take the strain. However, we wondered whether these would be enough whilst we were away from the island on a return visit to Perth.

"Can you help us out Peter?" Bjorn asked. "We would like to move *Mischief* to an inner pontoon, where she would be safer. And if possible have you keep an eye on her until our return from our travels in late February."

"No problem. I know of someone who has taken their boat out of the water, and I am sure we can borrow the berth." And before long, we moved *Mischief* to her new temporary home, tucked away safely further up the all-weather creek.

It was soon time to depart. We were eager to catch up with our extended family and friends. Thanks to Bridget's family, we had a terrific Christmas and New Year in the Margaret River area, some 250 kilometres south of Perth. This area is renowned for its wineries, boutique industries varying from cheese, chocolate, lavender to deer farms and breweries. We house-sat a beautiful home and garden in an idyllic setting surrounded by bush ('forest' is closest I can get for you non -Aussies; you have to look it up to get the full sense of the term!). We swam in the pristine beaches, explored the ragged coastline, walked the forests and of course, partied, whilst managing to avoid the 40-degree heat wave up in Perth.

But our reprieve from the heat was short lived. Perth proved to be a hot destination that year, and a very social one too, alternating between the vino and Adam's ale to keep hydrated. We had a wonderful time, swimming at the beach at Leighton in the mornings with our daughter and her gorgeous dog chasing us, or sundowner picnics at Cottesloe beach in the evenings. Apart from friends, including those at the Fremantle Sailing Club, we managed to catch up with several cruisers (*Sandpiper*, *Purr*, *Billabong*, *Pampero*) over a barbeque or sundowner.

◇◇◇

A Little Bit of MisChief

We returned to Malta in mid-March fully focused on getting ready for the next sailing season. We quickly got to know our neighbours on the pontoon, including Rolf and Wendy on *Vagabond* (Malta) and Philip and Henriette on *Waterdrincker* (Holland).

"Good morning!" Rolf greeted us as we introduced my 95-year-old dad, who looked nothing like his age. Rolf looked at my frail dad and at our boat, noting the distance between the pontoon and the boat stern. "Can I help?"

"Can you make sure he stays put? Don't let him try to get across on his own." I told Rolf. Meanwhile Bjorn and I prepared a harness to make sure dad navigated the passerelle or gangplank safely onto the boat. Dad, an ever-enthusiastic outdoor person, swimmer and lover of the sea would often forget that he was not as steady on his feet as he would have liked. Once safely on board, he was thrilled to go into the cockpit but gave up on tackling the steep stairs into the cabin. We spent a pleasant morning showing him our itinerary and photos covering our adventures over a cup of tea and Maltese cannoli - a speciality from a traditional Maltese confectionary just along the road from the marina.

Spring was upon us. It was time to start planning for the next sailing season just a few months away. We hoped to sail to the Ionian and explore the beautiful isles in peace, away from the mad mid-summer rush, before heading up the Adriatic to Croatia and on to Venice.

But before setting out, we decided on a quick visit to our friends on *Te Ara* who had moved to the marina at Ragusa, Sicily before Christmas. Ragusa was fifty nautical miles north of Malta and well serviced by ferry.

Georges came to pick us up at the terminal at Pozzallo and took us back to the Marina di Ragusa, where their boat was tied up.

"Good morning and welcome," Andi and their lovely daughter Lea greeted us warmly. After a cup of tea and endless chatter as we exchanged news, we were off exploring the quaint town with its lovely foreshore promenade and beaches.

'We have discovered a fantastic seafood restaurant in

Scoglitti." Georges said. "We thought we would go there for lunch tomorrow." Scoglitti is an active fishing village west of Ragusa.

"Sounds like a wonderful idea." And it was. We had a delicious meal consisting of an assortment of pickled fresh fish delicacies and a Sicilian version of the Japanese *sashimi*. The restaurant had commissioned a specially brewed beer to go with the seafood.

We spent a gorgeous couple of days together, eating our way through delicious Sicilian cuisine, washed down with good wine. We also met a number of other cruisers at the marina. We discussed the facilities as we were thinking of using the marina the following winter. We knew that the marina in Malta was scheduled to be overhauled and therefore not available.

It was back to Malta again. Out came the canvas, sails and ropes as we reversed our autumn packing away and prepared the boat for the summer. Bjorn and I worked out a rough itinerary from our Adriatic cruising guide. In early May we took *Mischief* out for a proper engine trial, motoring up the coast and back. We calibrated our trusty autopilot and associated compass which had steered the boat so faithfully all those miles from Fremantle, checked and tested the electronic equipment, and re-commissioned the water maker which had been pickled over the winter months.

"We are all set to go," Bjorn said.

"Adriatic here we come!"

A Little Bit of MisChief

Approach to Valletta, Malta

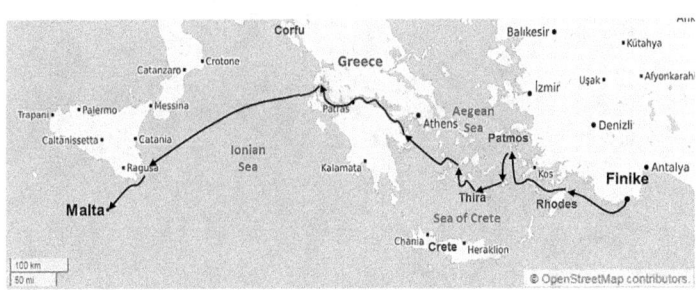

Finike to Malta Route

Christina Gillgren

19
Cruising in the Adriatic

We left Msida Marina at 6.00am on the fifteenth of May, after having checked out the previous evening. We headed due north to Sicily. Our plan for this year was flexible, and we expected to make our way towards the Ionian via the boot of Italy in the next week or two, then sail up the Adriatic to Venice. On the return journey in August, we wanted to stop in Ravenna to catch up with Mara, a long-time friend.

In company with Philip and Henriette on *Waterdrincker*, we motor sailed all the way across the channel to Sicily. Sea conditions were calm. With a gentle southerly wind blowing, we made excellent progress to arrive at the south-eastern tip of Sicily at around 3.00pm. Just as we were approaching the cosy marina at Marzamemi, on the east coast, we heard *Te Ara* call on the radio, asking for a berth at the marina.

"Excellent timing," I told Bjorn. We had agreed with *Te Ara* to meet at this marina and cruise the east coast of Sicily together before we each went our separate ways. Georges and Andi were headed westwards towards the Atlantic.

We had great fun trying to get into the tight berths at the marina. The wind suddenly picked up and naughty *Mischief* would not reverse as instructed. Well, really! …I guess I have to admit that I was also at fault, as I had not yet acquainted myself with the new propeller and its proclivities. With more than a little help from neighbouring yachts, we managed to coax *Mischief* into the berth. Now that our boat was safely ensconced in the pen, we watched *Waterdrincker*'s antics at berthing, shortly followed by the larger *Te Ara* trying to manoeuvre the tight little harbour. Despite the wind, they fared much better: both managed to reverse into their respective pens under their own steam.

Waterdrincker left the next day to make its way to the marina in Riposto, south of Taormina. Meanwhile we had a free day with Andi, Georges and daughter Lea. It was always fun catching up. Together we explored the little port town, famous for its tuna fisheries and by-products, including their famous Bluefin tuna *bottarga*, a delicacy of salted, cured fish roe.

Syracuse was next on our list. A glorious week flew by as we enjoyed the fabulous foods and feasted our eyes and bellies on the wonderful range of produce from the local market.

"Look at those cheeses!" Andi said, as we 'ooed' and 'aahhed' at the tantalising aromas and delicacies wafting around at the smallgoods shop (cheeses, salamis and more) at one end of the market. We bought fresh buns and mortadella. This made a hearty lunch, washed down with local beer.

One evening I cooked swordfish on the barbecue, served with my own version of ratatouille, which includes olives and capers, Maltese style. It was mid-May, a time when Bjorn and I celebrate both our birthdays that are only a few days apart.

"You must come on *Te Ara*," Andi called us on the radio the following morning. "We will celebrate your birthdays together!" And so we did, with these dear friends who prepared a terrific spread for us, cake and all.

Our next stop was at Giardini Naxos, a small anchorage with a pontoon just under Taormina, perched on the mountain overlooking us. After a final sundowner and meal together it was time to say goodbye. *Te Ara* headed north and west to get ready to tackle the Atlantic over the coming winter. Our route took us in an easterly direction, on a two-day crossing passing under the 'toe' of Italy to our next port-of-call. Our timing was excellent. As agreed via radio, we caught up with *Waterdrincker* on the way to Roccella Ionica, our destination.

A Little Bit of MisChief

"*Waterdrincker*! *Waterdrincker*! This is *Mischief*!"
"Go ahead, *Mischief*."
"Conditions look good for a stopover at Roccella Ionica. We will keep a lookout for the marker on shore we were told about, roughly 200 metres off the end of the breakwater. This is where we head towards the coast. Then we do a dogleg, only turning when the entrance is open due east."

We had been warned that with strong southerlies or with a swell, the entrance to this marina was dangerous. Even in calm conditions, we had to proceed gently as the channel shifts in strong storms and the entrance was subject to constant silting.

After an overnight stop, we set out on the next leg to the port of Crotone. Together with Philip and Henriette, we rented a car and toured the areas around Crotone, ending up with a lovely meal at a local tavern where we said our goodbyes. Early the next morning, we started out on the overnight trip towards Preveza in Greece. We wanted to see the parts of the Ionian that we missed out on the previous summer before proceeding to Croatia and the mid-season madness.

Greece is a place of contrasts. As opposed to the wonderful clear waters around the mostly hilly Ionian Islands, we approached the silty channel and the flat lands on the mainland at Preveza, carefully following the markers into the anchorage. We had been given detailed information on the Ionian by our friends Dominique and Claude (*Lobea*) in Finike, Turkey. We explored the town and sailed around the 'fjord' to the east of Preveza, with quant villages and more ruins to explore. However, I missed the clear waters, where I preferred swimming. So we moved on to what we were sure would be our highlight this time round in Greece, namely the lovely islands of Paxos and Corfu.

Gaios in Paxos turned out to be everything that Dominique said it would be, delightful in every way. We loved the mooring in the channel that wound itself round between the mainland and a small but lush green wooded islet (Nisida Agios). Nervously I motored towards the islet in preparation for reversing to tie up stern to the quay.

"That was perfect," Bjorn said, after we had tied up. "I think you really have cracked that nut and worked out the new prop walk. I was anxious when you started reversing, heading towards all those yachts. But the boat turned magnificently once the propeller bit."

"Not as nervous as I was when the wind suddenly picked up!" I muttered, under my breath. After all, why let my co-sailor worry needlessly.

The next thing we knew, a wizened gentleman approaching us to offer water and electricity - from his own house. Bjorn watched in amazement as he uncoiled miles of joined-up indoor extension leads, snaking along the quay, to our boat.

"We had better wear our boots ashore," he quipped. He shook his head in disbelief. Bjorn used to head the Occupational Health and Safety department in Perth, Western Australia.

"Too hot for that. I guess that the Med safety shoes will have to do," I replied, donning a pair of Crocs.

Our Greek friend turned out to be a retired architect, and quite a character. Many of the cruisers berthed alongside were headed north like us, and we enjoyed many a pleasant evening, exchanging information. Because it was still early in the season, being only the first week of June, the island was not overrun by tourists. Yet everything was open and accessible, touristic in a pleasant sort of way. We whiled away a whole week in the little town, took bus rides and rented a scooter to explore the island.

From Paxos we motor-sailed (we were in the '*Motorranean*' after all) to Corfu. The anchorage we selected lay under the old fort. Over a late light lunch, we admired the calm blue seas, enjoying the Greek music from the *taverna* on the beach. Albania lay a few miles across the water to the east. By late afternoon, however, the wind picked up. A thunderstorm came out of the blue, creating a swell in the anchorage to match any ocean crossing. It became so uncomfortable on board that we could not relax. We did not trust the anchor to have taken hold properly on the seabed. This was no good, as we wanted to explore the island. As a result, we pulled into the tiny marina nearby and tied up for a couple of days, so we could leave the boat and play tourists.

"I have dreamed of visiting this island ever since my

A Little Bit of MisChief

schooldays when I had first read Gerald Durrell's *My Family and Other Animals*. I will have to read it again."

We loved Corfu, with its colourful history spanning the ages, and medieval castles perched atop strategic locations. We rented a car for two days driving up and down the hilly terrain around the island and enjoying the magnificent scenery, beaches, monasteries and caves.

"And I thought the driving was crazy in Malta," Bjorn remarked, as yet another stupid driver overtook us with a blind bend in the road approaching.

We were on the way to the village of Palaiokastritsa in north-western Corfu. A monastery dating back over 800 years overlooked one of the most picturesque bays ever: it was reputedly the place where Odysseus, the legendary Greek hero of the Odyssey, had come ashore.

We had a long way to go north and it was time to move on. We took off early one morning as storm force headwinds abated, and ended up motor sailing to Montenegro. We had decided to give Albania a miss. We had heard that one was either welcomed with open arms and kisses on both cheeks or robbed and shot on sight - if you believe other cruisers' tales, that is. Being the daredevils we are, we opted against taking a shortcut through the minefields marked on the sea charts outside Albania, even though we had been assured no one had been blown up in recent times. We arrived outside the entrance to the fjord in Montenegro the next day around midday.

The 17-mile waterway to Kotor, an old Venetian trading town in today's Montenegro, is spectacular. We approached the narrow inlet and entered the channel. Menacing mountains rose dramatically on both sides of a long, thin bay that lead to the protected and secluded harbour and the old walled town of Kotor.

Kotor takes the picturesque prize of the region. Tucked away in the corner of the inlet, with the steep mountainous slopes seemingly dwarfing the bay, you could hardly spot the medieval old town at first, hemmed in as it is by solid, hefty walls. We were lucky to get to the main quay to check in just ahead of a cruise ship. Then we sped ashore to beat the tours that were bound to follow. Once ashore and through the gates at the old town, a lovely square presented itself. Open-air cafes and restaurants were dotted around, with winding streets snaking improbably up the surrounding slopes. It was time for a cup of coffee.

"The town seems to blend into the mountain slopes." I started out. "It is both dramatic and quaint at the same time: on the one hand the place resonates with the tumultuous past that was so characteristic of this region; on the other hand, there is this quiet elegance reflected in the Venetian's influence on the city's architecture." As usual, we had read up as much as possible on places we were visiting.

"Shall we walk up the cliffs tomorrow morning? There's the Castle of San Giovanni above." Looking directly above, on almost vertical cliffs, were the meandering upper town walls, with a promising view. The next morning we had a go at reaching the top, but only made it about half way.

"My knee won't take any more Bjorn. I have to stop and rest." And so we did, ironically taking a pew on the conveniently placed semi-circular stone seat in front of the Church of Our Lady of Health. Here we enjoyed the stupendous vistas of the fjord, as the inlet was often described, and a fabulous birds-eye-view of the Old Town of Kotor.

Kotor was a magical place. We lingered in the area for a week enjoying the old town, food and artsy culture. We took *Mischief* out to explore the fjord stopping at the artificial islet of Our Lady of the Rocks, created by sinking old ships loaded with rocks.

Another tick on our bucket list, and it was time to move on again. With no wind, we wove our way out of the inlet and continued for a further 20 or so nautical miles under engine to Cavtat, our entry port into Croatia. By now, we were quite pleased with our new engine that had already clocked over 100 hours.

Checking in to Croatia was a very different experience. After the quasi-casual approach to customs and immigration in

A Little Bit of MisChief

EU countries, the process in Croatia was organised, formal and pedantic. First stop was the harbour master.

"How many people can sleep on board?" he asked us. It seemed that there was a bed tax, because we had the audacity not to sleep in a hotel ashore. Bjorn and I looked at each other.

"Two beds," we replied. We felt that, as there were no planned visitors, which we would have had to declare, this was a fair answer.

For the first time since leaving Fremantle, we had to prove our sailing competency. This was laughable seeing how we had travelled over 13,000 nautical miles in *Mischief*. Bjorn and I were qualified ocean going sailors and provided our certificates to show this. After filling out endless forms and fritting to and fro between the various police, customs, immigration and harbour master offices - and in this case, the nearby ATM - we eventually got through the formalities.

We emptied our wallet in favour of the taxman for the pleasure of being in these waters for one month, to almost the end of July. In return, we received a visitors' map for cruising the islands, which outlined the marine national parks. Before we left the last office, we were warned that we could not stay in the bay overnight and needed to move on.

Next to immigration and customs was a post office cum stationery, which sold mobile phone chips. This was always one of our first purchases ashore in a new country. We could not miss the frustrated exchange as we entered the shop.

"I sent a message to my son in Australia and have now received about 400 copies or re-sends of the reply! This is driving us crazy. We have called Australia and it is not the network there that is causing this problem."

We introduced ourselves and struck up a conversation with Carola and Jim.

"Be careful about getting your telephone chip here. They don't seem to know a thing about what they are selling and can't fix anything," Carola warned. Jim did not mince any words about his thoughts regarding the service.

We still went ahead and bought a data chip for the computer, fingers crossed that we wouldn't have the same problem. And then we rushed back to move the boat to an anchorage around the corner. To our surprise, we found ourselves anchored next to three other antipodean yachts, two of which we would meet again later in the season.

This part of the Adriatic is a beautiful, diverse and great sailing ground with a terrific choice of islands and anchorages. And so we set off to the quaint islet of Lopud. We were joined by Carola and Jim from *Koza* (Australia), and then we headed to the island of Mljet, part of which is also a national park.

With very strong north-easterlies known locally as the dreaded *Bora* forecast, we sought refuge in the land locked, secure and spacious haven at Luka Polace, in the north-eastern end of the island. The heavily wooded island of Mljet is one of the most enchanting islands in the Adriatic. As usual, we hoisted our Boxing Kangaroo flag on the port spreader to show we were visiting Aussies. For the non-nautical among you, a boat under way should always run a number of flags, namely the country of registration flag on the stern, in our case the Australian Flag. The custom was to fly the courtesy flag of the country one is visiting on the starboard spreader. The spreaders are the arms sticking out of the mast to hold the shrouds (wires or ropes from mast top to deck to hold the mast in place). In the Mediterranean, we had noticed that some cruisers also flew courtesy flags on the port side to reflect the nationality of the people on board the boat at a given time, a practice we had adopted.

Anchored next to us was a boat called *Stefanija* (Australia). Seeing our Aussie flag, Gayle and Alec came across to introduce themselves. Over the usual sundowner, it transpired that they hailed from Perth and came out every year to sail in Croatia where they kept their boat. As these cruising grounds were their regular haunt, they were able to provide us with some wonderful tips as to where to stop and what to see.

'From the little village ashore you can take a tour to visit the lakes. The scenery is beautiful," suggested Gayle.

And this is what we did the next morning. The lakes visit included a boat trip to the island of St. Mary on which stood a derelict monastery.

A Little Bit of MisChief

On our last evening in the bay, we moved *Mischief* to the little pontoon attached to the restaurant ashore. We wedged in between Carola and Jim on *Koza*, and another Aussie boat. Then all of us gathered on *Koza* for a sundowner. On the other side of *Koza* was a huge ultra-modern motor yacht, some 21 metres in length, and of a soft gold hue.

"Fancy neighbours," I said to Carola, going on board.

"Yes, we have been entertained all afternoon. The owner is an elderly guy. And he has this rather interesting young 'lady' on board."

"She seems to be having quite a time." Jim added.

The other Australian couple had their children with them, one of them a young lad in his mid-teens.

"Cool," he said, "A real sugar daddy!" Out came his camera and he happily clicked away.

What followed next was bizarre. The woman went to the foredeck and laid out a lounge cushion. Then the owner came out and lay on the cushion in his 'budgie smugglers'. This is the Aussie name given to the triangular swim briefs.

Next, the young lady joined him - literally. She got on top of him. We don't know what was the more amusing: the young teen's excited commentary, or the actual goings-on - which provided ample fare for saucy comments.

But this was not all! The woman got up and walked towards the stern. She climbed into the cockpit and started snuggling rather suggestively against one of the other young male crewmembers, kissing him passionately.

"Hey!" I remarked. "Bet the owner doesn't know what's going on behind his back?"

"The other guys in the cockpit don't seem to mind, either," someone else quipped.

"Now you know why we have been so entertained," Jim laughed. "This has been going on all afternoon, and we are still trying to work it all out."

The next morning we motored out of the anchorage, heading north at a leisurely pace. We called into a few villages and anchorages along the way. In Korcula, we visited the house where Marco Polo is supposed to have lived. There were different theories as to whether the Polo family hailed from here. Marco Polo's birthplace is given as Venice in most of the literature we had come across. So, who knows?

We loved the island of Hvar, and the city port draped over the hillside. Ashore, in one of the narrow streets, we had our first taste of a traditional *Konoba* restaurant since our return to this country which we had cruised in previously. We had given the necessary 24 hours' notice that we wanted the slow-cooked lamb served under the bell as was traditional.

The reputation of turquoise waters in beautiful bays was not exaggerated. With more time to discover the surrounds than our one-month visit to Croatia some six years back had allowed, we enjoyed exploring this truly magnificent archipelago - a sailing paradise.

Our journey north was resumed with stops at various islands such as Drvenik Veli, Murter, Pasman, Ugljan, Molat to name a few. This was the 'inside' passage, tackling the islands closer to the mainland and then gradually moving to the outer islands. We kept meeting *Koza* and other Australian registered boats on the way. Nowhere else in the Mediterranean had we encountered so many 'down under' sailors.

With hundreds of bays and islands to choose from, we were glad to have been given the pick by Gayle and Alec (*Stefanija*) at Mljet. This knowledge was even more valuable as we approached July. In some of the more popular places, fees were levied simply for putting down your anchor. The fees increased if you chose to pick up a mooring buoy. As it was, we managed to avoid the overcrowded anchorages and opt for the more peaceful ones, though not always with great success.

At Muline, on Otok Ugljan (*Otok* being Croatian for 'island'), we set our anchor by lunchtime and settled for the day, happy to have found a serene location. We went ashore for a walk, a light lunch and a coffee. On our return, we found ourselves surrounded.

"What's this? Bloody charter boats on either side of us. And if you don't mind, they're speaking to each other yelling over our boat. And look at them, all naked, with their huge guts spilling over. Yuck!"

A Little Bit of MisChief

"They are not the most inspiring sight." Bjorn shook his head as we watched what he called the 'Wilhelms with willies' prancing around, with massive beer bellies and fog horns for mouths. I usually had my evening shower at the stern of the boat, and liked to strip and jump into the water. This evening I felt rather hemmed in.

'Bloody Hell! I don't like the look of them." I fumed. 'And we won't get anywhere saying anything to them. Fancy anchoring on either side of us when the bay is so large. They could have easily anchored side-by-side and further away. We'll have to move." And so we did.

We had been warned about the practices of some charter boats, but this had been the worst example of selfishness so far. We were mollified by the fact that the place we moved to, just up along the channel was even more pleasant and serene.

We continued up north, calling into the picturesque bay and town of Mali Losinj. We ran into more Australian cruisers with whom we had a lovely crab dinner at one of the local restaurants. From the local Lidl store we stocked up with wine and 'small goods'. Ahead lay the notorious Gulf of Kvarner, renowned for the ferocity of the *Bora*, the name given to the katabatic wind which originates from this area and howls south over the Adriatic. This type of wind is dangerous because it can be very sudden and strong enough to knock a boat over.

There was hardly any wind as we traversed the notorious gulf to Soline, an anchorage just south of the city of Pula.

Our ambitious program had us at the northern end of Croatia by the end of July for our ultimate goal of the year: Venice. From Venice, we intended to sail to a marina in Ravenna and visit Mara and Giovanni who lived outside Bologna. I had known them for decades and was looking forward to catching up. Then we hoped to resume our cruising down east the Italian coast aware that, with few anchorages available, we would have to go into harbours.

On entering the twin inlets behind the islet of Veruda, we veered right to the bay of Uvala Kanalic or Soline, as it is better known by cruisers. We immediately spotted *Koza* again. Not long after we put down our anchor and hoisted our Boxing

Kangaroo flag, we had more visitors, June and Pat on *Antares* (New Zealand). The unofficial Aussie flag had done its work this season. We spent some good times ashore, exploring Pula and the surrounds with them. Pula is known for its many ancient Roman buildings, the most famous of which is the amphitheatre, so much better preserved than its counterpart in Rome.

The inlet to the north of us housed a marina where Gerlinde and Martin - whom we had first met during our winter stay in Finike two years earlier - kept their boat *Mojo* (Austria). We had agreed to meet up in Pula when we sailed the Adriatic. Here we were finally. Our Austrian friends took us around the town and the surrounding Istrian countryside. The day ended with a visit to a lovely traditional local restaurant in the hills where we were served a delicious five-course meal.

Venice was not to happen, however. We attempted a crossing early one morning and were greeted with two to three metre breaking waves at the entrance to Pula Harbour. There was no option but to turn back. With unseasonal squalls and thunderstorms forecast for the next week or so, we decided the weather gods had turned against us. We were quite upset. It was, after all, meant to be the highlight of the season and our dream to arrive on our own boat to Venice.

After a management meeting over a bottle of good red wine to drown our disappointment, we redrew our plans for the 1000 nautical mile return trip to Malta. We signed up for another month of Croatia, forsaking the wonderful cities and towns in the northern part of Italy. The sad part was that we had to forgo catching up with our friends in Ravenna. On the plus side, it was enticing to spend the next month in beautiful anchorages exploring more of this wonderful archipelago, as opposed to overcrowded and busy harbours, and the muddy estuary waters of the Po River on the Italian east coast.

"We missed out visiting the Dugi Otok National Park on our way up. It's said to be stunning. And I wouldn't mind exploring some of the other anchorages and islands that Jim and Carola

A Little Bit of MisChief

mentioned."

We took the first break in the weather to cross the infamous Gulf of Kvarner, and enjoyed one of the few pleasant sails that season. We returned to one of our favourite stops at the delightful isle and town of Mali Losinj, which we had fallen in love with. We ended up staying two days in order to replace the starter battery. The weather was changing, with thunderstorms striking the mainland. Fortunately, they mostly missed the islands.

With August upon us, we found ourselves sailing south in company with hordes of Italian power-boaters. Some of them can be the scourge of the seas, cutting across us when we were under sail, instead of giving way and going past our stern.

We made our way to Uvala Cuscica, a large bay at the south end of Dugi Otok. A ranger came by in the evening to collect our fees and give us a three-day pass to the National Park. In the morning, we navigated through the narrow channel to reach the large and fully enclosed inlet of Luka Telascica. We started by heading towards the northern anchorage, nestling in between two islets in the middle of the quaint little bay. The landscape around us resembled a moonscape. It was a startling change to the wooded islands we had visited on our trip north, and dramatic in its own way.

After a couple of days, we left the island group of Dugi Otok and sailed to a nearby island group around Murter. It is amazing how one can go from a totally barren landscape to such lush greenery in the breadth of a few nautical miles. With yet another *Bora* forecast, we decided to tuck in to the large bay outside Murter town where we spent a pleasant week, catching up again with *Koza* and meeting Helve and Rick on *Tangaroa* (Australia).

We braved it in strong northerlies all the way down to Rogoznica, on the mainland and then crossed to Vela Luka, a pretty town on the western end of the island of Korcula. Early one morning in mid-August, we checked out of Croatia from the picturesque island of Lastovo. What followed was one of the best sailing days that summer: a magnificent ten-hour sail across to Vieste in the Puglia region on the east coast of Italy.

Christina Gillgren

A Bit of Fun with the Spinnaker

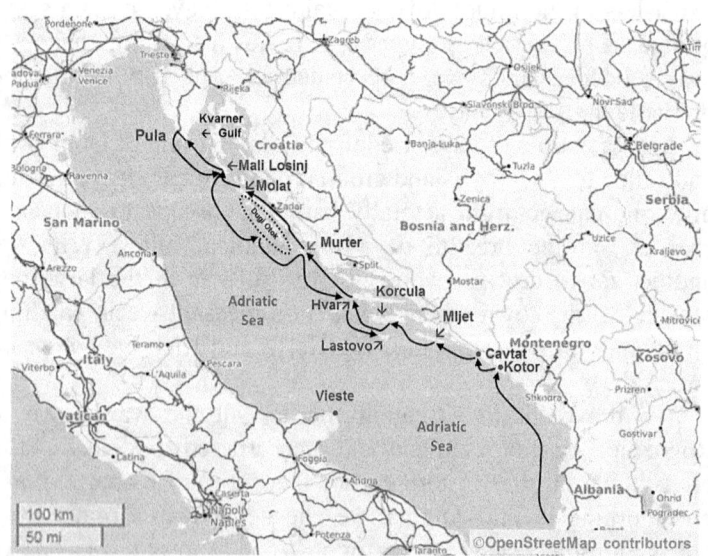

The Adriatic

20
...With a Taste of Italy

The contrast between Croatia and Italy could not have been greater. This region of Italy, known as the Puglia, is favoured by a mild climate. The weather and water temperature were a few degrees warmer on this side of the Adriatic. Our sea chart showed a predominantly shallow sandy stretch of coast to the southern tip of the heel of the boot of Italy. Yet instead of lovely turquoise waters, we would now be confined to harbours, as there are hardly any sheltered bays on the Italian east coast. Vieste was meant to offer one of the rare havens along this coast, but the anchorage on the south side of the town shown on our cruising guide turned out to be silted. With the depth beneath the boat decreasing rapidly, we decided to go into the marina instead.

As soon as we had tied up on a pontoon, we went ashore to check into Italy. What greeted us was surprising: we were introduced to what the French may have lent the name to but the Italians have perfected, namely bureaucracy. As a non-EU registered yacht, we were expected to fill in copious forms and to sign in and out in every port we intended visiting. This involved registering with the coast guard, the *Guardia Costiera*. This mob also included the harbour master functions. In addition, we had to inform each port of our next port-of-call.

"This is absurd. So unexpected." I started out, amused by

our reception. "Very different to what we encountered when we sailed up from Malta via Sicily and the boot of Italy to the Ionian. Nobody along the way was interested in our comings and goings."

"It was the same in Greece. Very few islands actually bothered with our boat papers."

I love Italy and everything Italian. I particularly enjoyed listening to the weather forecasts. What other language in the world would describe poor visibility (light fog perhaps or humidity) using such poetic words as '*visibilita discreta*'.

We were looking forward to exploring many of the medieval towns and villages as we made our way south. Off we went to explore the town of Vieste, perched on the scenic Gargano peninsula. We made our way up hill through the narrow alleys of the old town, draped with lines of clothing drying in the gentle breeze.

"We should also find a phone shop to get a SIM card for our telephone for Italy." Bjorn said, ever the practical guy.

"And then its dinner. So let's look out for a trattoria."

The next day, after a leisurely mid-morning breakfast, we went ashore again to check out as we had been instructed, taking the paperwork along with us. We had decided to do things 'by the book' and see how it would work out: whether the authorities would somehow manage to match up all the bits of poor photocopies of our papers we would leave in randomly selected ports.

"What is your next port of call?" the harbour master enquired.

"I think we will try Manfredonia next," I replied. "Our cruising guide says we anchor in the harbour. Is this correct?"

"No, No. You cannot anchor in a commercial harbour. You must go and tie up. We will inform them that you are coming. They will tell you where to tie up when you call them on the radio."

"We may be on to something here," I told Bjorn as we left the building for our boat.

With no wind and flat seas not more than a couple of metres deep, we motored the eleven miles to Manfredonia, founded by

A Little Bit of MisChief

King Manfred in 1263. Although instructed not to anchor, we still did so, alongside two other Italian flagged boats on the south of the harbour. We found it to be a commercial and industrial town, so we jumped on the local bus to visit some of the surrounding towns. One of our stops was Monte Sant'Angelo, on the mountains to the east of the city. Local lore has it that St Michael the Archangel appeared here. The grotto that houses the sanctuary that was built in commemoration has been the focus of many religious pilgrimages. Proud locals told us that it was added to the UNESCO World Heritage List in the previous year. Of interest was the memorabilia on sale regarding Padre Pio, also known as Saint Pio of Pietrelcina. He evoked childhood memories, as he was well known on the island of Malta where he was venerated.

Our next stop was Barletta, a medieval fishing town with narrow streets and few shops, beyond which sprawled a huge modern city. Apart from the local yacht club which was very welcoming and where we enjoyed an evening meal and dance with the locals, there was not much to this place to entice us. We stayed a couple of days before moving on.

It was at this point that we found out how much checking in and out, however tedious, worked out in our favour. We used the *Guardia Costiera*, with whom we were meant to check in at every port of call, to 'book' a spot on the next port's town quay. This met their requirement that we stop where we said we were heading. And there were no fees. This arrangement worked out so well, that we decided to stop at almost every harbour on the way south.

We enjoyed five days in quaint Bisceglie, strolling along in the old town with its arched alleys and hidden courtyards.

"You see how the narrow streets are hardly ever straight?" Bjorn started out. "They are built that way so that it limits the number of soldiers that can push through in battle. If there are archers among an invading army, their 'reach' is limited by the curvature of the wall."

We had a ball running around. The local buses and trains ran on time and were excellent value for money. We went past cultivated fields in a mosaic of colours. Agriculture seemed to thrive in this region. Olive groves, vineyards and a plethora of orchards lined the way. Among the places we visited was Trani with its distinctive cathedral overlooking the harbour.

We had an unexpected surprise at Molfetta. We were once again the only yacht to tie up at the town quay, courtesy of the *Guardia Costiera*. Since crossing to the coast of Italy we had hardly met any sailors, and no foreign cruising boats at all. Bjorn and I figured that the reason for this was that the Italians had made their way to the Ionian and to Croatia.

As we were about to leave the boat to go for a swim on the other side of the harbour wall, the friendly official at the *Guardia Costiera* office nearby waved us over. He said he would keep an eye on the boat for us. Meanwhile, word seemed to have spread regarding the arrival of a sailing boat flying an Australian flag. At sunset, the time for the evening *passeggiata*, we had a small stream of *Molfettese* coming up to our boat. They would invariably check out the flag, the name on the transom with the home port of Fremantle, the size of the boat and everything else about it.

"You come all the all the way from Fremantle, Australia?" one elderly gentleman asked, in heavily accented Italian.

It did not take long to discover the reason. Molfetta was the place of birth of numerous Italian fishermen in the Western Australian port city of Fremantle. It seems that they had migrated from this fishing village *en masse*. For this reason Fremantle and Molfetta had been named Sister Cities. Over the next few days, a couple of them would turn up on the quayside, chairs at the ready, to relate stories of their days in Fremantle.

"You come all the way by boat. *Solo due insieme. Siete pazzi*! I live in Fremantle many years. Now I retire here!" another wizened local told us.

"What did you do in Fremantle?" I asked.

"Fisherman! I, fisherman. Now too old. I, retired. Look I have pension from Australian Government." This wonderful gentleman would then relate an anecdote from his life in Fremantle.

From our stream of visitors, whose fluency in English probably matched my rusty Italian, we learnt that the traditional

A Little Bit of MisChief

blessing of the fleet in Fremantle was based on the Molfetta tradition of this annual feast day. We were taken over by these friendly locals who would show us around the market or point us to the 'best' shops every time we stepped ashore. This was apart from their generosity. They showered us with everything from fresh fish, vegetables, homemade high quality olive oil and many other local produce, including wine.

One afternoon, a local fisherman presented us with a bucket of two types of fresh prawns, the giant red prawns they fish in southern waters, and the more traditional prawns of the area. After he left, I turned to Bjorn: "So many! How are we going to do justice to all this?"

"Our gastronomic inventory is certainly looking good! We now have over six litres of home-made extra virgin olive oil as well."

Meanwhile an Italian yacht also called in at the quay. Its owners came over. "Hello, welcome! *Mi chiamo* Francesco. My friends call me Cicco!" he started out. "Welcome to our town. How long are you staying?" It transpired that Cicco and his friends ran a sailing charter service out of Molfetta.

"Only a few days more. Then we move on south." It was a Monday.

"Ah, no, you must stay for the blessing of the fleet. It is this weekend."

Cicco and his sailing friends practically adopted us, showing us around the town and the area. One evening, they treated us to a spectacular seafood feast at one of the renowned local restaurants. In return, we shared the incredible array of fresh produce, including the prawns, some of which we cooked and ate together, over a bottle or two of excellent Puglia wine. We enjoyed several balmy evenings in *Mischief*'s cockpit, getting to know each other, swapping sailing anecdotes and learning about the region. Towards the end of the week, we discovered from the *Guardia Costiera* official that the local blessing of the fleet would see the harbour overrun with fishing boats and other craft. He recommended that we move the boat, and we decided it was best to be on our way beforehand.

The evening before we sailed out, Cicco and his friends

turned up on the quay to bid us farewell, in their hands a huge hamper full of wine and local delicacies. The friendliness and warmth of the *Molfettese* is something we will never forget.

We were not too excited about our next port of call, the large commercial harbour of Bari. The *Guardia Costiera* guided us to a part of the quay, which looked fine to start with. However, as evening and the night rolled on, we realised the downside. To begin with, the constant stream of ferries stirred up the water and had *Mischief* bobbing up and down along the quay, chafing the fenders and tugging at the mooring lines. That was not the only snag. We were not far from where the tugboats were moored. Their comings and goings all night stirred up the harbour waters and caused a huge surge that tested our mooring ropes further, the fenders squeaking away in protest.

"We have to move," I told Bjorn. "Let's try the Lega Navale's marina." The Lega Navale, or Italian Naval League, is an organisation established to promote a love of the sea and all things maritime among Italians and young people in particular. We knew from other sailing friends that they operated a marina or some pontoons in most harbours around the Italian coast.

We were lucky to find a berth at this marina, but it was another thing manoeuvring into the pontoons. With *Mischief* secure, we ventured to explore the old town inside its protective walls. But we did not enjoy being cooped up in this big, dirty and busy harbour with the sea - and a swim - so inaccessible.

After the hustle and bustle of Bari, our next stop was a real delight. Monopoli turned out to one of be the prettiest port towns we had come across. Once again, thanks to the *Guardia Costiera*, we were allocated a spot on the quay under the abbey of Santo Stefano. It was only a short stroll away from the charming historic walled town dating back to the Middle Ages. We were intrigued by its name, guessing that it stood for one/only (mono) city (polis). Unique it was, with its charming historic centre and strong fishing tradition.

For the first time since crossing to the Italian side of the Adriatic, we had company. The day after we had arrived, another Italian yacht, *Enrica*, pulled in ahead of us at the quay. After helping our new neighbours tie up, we struck up a

A Little Bit of MisChief

conversation. We were invited on board for a drink, where we exchanged stories.

"This music is lovely. I am no longer familiar with Italian songs after living in Australia for such a long time," I started out.

"It's one of my songs!" Anna Fina told me proudly. She went down into the cabin and came back with a CD of her songs.

Anna and her partner were keen architecture enthusiasts. They offered to guide us around the walled city, explaining the façade and building designs. The narrow streets were decorated with pots full of colourful flowers, and bougainvillea in particular, set against whitewashed walls or hanging from balconies. The old town had just enough history and ruins to keep us happy between feasting on fabulous Italian food, from land and sea. Every afternoon, we would go on the other side of the breakwater, just next to an old castle to swim in the clear azure water. We also enjoyed a number of trips just inland of the town. The area is charming, with miles of olive and almond trees spread out across the countryside.

"I can't understand why all those fishing boats are tied up along the north breakwater. Shouldn't some of them be out fishing?"

Chatting to the locals, we learnt that the fishing boats were all in harbour patiently awaiting their turn to go fishing after the end of the month. It was explained to us that, for sustainable purposes, the east coast of Italy was divided into maritime districts. Boats were allowed to operate within the waters of the maritime district in which they were registered, as well as in the waters of the two neighbouring districts. They were allowed to fish for two months of the season.

"The Romans complained that there was not much fish left in the Mediterranean," Bjorn stated. "And it seems this is even more the case now."

As we strolled along the quay, we came across many a fisherman tending to their lines in an unusual fashion. A plastic drum, not unlike a giant bobbin, was used to line up hundreds of hooks along the rim. One of the fishermen explained that this was for long line fishing.

A month on this coast of Italy flew by, with the telltale signs of good living now starting to show up in waistlines. Reluctantly we headed out of Monopoli to our final port of call at Brindisi.

After our bad experience at the port of Bari, we decided to avoid the town quay and opted for the marina on the northern side of the outer harbour. Armed with maps of the area, we set out to explore.

Brindisi, a port town, has been branded the 'Gateway to the East', the local brochure informed us. It served as an important port for the Roman Empire, and later for the merchants of Venice. It is where the famous *Via Appia* or Appian Way, ends, connecting Rome to Italy's south-east.

We spent a week in Brindisi. We set out to explore the town going from one church to the next. But our enthusiasm for all things historical was waning. We had overdosed on castles, churches and cathedrals to the extent that Bjorn was now pointing out cats on the prowl rather than look at more buildings. We rented a car for a few days, and drove around, visiting some of the natural reserves and wetlands in the area.

One of our most pleasant discoveries was Ostuni, Puglia's White City, about eight kilometres from the coast and mid-way between Brindisi and Monopoli. Ostuni reminded us of the Greek Cyclades island town with its dazzling, whitewashed houses. The difference was the elegant historic features such as the Town Hall and St. Oronzo's Column interspersed with the everyday traditional dwellings. We roamed up and down this stunning hilly city, exploring picturesque stairways, alleys and archways before selecting a trattoria for lunch.

Lecce was another highlight. The tourist office's pamphlet described the city as the Baroque masterpiece of southern Italy with its 'riot of cherubs'. This was borne out in many of the city's extravagant architectural facades.

September was upon us and we were now watching the weather maps on a daily basis. "Look Bjorn, light northerlies are forecast over the next few days. This may be a good time to leave. If the weather holds we can head straight to Sicily."

A Little Bit of MisChief

It would take us three days to reach our destination. And so the following day we got up for a leisurely breakfast, paid off the marina and after lunch hauled in the mooring lines to depart on our next leg. We could now tick the Adriatic off our bucket list.

Christina Gillgren

Vieste from the Sea

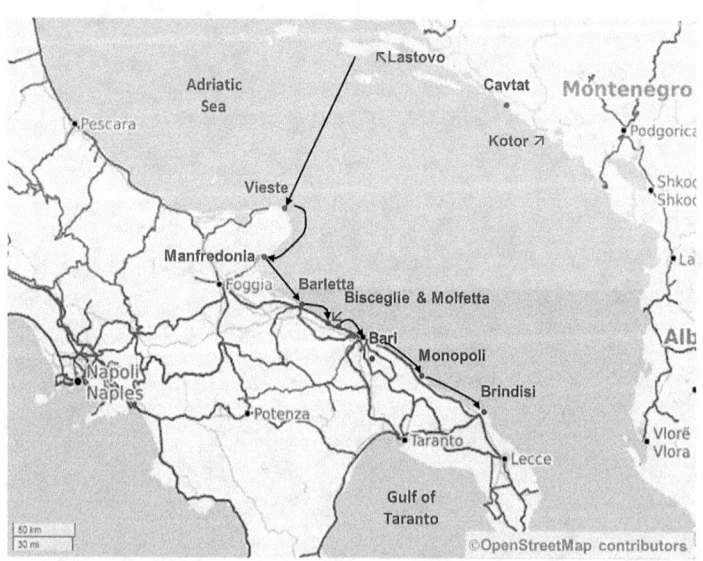

Italian East Coast

21
Sea Change: Malta and Scrumptious Sicily

The three-day trip from Brindisi was uneventful with gentle northerly winds propelling us eastwards. We turned on the motor when the winds were too light, motor sailing whilst running the water maker. And of course, keeping the house batteries charged.

We arrived at Syracuse, Sicily at midday and did not bother to go ashore. Instead we opted to have a siesta. We intended to leave for Malta in the evening for an overnight sail to the island. This was so that we would arrive in the morning and have all day to sort out where we could tie up. We anticipated staying in Malta for a month to catch up with family and friends before heading back north to Marina di Ragusa, at the south-eastern end of Sicily, where we had booked to keep *Mischief* for the winter.

We sailed into Malta in early-mid September to suss out the marina situation. With the planned upgrade to Msida Marina, berthing in Malta over winter was not an option. But we succeeded in securing a temporary berth for a couple of weeks. We caught up with family and my dear friend Johanna. We also met other cruisers who were visiting the island, either looking for a berth, or on their way to winter berthing in Tunisia. One morning, we had breakfast with Vicki and Jeff on *Wraith* (UK), just before they headed out to sea to cross to the sole of Italy to spend the winter in Roccella Ionica (more on this later).

In early October, and with a favourable weather window with southerlies blowing, we left for Marina di Ragusa, exactly due north of Malta. The name 'Marina' can be confusing, as in Italy it often refers to a seaside village or town. Marina di Ragusa is a southern Sicilian beach resort, which also hosts a yacht marina.

It was a pleasant crossing with enough wind to sail almost all the way across. The wind died down just as we approached the marina.

"Marina di Ragusa! Marina di Ragusa! *Questa è Mischief!*"

The wonderfully efficient young lady at the front office, whom we had befriended when we had visited our friends on *Te Ara* at the marina the previous Easter, immediately recognised us.

"*Benvenuti Mischief*! Come into the marina. Make sure you keep to the port breakwater, as there is some silting on the starboard side. The *marineros* will meet you and guide you to your pen."

I guided *Mischief* to the pontoon indicated, going just past where we were to be berthed to be able to reverse into the pen. This went ever so smoothly as our beloved boat slid gently between two yachts.

"That was amazing. You tucked her in so perfectly," the lady from the boat to our port called out, to my delight.

Little did she know that the *marineros* were on our starboard bow and had used their rubber dinghy to coax *Mischief* right into the groove. And after that wonderful applause, I was not going to set her straight.

I noticed that our new neighbours flew a Silver Fern, the unofficial flag of New Zealand. To our other side was a New Zealand catamaran flying the same flag. I could not resist!

"Bloody hell! Bloody marina! Tucked in between two Kiwi boats! Gosh the marina must be desperate to bring up the standards, sandwiching an Aussie boat between you guys!"

"Bloody Aussies!" our new friend Helen was quick to retort. "Now we're in trouble!"

A Little Bit of MisChief

I immediately ran forward to hoist our Boxing Kangaroo flag on the port spreader.

Helen and Kerry on *Geronimo* turned out to be a lovely, friendly and lively couple and we took to each other immediately. We would hurl friendly insults about the alleged habits of New Zealanders and Aussies on many a sundowner over the course of the few weeks we were there.

"You are utterly wicked and leading me astray!" I would moan, grinning from ear to ear, a glass of G & T in hand. "Here I am a 'shy and retiring' Aussie, trying to bring up the standards!" At which Helen would almost choke, as she spluttered "What!!!"

Walking along the pontoons to see who was around, we were delighted to discover that we knew many of those who would be wintering in the same marina.

"Look, Kit and Belinda on *Quilcene* (UK) are here." We had first met them over the winter at Finike and had not seen them since. And further along on other pontoons, "there's *Orca Joss* ...and Alan and Holly on *Summer Wind* (New Zealand) and look, the large black yacht that gave us such a hassle in Turkey!" It was great fun catching up with everyone, and meeting new cruisers on our pontoon.

"What's *Wraith* doing here?" I told Bjorn as we came across the boat on one of the outer pontoons. "Weren't they meant to go to Roccella Ionica for the winter?"

There was nobody on board that morning but news travels fast among sailors. Helen told me that the yacht had been damaged when it was involved in a collision with a tanker some 20 nautical miles northeast of Malta.

We caught up with Vicki and Jeff on *Wraith* later that week. The owners described their harrowing experience, only a few hours after waving us goodbye in Malta. They had encountered heavy seas. They were busy controlling the sails in the rolling swell, running in and out of the cabin when a tanker approached at speed. It motored right in front of them oblivious to their presence. The yacht, unable to take evasive action, crashed into the side of the tanker and lost its anchor and chain. It started taking in water but the situation was controlled by inboard pumps. After calling Valletta Radio for assistance, a Maltese aircraft was dispatched and the tanker was directed to turn around and give assistance. The yacht owners, unhurt but badly shaken, opted to head for Ragusa where there were better facilities for the necessary repairs.

With Bjorn's parents in Stockholm not doing so well health wise, we were under pressure to visit as soon as possible. The marina was well planned and safe, and we had no hesitation in leaving *Mischief* there over the winter months. We took the ferry from nearby Pozzallo to Malta from where we flew to Sweden. We spent three weeks there and watched Bjorn's dad deteriorate. Within three days of our return to Malta, he had passed away.

On a visit to my parents, it was becoming increasingly obvious that they also needed greater attention. Their days of living independently were ending. Things were brought to a head when my mum fell and broke her hip, and whilst she recovered well, it was obvious that residential care was called for.

This state of affairs gave us good cause to think. We couldn't very well just up and continue sailing at this critical time in our parents' lives. With the decision to stay in the Mediterranean for a couple of years until things settled down, we decided to make Malta our temporary base and bought a small runabout (i.e. car). Our wonderful friend, Daniel, offered us the use of his lovely home again.

Autumn had brought along the usual swag of storms, and we were eager to return to Ragusa to check on the boat. Bjorn and I decided to spend Christmas in Sicily. We took the car across on the ferry. In company with our friends, most notably Helen and Kerry (*Geronimo*) and Jannine (*Orca Joss*), we took advantage of every fine day. We drove around some of the scenic surrounding countryside and vineyards, and visited the well-known Baroque towns of Ragusa Ibla, Modica (where we sampled the endless variety of local chocolate, my favourite being the chocolate with sea salt), Scicli and Noto, all of which

A Little Bit of Mischief

are UNESCO World Heritage listed.

We had a very 'merry' Christmas, a wonderful break, and reluctantly headed back to Malta to 'dry out'.

And now the serious albeit reluctant thinking started: on the one hand, we loved our *Mischief*, but it was impractical to keep the boat in a marina in another country. A glimmer of hope on the horizon was that our good friends on *Te Ara* were crossing the Atlantic to Brazil, and their itinerary looked appealing. We yearned to follow in their footsteps, but there were many challenges working to separate us from our beloved boat.

Space at Malta marinas was at a premium and it was impossible to obtain a permanent berth at Msida Marina. Things became further complicated by constantly changing laws in Europe. Italy had just introduced a tax for boats cruising in Italian waters, and Greece had its own raft of taxes, interpreted differently depending on where you were and how officious the locals were. Another complication was the boat registration. *Mischief* was an Australian registered boat. Under European Union (EU) laws it could stay in EU waters for two years before having to leave for a non-EU country. A quick nip over to Tunisia would have done the trick in previous years. But it was not an ideal option with the upheaval brought about by the 'Arab Spring', the series of demonstrations in the Middle East and Northern Africa.

A further challenge was our Australian nationality. We could reside in the EU for 90 days out of 180 days. To overcome this, Bjorn had, prior to departure from Australia, sought Maltese citizenship as my spouse, giving us both dual citizenship for Australia and the EU via Malta. However, as EU residents we could not maintain an overseas registered boat for more than 30 days, and would have to register the boat in the EU. There were two problems with this choice: the first was that not only was the tax prohibitive, but we would have also lost our Australian registration. The second was that *Mischief* was designed primarily as a blue water boat, built and certified for ocean crossing. It was not a suitable boat for the type of coastal cruising in the Mediterranean, where a boat with an open rear cockpit would be more in tune with the coast hopping lifestyle.

Whilst moving from country to country *Mischief*'s Australian registration had not presented a problem. Now that we would be based in Malta, this was a real headache. We explored the possibility of shipping her back to Australia or to some other part of the world such as Asia.

Both the EU and non-EU options were fading fast. An emerging refugee problem in the Mediterranean and political developments in Turkey muddied the waters further.

It was time for a literal sea change or, to our dismay, 'land change'. Given our decision to spend a couple of years in the Mediterranean, we opted to test the boat market. *Mischief* was listed for sale. Everyone warned that with a depressed boat market, prospects were dismal.

Imagine our surprise - shock actually - when our boat broker called us, two weeks after listing the boat on their company website. A couple had expressed interest. Of course we did not take this seriously. Then we received another call telling us that the potential buyers had decided to fly to Ragusa in March to inspect the boat. We were totally unprepared for this. There was no alternative but to head back to Ragusa to prepare *Mischief* for her not really very welcome visitors.

To our distress, the young Spanish couple fell in love with our beloved *Mischief*. They were looking for a boat to sail across the Atlantic. I am sure they must have thought we were mad - or madly in love with the boat - because Bjorn and I kept on exchanging looks, unsure if this was what we truly wanted. The couple upped their price to the extent that, given the state of the second-hand boat market, we could not justify saying 'no'. But neither could we believe what we had actually done.

Our Sicilian Spring turned out to be very different. Instead of joining our cruising friends prepare their boats for another summer cruising season, we started going through our possessions to work out what to take off the boat and what to leave behind.

We still had a few months up our sleeve at the marina, and were determined to make the best of it.

It had been a long, cold and wet winter. For a few weeks, we revelled in marina life, immersing ourselves in the pleasures of

A Little Bit of MisChief

being among our friends. We may have been about to lose *Mischief*, but certainly the 'spirit' stayed with us.

◇◇◇

Marina life in Ragusa was significantly different from our experience in Finike. Being a newer marina, there was not yet a 'resident' population to organise the diversity of activities we had enjoyed in Turkey. The marina itself was beautifully designed to ensure calm waters, but whoever planned the site had no inkling of cruisers' needs. My biggest gripe had to be the toilet facilities and shower rooms. Beautiful new buildings they were, and kept very clean, but some idiot had situated each block at either end of the large marina. This meant that when nature called, you had to hopscotch cross-legged along your pontoon, down the main pontoon and then around the marina perimeter to get to the blessed building: about half a kilometre's walk. And let's hope you remembered to take the key card to open the door.

It was for this reason that we came up with an arrangement to borrow our neighbours' bikes, kept on the pontoon, for cases of emergency.

There was no clubroom or common room, so the resident cruisers came to an arrangement with one of the local cafés in the marina (yes, they did have a line of retail shops and a small mini-market and restaurants) to set aside space for us in an adjacent room to gather on certain nights. One night a week, they would cook special meals at a reasonable price. The cruising community organised a morning radio session so that we could exchange information on what was happening in the surrounding areas, plan activities, arrange to meet up and generally keep in touch.

Ever creative, the cruisers found plenty of opportunity to have an unforgettable time together. We explored several restaurants at the Marina di Ragusa town and surrounds, tasting some of the most delicious fare. When it came to food, Sicily won the prize for scrumptious dishes. We rented a coach and visited nearby towns, attending local festivals, including a memorable festival of the very ornate Sicilian horse and cart display in Donnafugata. Also, around us were various local centres where ceramics, produce of all kinds and other art were on display. At the marina, the boat cockpits came into 'wet' use again whenever the heavens dried up. Belinda would enchant us playing the flute in *Quilcene*'s cockpit whilst we imbibed, nibbling away on dips, olives, cheese and whatever goodies we each took along. John (*Orca Joss*) would strum his guitar, alongside other musicians, in the bar area ashore.

That particular March, sunny days were few and far between, and you were left in no doubt that this was laundry time. A queue would form to the laundry room - yes, at least the marina had thought of that. But with no place to hang out our washing, you were serenaded by the breeze blowing through the endless lines strung up between mast and spreaders with clothes flapping away as you walked down the pontoons.

"Where are your undies?" Helen asked me one bright morning. In addition to the clothesline, I had taken out the little clothes hanger that was very much like an inverted umbrella frame, on which you could hang small items such as socks and underwear. Though my lines were full, the clothes hanger was empty save for a few socks prominently displayed on the stern of the boat.

"Hmmm!" I answered mischievously. "Obviously, I do not wear any."

"You dag!" she cried out. For the non-Antipodeans, 'dag' actually refers to the soiled, matted wool on a sheep's rear. Down under, and particularly among the Kiwis (referring to New Zealanders), it is commonly used almost as a term of endearment when friends tease each other - especially when you succeed in pulling their leg.

I won't repeat what else she called me. Let me just say that I narrowly avoided a swim that morning.

The laundry room was the source of much fun in other ways. For example, with no library available, the laundry sprouted bookcases and soon, books in a variety of European languages lined the shelves.

However, the prize went to the super yacht that donated a massage machine to the laundry room. Why anyone would have

A Little Bit of MisChief

that on a yacht is beyond me. I'm not too sure what it was meant to 'massage', but it was quite funny to approach the laundry room to hear screams of delight or horror - depending on the person - emanating from this innocuous room. Sure enough, on entering, you would come across a group of mostly women, falling about the place with laughter. Everyone had their turn riding this monstrosity, more like a powerful 'bucking bronco' type of massage machine. I leave it to you to work out what we actually called it.

We managed a few forays to explore more of Sicily, which we had grown to love, even 'discovering' the largest Roman villa we have seen so far. This came about after an enjoyable excursion to the centre of Sicily when we set out to find the famed 'Bikini Girls'. The trail led to the Villa Romana del Casale near Piazza Armerina, belonging to an influential Roman family. This majestic villa is extensive, and parts of it were still being excavated when we visited. It is renowned for its well-preserved, captivating mosaics. Sure enough, in one of the rooms we found the depiction of a group of young women wearing bikini-style outfits for sporting events.

To be honest, though, many of the 'happy' times with our friends felt almost like wakes, so shell shocked were we with the way things had turned out with *Mischief*. I have to confess to staggering between boats on some late evenings, as I may have been a tad unsteady to tackle the gangplanks. Well, who could blame us, as every evening these walkways seemed to take on a life of their own?

Bjorn and Kerry sailed *Mischief* back to Malta in mid-April, while Helen and I drove a laden car back via ferry. It was good to have friends who understood what we were going through at such a time, and we spent a wonderful week or so together as we showed them around the island. Our transition to land was further eased as quite a few of our yachting friends called into Malta on their way around the island. Among them were Jane and Clive on *Jane G* (UK) whom we had got to know so well in Finike, Turkey.

"One adventure finishes," Clive consoled us, "but then you go on to the next one." How right Clive was!

Syracuse Fish Market

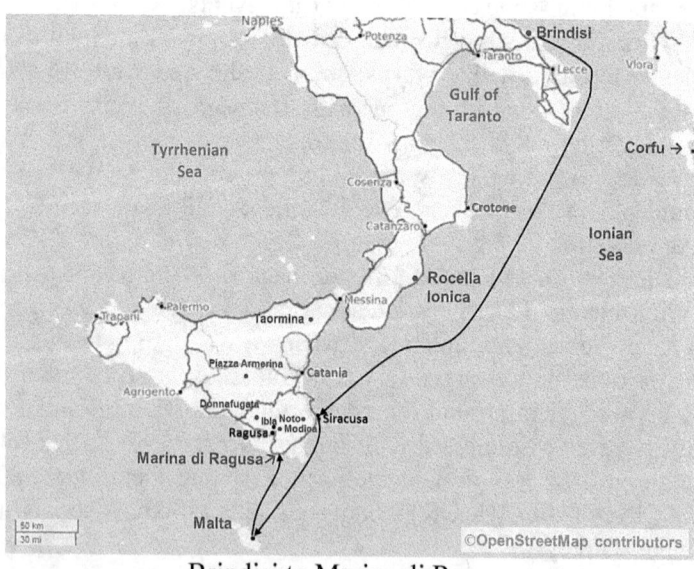
Brindisi to Marina di Ragusa

22
...And Everywhere Else!

It was time to take stock of what we wanted to do now that we would be land bound. And so Bjorn and I turned our attention to renting an apartment in Malta to have as a base for the next couple of years whilst we enjoyed time with our parents and families in Malta and in Sweden. We hoped to use this time to concentrate on land travel until we worked out whether to resume sailing or take on a new adventure. We were fortunate to find a lovely airy apartment just on the seafront in a quiet part of St Paul's Bay, with a grandstand view of the bay and of St Paul's Island, where the apostle Paul is said to have been shipwrecked on his way to Rome.

"At least the first sound in the morning will be of waves lapping the shore, and our first sight that of the sea in all its colours and glory." I told Bjorn. It was as close as we could get to being on a boat.

To celebrate our joint birthdays in May we decided on a visit to Venice, known also as the *Serenissima*, before the floods of tourists descended on this archipelago in mid-summer. We started out with a glorious week going around the city that had so eluded us on our cruising trip up the Adriatic. This turned out to be an old-fashioned romantic holiday. We strolled through the city day and night, arm in arm, taking in this enchanting city, with its palazzos, canals, bridges and iconic gondolas, savouring all that the city had on offer.

"Finally, Piazza San Marco; you certainly can't miss the Basilica and Campanile." Armed with a Square Pass we spent the better part of two days alternating between exploring buildings and replenishing our energy in one of the surrounding coffee shops before we faced the next queue.

We visited a few of the islands of the Venetian Lagoon: we loved walking the streets and galleries of Murano with its famous glassblowing industry, yet in a way felt more attracted to Burano, an island of fishermen, lace makers, and colourfully painted houses. We took the train down to Chioggia, an unpretentious fishing town at the southern end of the Venetian lagoon. Like Venice, it is built around canals and boats. Yet Chiogga enjoys a slower, more conventional, pace more in tune with our lifestyle. Reputed for its seafood, we splurged out on a delicious and unforgettable fish banquet.

Frances and Bill on *Tulameen II* had wintered in one of the marinas east of Venice, and we had arranged to meet up.

"This is for you," Frances said, handing me a bag. Imagine my surprise when it turned out to be a painting of our beloved *Mischief* at anchor at Fethiye.

"I can't believe this! I had given it up for lost!" Frances had sent the painting to an address I had provided in Malta, but the parcel had been returned to her with a note that read: 'unable to be delivered due to dog!'

Our next stop was the Emilia-Romagna region in north-eastern Italy to catch up with friends Mara and Giovanni whom we had known before migrating to Australia in the early 1980s.

"*Ciao, carissimi!*" Mara and Giovanni greeted us, hugs all around. With old friends, no matter how much time elapses between catching up, it always feels like yesterday.

The beauty of knowing people in places you are visiting is that you get to see so many sights that occasional trippers and tourists may miss. In our case, we had a wonderful yet leisurely week exploring the magnificent Po River delta and some of the surrounding countryside, towns and villages. Giovanni explained fishing techniques and the types of crops. At one stage, we passed by a distillery which had a mountain of what

A Little Bit of MisChief

looked like grape skins on the road verge. Giovanni explained that this was used to produce grappa, made from grape skins, seeds and stalks, after which I resolved never to drink the stuff again.

We did not ignore the surrounding cities, and enjoyed nearby Ravenna admiring the colourful mosaics adorning many of its central buildings. We visited Bologna, the lively, historic capital of the region, and completed our tour with a trip to the beautiful city of Florence, capital of Italy's Tuscany region, which is home to many masterpieces of Renaissance art and architecture. You need at least a week to see Florence, but with just a day at our disposal, we only managed a walk through this magnificent city, viewing iconic sights such as the Duomo. Seeing that the queue was not too long, we also managed a visit to the *Galleria dell'Accademia*, which displays Michelangelo's 'David' statue.

Of course, no holiday would have been complete without sampling the local cuisine. "*Domani*, we go to a special place for dinner. They make their own pasta, but it is *una pasta speciale* from this region." Giovanni explained.

"Yumm, definitely," Bjorn and I answered in chorus. Who would be *pazzo* enough to pass on such an opportunity? And a lovely, cosy little restaurant it turned out to be, in one of the quaint neighbourhood villages.

On our return to Malta, the summer season beckoned. With the temperature rising, the sea became our second home. We usually took an energetic morning swim. In the afternoon, we would paddle out with friends for about half a kilometre, chatting away for an hour or two, until the skin became all shrivelled. This was often followed by playing cards sometimes into the evening at the Simenta: the conveniently located kiosk on the quay and bathing beach beneath our apartment building. Here we gorged ourselves on the delicious *Ħobż biż-żejt*, made with the local crusty sourdough bread. The bread is rubbed with tomatoes or tomato paste, drizzled with olive oil and filled with a mix of tuna, olives, capers, onion. Additions include white beans, herbs, lettuce and perhaps a *ġbejna*, a local hard goat cheese. Of course, this was accompanied with frequent sips of the local plonk to keep us hydrated.

Given the car traffic hell and the rising temperatures on this island during the summer months - reflected both in the weather and in people's temperament - we did not venture far from St Paul's Bay. Often our weekly outing entailed bringing mum and dad over to the beach for a couple of hours to enjoy the sea air and view over a light meal. Our placid pace was interspersed with the arrival of visitors. There was a string of them that summer starting with two of my sisters, from northern Europe and Australia respectively, and followed by a short visit from our daughter. In the midst of all this we were delighted to attend our nephew's wedding in mid-June, having practically witnessed their budding romance - yes, this was the couple who had visited us on the boat in Greece.

In August, with sweltering temperatures forecast for the Mediterranean, we packed our bags for a short visit to see Bjorn's mum and the rest of his family in Sweden. We returned to Malta in time to do another side trip to Sicily, and to the Marina di Ragusa where we had spent the spring on *Mischief*. This trip came about because, whilst in Perth earlier in the year, we had waxed lyrical about our stay at the marina. This had enticed our Australian visitors (in-laws, actually) to come and visit for a wonderful week of food, wine, swimming, touring and sampling the local Sicilian village life.

"Look at all that fresh seafood!" Richard started out. "Prawns tonight!" he said as his eyes feasted on all the offerings, fresh off the boats. We were in one of the tiny fishing hamlets along the coast from Marina di Ragusa.

"Let's go to the marina and catch up with Helen and Kerry on *Geronimo*. See who else is around," Bjorn said. Sure enough, our friends were on board and soon there were introductions all round.

"You must come by tomorrow for a sundowner with us!" Helen said. "Find out more about living on a boat," - this to our visitors.

We had a wonderful evening reminiscing, with promises to

A Little Bit of MisChief

catch up soon. Then it was a rush back to Malta in time to greet friends who were travelling through Europe and flying down to visit us.

It was soon time to fly up to Stockholm again where we intended to spend Christmas and the New Year with Bjorn's family. We were greeted with a metre of snow outside Bjorn's parents' house and spent the first morning shovelling snow so we could get out with the car - a far cry but welcome change from the quasi-continuous summers we had enjoyed for almost a decade.

On Christmas Eve, when Christmas is traditionally celebrated in Sweden, we caught up with the family and had a sumptuous dinner. This included a great variety of pickled *sill* or herring for starters, then a course of *lutfisk* which is aged stockfish (air-dried or dried/salted whitefish), baked pork, Swedish meatballs (yes, they're different!), salted cured pork and brown beans and potatoes. The dessert included a selection of sweetbreads, biscuits, creamed rice porridge and rhubarb jelly, and followed a few hours later with coffees and teas and my favourite: the yummy 'Princess' cake and more sweetbreads!

At New Year's Eve, which we celebrated at Bjorn's sister's house, the normally placid Swedes go Viking berserk. All the neighbours go out into their gardens and let up an endless stream of fireworks which light up the sky.

2013 was a special year for us as Bjorn and I were to celebrate our 60th birthdays in the middle of the year.

"One we will remember;" I told Bjorn. "And we have to do some sailing, as I am going mad without a boat."

We sat down to work out a rough itinerary that would see us traverse the globe. First we made our annual trek back to Perth to family and friends who had stood by us all these years during our travels, encouraged us and welcomed us back each time with open arms. They say that distance makes the heart grow fonder. On each return trip, we felt Western Australia call out to us. The more time we spent in Europe and elsewhere, the more we grew to love and cherish Perth with its magnificent weather, clean air and eclectic lifestyle. We had come to appreciate the size of the State, having sailed half way up the coast on our departure. It had brought home its majestic and rugged beauty.

As usual, we caught up with as many of our friends as we could manage, and even fitted in a trip to the eastern seaboard of Australia. A special highlight had been catching up with Joe and Helen (*Dreamcatcher*) with whom we had sailed across the Indian Ocean and up the Red Sea to Turkey. We returned to Malta in late March after a hectic 10-week visit.

As spring established itself, many cruisers north and south of us did what they usually do: come to Malta for repairs and any significant maintenance required, as the island was well equipped to cater for yachts, large and small. The phone would ring in our apartment and I would tell Bjorn, "Wonder who it is this time?" as sure enough, another cruising couple we knew would have called into the island. Bjorn enjoyed a reputation of being a 'Mr Fix-it' who knew his way around all things marine. More importantly, he had befriended many of the chandlers and service agents on the island, from electronics to boat rigging. Bjorn was ever willing to help, especially as it meant being close to boats.

Meanwhile our ex-marina neighbours, Helen and Kerry from *Geronimo* also decided on a visit.

"We have to go back to Australia, perhaps for a couple of years," Helen told us. "But we are not happy about leaving the boat in a shipyard, unattended." Helen and Kerry had decided to bring *Geronimo* to Malta and put her up on the hard (this means having the boat hauled out of the water and leaving it propped up on land) at the boatyard.

"Oh, don't worry. We will keep an eye on her and look after it for you."

"You can do better," Kerry said. "It's not good to leave her out on land for too long. We haven't yet worked out when we will be back in Europe. Put her back in the water whenever you want and sail her around. Much better for her - and you can enjoy her too!"

Bjorn helped Kerry pack up *Geronimo* in readiness for going

A Little Bit of MisChief

on land; in the weeks that followed, he enjoyed going down to the yard to potter around on the boat seeing to a few things that needed attending to. He was also kept busy helping Holly and Alan on *Summer Wind* who had come to Malta, also from the Marina di Ragusa. Their plans included changing the engine, a mammoth undertaking that Bjorn and I had gone through with *Mischief*.

Holly and Alan's long stay on the island helped cement a friendship. Many a pleasant evening was spent enjoying a glass, or two, er …or more, of vino sometimes at our place, sometimes in *Summer Wind*'s cockpit or at one of the local restaurants.

"We are looking for crew to help us sail across the Atlantic at the end of this year," Alan told us.

Bjorn and I looked at each other. "Yes, we're in!" we replied in unison. It was so wonderful to have sailing back on the agenda. Crossing the next ocean was too good an opportunity to miss, and would complete an excellent year.

We received the best birthday present ever on our birthdays when Mark and Bridget (our son and his wife) announced the expected arrival of junior in January 2014. This dovetailed comfortably with our sailing plans as the Atlantic crossing would take place between December and January and we could then head off to Perth.

With *Geronimo* at our disposal, we managed some wonderful cruising around the Maltese Islands - and learnt the hard way that the best time to be out on the water was during the week. On weekends, the anchorages would simply overflow with local cruisers, some of whom turned out to be extremely territorial.

On one occasion, we went for a couple of days sailing to the top end of Malta and around the little sister island of Gozo. On board was my sister Josianne, with whom I share a close bond. We promised her one of the most exotic anchorages the Mediterranean had to offer.

We called into the bay of Santa Maria on the islet of Comino, and tucked into a corner, dropping our anchor in the shallow, crystal clear aquamarine waters. There were three other boats in the bay and the day passed away peacefully, swimming, snacking and snoozing. As evening approached, so did a whole flotilla of boats. It was Friday and we were about to witness the local race to get to an anchorage first, somewhat reminiscent of our Ionian experience. This huge powerboat came in, almost ramming us as it drove past, its wake rocking the boat so much that we had to hold on. It dropped its anchor next to us and reversed up to the shore to tie up.

"Hey!" I called out. "You can't tie up here." It was obvious our boats would soon be bumping into each other. Boat etiquette was 'first come, first served'. We had spent the last years sailing in the Mediterranean, making sure we got to anchorages as early as possible in the day to secure a good place. We did not get a response as a slinging match had broken out between this boat and another smaller powerboat, the larger boat who claimed that this was "their regular place."

"Come on Bjorn, let's move!" I urged. "You don't argue with types like these." We pulled up our anchor and headed across the small bay to drop our anchor once again.

The next morning, with little or no wind, we motored first to the picturesque and aptly named Paradise Bay on the northern shore of Malta. We then went across to Comino once more to the majestic Crystal Bay, surrounded by cliffs and a choice of caves and tunnels to snorkel through and explore.

With more boats arriving, we upped anchor and made our way around the northeast coast of Gozo to San Blas Bay, a small, yet picturesque beach with vibrant reddish-orange sand. What makes it more special and unique is its location, set in secluded and green countryside at the end of beautiful valleys, and with no sealed access roads. Visitors have to proceed to the beach by walking down a steep hill.

We were now closing in on our final coup as we travelled over the northern end of Gozo to the west coast and to the almost circular sandy lagoon with overhanging limestone cliffs in Dwejra.

"We're going in behind that rock," I said to Josianne, as we approached what appeared to be a narrow passage between the rock and the cliff face.

A Little Bit of MisChief

"Can we get in there?" she replied.

With calm waters, it was no problem to get through the narrow entrance into the lagoon. The depth metre jumped from 45 metres to about seven metres as we entered the opening, and then to around 11-12 metres of clear water inside the lagoon. It lay behind the islet called Fungus Rock, sometimes known as Mushroom Rock. The Rock got its name from the Knights of Malta who discovered a plant thought to be a fungus, but which was actually a parasitic flowering plant (*Cynomorium Coccineum*) that could cure medical conditions such as dysentery, bleeding and impotence. Growing up on the island, I had been told that Napoleon himself had sought this fungus, reason unknown, which is why it got its local moniker as *Il-Ġebla tal-Ġeneral*, The General's Rock. Another local tale? I have not been able to shed any light on this, though I have not tried hard.

I had set the anchor at the northern end so that we could watch the sunset through the gap between the rock and the mainland. It was a magical night, starlit and with a good waning moon, as we settled down to a dinner of baked macaroni which I had prepared for this trip.

"This is stunning; very dramatic and yet so peaceful and calming after the hustle and bustle at Comino. You wouldn't know this existed from just motoring past," Josianne said, as we all lay around the cockpit, enjoying the serene evening.

"We have been sailing in the Med for about four years now, and this anchorage ranks among one of the most beautiful." We were lucky in that only one other boat had joined us in the spacious lagoon, anchored at the far side.

We motored round the south-western end of Gozo the next morning to get a peek at the renowned Blue Lagoon in Comino before the tour boat flotillas arrived. They came in laden with tourists, transforming the tiny bay into a nightmare as powerboats whizzed up and down offering cave trips, joy rides and the lot. Even at this early hour, we did not have much luck. The bay was already filling up, and we just managed a quick motor through its dazzling turquoise waters.

◇◇◇

Towards the end of July, *Geronimo* was returned to the boatyard. We packed our bags for a lengthy visit to northern Europe. Our journey started out with a visit to Bjorn's mum and family in Sweden. We succumbed to the lure of a cruise ship to visit a number of cities around the Baltic Sea. This was quite a re-adjustment from our independent travels and not our cup of tea. Except that at least it got us past the visa problems and into Russia without a hassle, and without having to cart luggage about from one country to the next. An unexpected bonus was the five-hour trip from the city of Stockholm through the archipelago of nearly thirty thousand islands, islets and rocks to reach the Baltic.

"Let's go up to the lounge above the bridge. We'll have a bird's eye view from there." Bjorn told me.

We chose a table close to the viewing platform. With champagne in hand, we 'aahed' and 'oohed' as the ship was competently guided through the islands.

"There's hardly a hair's breadth between ship and shore."

It was amazing to see a ship this size handle the narrow passages and sharp turns.

Our first destination was Helsinki, Finland's capital, a gracious town where we opted for headphones and did our own touring. Next on the agenda were three days in St Petersburg, which had been on my to-visit wish list for decades. Founded in 1703 by Peter the Great, the Russian port city had been renamed first as Petrograd and then Leningrad before reverting to its original name about 25 years ago. We thought three days would suffice, but we hardly had enough time to visit the Hermitage Museum, and the Peterhof and Winter Palaces, attend a ballet at the famous Mariinsky Theatre, do some day and night river cruises and appreciate this city with its turbulent past. The grandeur is there, but it is no wonder the peasants protested.

We were pleasantly surprised to discover that the cruise highlights were not over as we stepped ashore onto the quaint town of Tallinn, Estonia, followed by an equally enjoyable tour of Visby (capital of Gotland, another Swedish island). From there we visited Warnemunde and Rostock in Germany and ended our cruise in Copenhagen, a city we loved and a favourite

A Little Bit of MisChief

destination, as this was where my youngest sister Josianne lived.

After two weeks on a cruise ship, it was wonderful to be able to get back on a sailing boat. Thanks to Josi, we enjoyed a lovely, lively sail in Køge Bugt in the Sound, the waters between Denmark and Sweden. A week later we drove down south to the environs of Nykobing (island of Falster) in the south of Denmark to catch up with Birte and Jorgen (*Circe*), who had completed a circumnavigation. To our delight we found them in great shape. It was great fun catching up with sailors and mentors with whom we had shared so many adventures. Jorgen had purchased another boat to keep him occupied; this was a trend among many returned cruisers unable to let go of the bond with the sea.

We had a wonderful time exploring the area. Although the countryside and surrounding villages and buildings are typically Nordic, some human attributes are universal.

"Can you see those mirrors?" Jorgen said, pointing to little mirrors mounted on the outside of window shutters, similar to the rear view mirrors on motorbikes. "It is so that those inside can see what is going on - and who is passing by - outside!"

"In Malta, there have enclosed balconies with louvered shutters on windows, but they serve the same purpose," I laughed. "And in Australian country towns, it is the curtains that are often put to this use."

Our next stop was Provence in south-eastern France, where we caught up with Andi and Georges (*Te Ara*) and their delightful daughter, with whom we had had such a wonderful time catching up in various destinations. Their tastefully converted farmhouse was set majestically among gracious hillocks and farmland, mostly vines. Georges and Andi took us for a stroll through the university city of Aix-en-Provence, Post-Impressionist painter Paul Cézanne's birthplace. Georges tirelessly drove us through the tiny winding roads through rolling vineyards, olive groves, almond trees and lavender fields to visit the most gorgeous little towns. In Lourmarin we could immerse ourselves in the *gentil Provencal* ambience in the narrow winding streets. We visited Bonnieux, perched on a plateau above the valley and then drove on to Menerbes, a walled hilltop village in the centre of the Luberon region dating back to the 16th century. Lacoste, with its château belonging to the infamous Marquis de Sade, was another pleasant little village. Our trips included a number of country markets, where we sampled the local fare, sipped coffee at the street side cafes, and imbibed in the local wines for a full and terrific week.

"Why don't you join us for a sail in the Caribbean?" Georges started out one evening. Georges had sailed *Te Ara* across the Atlantic to Brazil and then northwards towards the Caribbean and to Central America to Guatemala. This is where they had left the boat during the hurricane season.

"We are crossing this year with *Summer Wind*. It would be so much fun to see more of Central America whilst we are there." Bjorn looked at me and read the eagerness and enthusiasm in my eyes. "And yes, we would love to join you for some sailing."

What a way to end our summer tour and to celebrate our 60th!

We returned to Malta well and truly ready for a short rest before welcoming more friends from Australia. It is no wonder that our apartment was being referred to as the "Gillgren hostel." We enjoyed our visitors, including a special visit by Mark and Bridget and Bridget's parents, a brief but much appreciated stay, where we could admire the growing 'bump' that would be our grandchild. It was a busy time as we tried to show our in-laws as much of Malta and the sister island of Gozo as possible. We even managed a family reunion so they could meet our side of the family.

In early autumn, we heard from Holly and Alan on *Summer Wind* that Holly's brother wanted to join them for the trans-Atlantic crossing. This meant that there would not be enough space on board for us. Instead, they invited us to join them for a sail through the Caribbean islands. "This is even better," I told Bjorn. I would have enjoyed the trans-Atlantic trip, but we've experienced crossings. The Caribbean is definitely more

A Little Bit of MisChief

enticing."

"And it fits in neatly with sailing on *Te Ara*."

It was a busy but hugely enjoyable couple of months as we worked out an itinerary that would fit in with our friends. On our bucket list was a visit to one of the best Maya temples that our son had assured us was undisputedly Tikal. Accordingly, a visit to Guatemala headed our list, followed by meeting up with Georges and Andi somewhere in the eastern Caribbean waters outside Guatemala or Nicaragua for a couple of weeks, then fly over to the Windward Islands to join *Summer Wind* for another couple of weeks. As our flights back and forth from Europe took us through America, this was an opportunity to look around Florida and wherever else we landed. As news spread of our plans, we received another invitation from our French friends in Finike, Dominique and Claude on *Lobea* to join them in the Windward Islands.

"This has worked out well," I said. "The baby is due in late January, and we have to give our kids space to get used to a little one in the home. If we are away until March, we can return to Malta and re-pack for our visit to Perth - and to family and our first grandchild - in the beginning of April."

Christina Gillgren

Glass Garden in Murano

Traditional Swedish Christmas Buffet

23
The Caribbean

The first two years of being land-based had worked out well. Coupled with our 60th birthday celebrations, our travels had taken us in various directions. We had seen many new places, caught up with family, and reconnected with and reinforced long time friendships.

We had heard much about Central and South America from both our children. This was a good opportunity to base our forthcoming trip around the Caribbean to be able to tick a few items off our bucket lists.

No trip to Central America can be complete without exploring the amazing indigenous cultures of the region. With this in mind, our first stop was Guatemala. This part of the world can be a dangerous place, but we were not prepared for our greeting at Guatemala City. We arrived there, via the USA, before sunset to be greeted by machine gun toting youth all around us. People and noise filled the airport and surrounds; in fact, total chaos prevailed. We were careful to take a registered taxi to get to our hotel. After much research on the internet, we had booked a hotel in what we hoped was the safest quarter of the city for an overnight stay. When we got to our hotel, Bjorn and I looked at each other.

"Where on earth have we selected our hotel?"

The taxi stopped us in front of a large iron gate around a

high-walled compound surrounded with barbed wire. Our cabbie rang the bell and waited for a response, which was not immediate.

When finally the doorbell was answered and the side gate opened to let us in, we entered a charming, colourful courtyard. We were soon to discover that with the warfare that goes on as part of daily life in this city, this barricading was the norm.

We had a pleasant room in which to spend our first night. In the morning, we enjoyed a traditional breakfast, which included eggs, tortillas, beans and plantains. And of course, no Guatemala breakfast is complete without a mug of world-class Guatemalan coffee. Bjorn was in heaven.

We had the better part of the day to pass before getting onto our next plane that would take us to the ancient Mayan city of Tikal. A walk was called for to while away the morning and to explore some of the city - well, at least the 'tourist' quarter. We were warned to stick to the main road, which we did, but were quite unnerved with the sight of a machine gun toting private security every two steps. Chemists, drug stores and the like were heavily barricaded and guarded. Even a modest hairdressing salon had a sentry posted outside the door, often a young man hardly out of his teens, and machine gun in hand.

Such was the state of anticipation of trouble that one could be forgiven for missing the highly colourful life of the Guatemalans. The buses especially were a delightful sight: colours splashed all over and lights flashing away merrily, people crowded in like sardines and the rooftop full of luggage as they sped down the roads, hooting their horns at everyone. We finally found a shopping centre, behind heavily barricaded walls and the usual periphery of guards, where we could relax and have a cup of coffee. We were not at all sad to fly out of this city in the evening.

Fortunately, tourist places such as the ruins at Tikal in north-eastern Guatemala were safer places where we could roam around at leisure. We commenced our laid-back tour spending three days in the vivacious island town of Flores, situated on Lake Peten Itza, and connected to the mainland via a causeway bridge. The compact town is dense with colonial, red-roofed

A Little Bit of MisChief

buildings and narrow cobblestone streets. As we strolled through the city's charming streets, we came across numerous restaurants, reflecting its popularity as a tourist safe haven from which to take the trip to Tikal. We were also lucky enough to see a mini carnival one morning. Following the procession around, we ended up joining in the street party.

Our son had recommended Tikal because apart from being one of the most magnificent examples of Mayan civilization, it also lay in the middle of a jungle. We set out early one morning for the hour-long journey. As we approached by coach, we were soon enveloped in lush vegetation. Dressed for the occasion in hiking boots and anoraks, we ploughed through the dense rainforest paths. These would suddenly open up to reveal spectacular temples and other public buildings with steep steps or ramps to access the edifices. We spent the better part of a day trekking through this outstanding archaeological site. The size and scope are amazing, and the temples themselves a real wonder and tribute to human endeavour. We climbed to the top of one of the highest temples, hoping for an overall view, but could only see the odd temple peeping between the treetops. The jungle itself provided an impressive display, as our guide pointed out the wonderful array of plant, animal and bird life.

"I can hardly stand up!" I told Bjorn as we were driven back. "My legs ache and my knees feel as though they are about to give way!" That evening, we chose a restaurant where we could lie back on couches and rest our exhausted legs, snacking on a tasty assortment of *tamales*.

From Flores we flew back to Guatemala City. A taxi took us direct to the ancient city of Antigua. This former capital of Guatemala is charming. However, it is located in an earthquake prone region and is surrounded by active volcanoes. This combination led to its being abandoned as the capital some 250 years ago following an earthquake that devastated many parts of the city.

A tour of Antigua showed off the strong Spanish colonial influence, and the graciousness of the city. We spent a couple of days strolling through the markets and surrounds discovering, to our surprise, numerous Spanish language schools which attracted visitors from all over the world. Our stay included a trip to Lake Atitlan in the mountains, where we visited a number of Mayan villages on its shores who still follow a traditional lifestyle.

"For the first time ever, I feel tall," I laughed. "Even the men are shorter than me."

We were sorry that we had not planned to stay longer and visit more of the sites in Central America, but we had a date with sailor friends Andi, Georges and daughter Lea on *Te Ara*. And so, we took a taxi back to Guatemala City, after which we flew via San Salvador to Panama City. It was almost impossible to get from one place to the next on a direct flight in Central America, and we had numerous stopovers in some dodgy airports to look forward to.

◇◇◇

Panama City, the capital of Panama, is a modern city framed by the Pacific Ocean and man-made Panama Canal. We arrived late in the evening and settled down for the night.

"Good morning Mum!" our son's excited voice came over the phone, very early the next morning.

"Everything all right?" I asked, still groggy with sleep.

"Yes, absolutely. You and dad are now grandparents. We have a son!"

With the better part of a day before our next flight, we set out to explore the city's cobblestoned historic centre, *Casco Viejo*. Beaming with joy as we took in the morning's phone call, we practically waltzed through the centre, strewn with colonial-era landmarks, and plazas lined with bougainvillea, cafes and bars. It was safer than other cities in Central America, but we were mindful of where we were.

Our next flight took us south to Columbia and then back north again to the island of San Andres, which lies off the coast of Nicaragua, but belongs to Columbia.

"It looks gorgeous!" I told Bjorn as we approached for landing. "There are reefs all around, awash with surf. And the sea is a startling shade of turquoise."

At the tiny airport in San Andres, immigration officials

A Little Bit of MisChief

greeted warmly and informed us that we needed to pay an entry/tourist tax.

"That's fine! Where's the ATM?" Bjorn asked. And so it was that our friends Andi, Georges and daughter Lea saw us approaching, accompanied by an official.

"What happened? What have you done now?" Georges asked, waving his arms. I could see that he was not alarmed as there was a broad smile on his face.

"It seems that the ATM is located here at the arrivals area," I grinned, "and we need to pay for the pleasure of visiting!"

I made sure we made good use of Georges' arms by giving him and his family a big hug.

San Andres was a pleasant surprise: very much a Caribbean island, with picturesque tropical beaches, and seductive, warm waters in which to explore the rich coral reefs. Georges told us that the area was famous for its diverse ecosystem, which had resulted in the region being declared a UNESCO Marine reserve. San Andres was popular with Central Americans. As we found one evening, it is also well known for its reggae music.

One of the delights of cruising is going around the local towns: inevitably the girls would go shopping for boat provisions (when cruising in company, that is) and the guys trotted off to the local chandlers or ironmongers or whatever place sold marine equipment to get the never-ending bits and pieces that needed replacing or fixing. Andi and Lea showed me their discoveries of best baker, grocer and a gourmet shop, which sold a wonderful array of cheeses. Thus fully loaded, we met up with the men to return to *Te Ara* for our daily sundowner.

"You must also cook your famous 'passage chicken'!" Andi told me. Well, I had over the years waxed lyrical about this dish I would cook in the pressure cooker in preparation for or during ocean crossings.

After a few days on the island, the plan was to sail down with our friends past the coasts of Nicaragua and Costa Rica to the Bocas Del Toro archipelago in Panama. Leaving the San Andres anchorage proved to be quite an art form - and a little bit hair-raising - navigating the narrow passage through the reefs, with Andi down in the cabin following the sea chart on the computer and passing on instructions to the helmsman, Georges.

"Ah, it is wonderful to be back on the water again!" I told Andi and Georges. *Te Ara* is a lovely and fast sailing boat, much bigger than what we had been used to. However, we soon settled in to the motion of the boat in the swell that seems to build up in this area, trimming sails and chatting away until nightfall. To begin with, I was a bit unsure of handling a boat this size on my own, so I was pleased when Georges suggested that Bjorn and I would take one of the night watches together. It turned out to be a pleasant overnight sail. By morning, the swell started to subside. We arrived at the entrance to the Bocas Del Toro archipelago in the afternoon to find quite a number of boats in the bay behind the entrance. Soon Georges and Andi were waving to a number of boats and organising sundowners.

Bocas Del Toro is a large inlet surrounded by rainforest, with several islands strewn through its waters. The main island of Isla Colon hosts the capital, Bocas Town, a quasi-ramshackle hub full of cheerful Caribbean style clapboard houses with restaurants jutting out over the water, colourful shops and a lively nightlife.

We enjoyed the friendly, relaxed atmosphere of the town where we provisioned the boat in readiness for cruising around the bays and coves. We spent the next week or so exploring various anchorages around Bocas, and catching up with other cruisers. Then we called into Red Frog Marina - so called after the small red frogs that inhabited the local jungle - to check out the place. Every day, Andi, Lea and I would set out through the jungle path to the beach on the ocean side. We were greeted with the sound of waves pounding the beaches. The beautifully warm waters were very inviting, but we had to be wary of the strong surf and currents when we went swimming. On calmer days, Bjorn took the opportunity to teach Lea boogie boarding. Sometimes all five of us went across to the beach to enjoy a

A Little Bit of MisChief

delicious laid back light lunch, sprawled on couches at one of the beach *cabanas*. It felt like a modern version of Robinson Crusoe, but with all the comforts.

During our stay on *Te Ara*, I had the pleasure of helping not-so-little Lea out with her English lessons, which I can proudly report we both enjoyed. In addition, our host Andi celebrated her birthday, and so we girls took off arm-in-arm for a luxury massage at a nearby resort for a good pampering. That evening, Georges organised an excursion via water taxi to one of the other islands for a sumptuous meal in a lovely restaurant built on a platform over the water with the rainforest in the background.

It was soon time to say 'goodbye' to our cherished friends, who over the years had become like a second family to us, but not without one final adventure. We had booked one of the local water taxi guys to take us across the five miles to the main island of Isla Colon where the airport was located just outside Bocas Town. We were up and ready to go at about 5.00am, anxiously hoping the guy would turn up. Well he did, but the motor kept conking out along the way. Bjorn and I wondered if we were going to make our plane and the endless flight connections that would take us to Grenada in time to meet our next lot of friends. Imagine the relief when we finally reached the main island - soaked to the skin as, of course, it had started raining.

After country hopping via Colombia and Trinidad our last flight approached the island of Grenada late in the afternoon, the indented southern coast was set out below us in all its glory.
"A sailor's paradise," I said to Bjorn.

The airport was on the south-easternmost tip of the island. It was a short trip by taxi to the marina, where we had planned to meet our friends Holly and Alan on *Summer Wind*.

And what a welcome it was! There we were, lugging bags, to be greeted by a loud local band playing on oil drums. Beyond them, spread over a number of refectory tables, were many of the sailors in the marina or at anchorage. We celebrated our arrival in style as we joined in the barbecue and festivities. To our surprise, we came across yachties we had last seen in south-east Asia. These included Martha and Bryce on *Silver Fern*, whom we had farewelled in Langkawi, Malaysia.

Of course, we were introduced to Pina Coladas - the Caribbean staple. Well, when in Rome…

Grenada lies in the south-eastern Caribbean Sea, part of the Windward Islands chain. The Grenadines consist of the island of Grenada, and a chain of smaller islands weaving their way northwards leading to the main island of St Vincent. Grenada is dotted with numerous fruit and spice plantations, hence its moniker as the Spice Island.

The next morning we woke up to a glorious day, sunny with calm waters all around. "Hello Grenada!" I started out.

Alan gave me a mischievous look and, grinning, told me, "That is in Spain. This is Grenada." Which he pronounced 'Gree-nay-da'. It would take me a couple of days to get the intonation right.

Day one was very promising as we were treated to Holly's breakfast in style: I could not compete with Holly's magnificent *Cordon Bleu* cooking and food presentation, so took on my role as sous-chef. At breakfast this had me peel and skin the local oranges and then, using a paring knife, separating the 'skinless' segments. Holly and I worked out a menu to get us started. This was followed by a foray into the local town market to provision the boat with as much fresh produce as possible.

Summer Wind was a nostalgic boat for us. Designed by another great naval architect of the same vintage as *Mischief*, she was remarkably similar in some ways, and remarkably different in others. She handled so very much like our beloved boat that, at first, I kept my distance from the helm. Truth is I was missing our boat.

"The good thing about the Caribbean," Alan started out as we hoisted the sails, "is that you can rely on the wind. It generally blows from the east to north-east around here in the sailing season. It means you can usually sail north or south along the chain of islands." For the sailors among you, this means a steady supply of 10-25 knots of winds, with the wind

A Little Bit of MisChief

shifting from south-easterly to north-easterly between November and April. Definitely sailing heaven!

"That's great!" Bjorn continued. "I, for one, have had enough of the motoring we did in the Med. It either blew a gale or else we were becalmed."

Our first stop was just around the corner, and we called into the marina next to the capital, St. George's, whose colourful homes overlook the harbour. A problem had developed with the in-mast reefing (when the sail rolls into the mast), so Alan and Bjorn had to wait until the wind died down to tackle the problem.

We spent a glorious couple of weeks with our friends - sometimes sailing in company, and often catching up with other cruisers as we made our way north through the beautiful Grenadines archipelago. Our first stop was at Union Island. After we dropped our anchor, just off the Yacht Club in Clifton Harbour, we were startled by a loud engine sound overhead: So loud, we almost jumped out of our skins. A plane flew really close to the top of our mast as it positioned itself for the approach to the airport. The skill of the pilots and the little planes taking off and landing became a remarkable sight at almost every anchorage in the Grenadines. Tiny airstrips were built on whatever small flat promontory was available, usually set against tall mountains.

We explored the quaint, quirky port town on Union Island, which was colourful and lively, walking up the short main street to the hilltop behind the town to see the view. Inside the adjoining reef, kite surfers were making the most of ideal conditions: good wind with no swell, as they zigzagged across the iridescent waters at high speed, their wakes competing with the white horses stirred up by the wind.

"Hmm... Union Island... the name really does not do justice to this small island paradise: beautiful sandy beaches nestled in between palms and lush vegetation. I just love the little town. So charming."

"Wait until we get to Tobago Cays," laughed Alan in response. I was now very curious. Georges and Andi had also waxed lyrical about this location.

At a leisurely pace, we wound our way northwards past sun-drenched islands towards the coral reefs of Tobago Cays Marine Park. As we wove our way into the anchorage, Alan pointed out a freighter wedged in between two small islands.

"Must have been a hell of a storm to do that," Bjorn mused.

It was blowing around 18 knots with white caps splashing against the outside of the reef when we set our anchor. Accompanying us were *Silver Fern*. We took the dinghy to the sandy bank at the tip of a small island, marvelling at the glistening water colours.

"There are no words to describe the different shades of blue," I said. "This is breathtakingly beautiful!"

We spent the better part of the afternoon snorkelling on the coral reef, tackling a somewhat strong current. You had to choose the right moment to climb onto the steep sandy beach as the swell had worked its way into the anchorage.

We sailed past several islets as we headed for Bequia, the second largest island of the Grenadines. Of course, as always, Alan had to correct my pronunciation. "It's Bek-way," he teased.

The anchorage was spacious and popular. I counted up to 40 yachts spread out along the beach. Ahead lay hilly terrain covered in thick vegetation leading down to the port town where we were headed to stretch our legs and explore. A lovely promenade flanked the beach that contained beach residences, colourful shops selling the usual sarongs and souvenirs, and restaurants offering the local fare, usually delectable seafood: you could not forget you were in the Caribbean.

At the general store, we replenished our supplies of the local rum, pineapple juice, and coconut cream. We won't give away the secret recipe for this tasty version of Pina Colada expertly made by Alan, which we had to keep on sampling night after night to make sure the standard was maintained.

We then headed north to the volcanic island of St Vincent. With reports from other cruisers of theft from yachts at anchor in this part of the Caribbean, in some cases armed robbery, we had been warned to be vigilant. We were still sailing in company with *Silver Fern*, whom we followed to a small

A Little Bit of MisChief

anchorage in the south of island. This time we rafted up, which means, we anchored alongside each other.

"There's only the one restaurant ashore which serves seafood. Although the decor is basic, the food is really good," Bryce told us.

Soon we were all headed along the beach to book a table for the evening... not so much because the venue, a large room leading on to a spacious veranda, would be crowded, but more to let them know that they had patrons for dinner that evening. We were not disappointed. With platters of lobster, giant prawns and the like, we had our fill of the delicious seafood feast they set out for us. With the place to ourselves, we lounged on the veranda, replete, fully enjoying the peace and serenity of this tranquil bay.

Early the next morning we set out to cross over to the next island of St. Lucia. As always, we set the sails and then sat back to enjoy a fresh and sometimes frisky sail in the strong breeze.

"This is heaven!" I shouted out, sitting in the cockpit. I watched the sails to ensure they were trimmed to get the best out of them, water whooshing along the hull, with windblown hair and a grin from ear to ear. "I have to say, having come so far, the Caribbean is unbeatable from a sailing point of view."

As we approached our first stop on the western - and lee - side of the island of St Lucia, two dramatically tapered mountains came into view.

"Look at that!" I started out.

"That's the famous Pitons of St Lucia," Holly told me.

This time I paid attention to the alien pronunciation.

"Saynt Loo-shya?" I queried.

Holly gave me a smile. "Hmmm...yes, that's right!"

The next day we went ashore to explore the fishing village of Soufriere, as always with a side trip to the local market for fresh produce.

We made another stop over before heading to our final destination on the island. This was the quaint inlet at Marigot Bay. A sand cay jutted out into the middle of the inlet, and a cosy resort and marina lay beyond, tastefully blending into the hillside. It was another heavenly anchorage where we enjoyed two pleasant, relaxing days.

Our time with Holly and Alan was coming to an end. And so, we headed to Rodney Bay at the north-westernmost point of the island. We came across several old friends at this large, popular anchorage. That evening, Bjorn and I treated Holly and Alan to a meal ashore, at the Gros Islet quarter of the town. An internet search had identified a potential restaurant called very promisingly 'Flavours of the Grill'. I can happily report that we all came out satisfied customers after another lovely, well-presented and delicious meal of more fresh fish and lobster.

After two days at anchor, Alan took *Summer Wind* into Rodney Bay Marina so that it would be easier for us to disembark and transfer our belongings on *Lobea* where we would spend the next fortnight. It was all excitement as we met up with Dominique and Claude. We exchanged news, reminiscing on the wonderful winter we had spent together in Turkey. Whilst at the marina, Dominique and Claude, and Holly and Alan took us around to meet other cruisers we had met in the Mediterranean, namely Linda and Frank on little *Interlude*. We called it 'little' because whilst it was the same size as our boat, it had acquired this nickname to distinguish it from the larger *Interlude* owned by Katie and Kurt, when all of us had wintered at Finike Marina.

"What a lovely surprise? Linda! Frank! How good to see you both? But why are you wearing a sling?" I queried.

"Bit of a story. I was mugged in Martinique and my shoulder ligament was pulled out. It is a real bother as of course I cannot sail for the next six to eight weeks whilst I wear this plaster cast."

"Ouch! Nasty experience."

The eastern Caribbean is a relatively safe place when compared to the western end. It was not, however, without incident. In the month we were there, an English yachtsman was murdered on his yacht in a burglary gone wrong whilst in an isolated anchorage on one of the islands.

We had been planning a tour of the island, and so this was a great opportunity for all of us to hire a minivan and guide, and explore St Lucia. Our day trip included a visit to some banana plantations. They grew various species of bananas which had different uses. Our guide described in detail the growing process, which included 'bunch sleeving', when a banana bunch is covered by a polythene bag - usually blue - to prevent disease. In between all the sightseeing, we chatted endlessly about our collective cruising past and future plans, sharing anecdotes and jokes. We were taken to various viewing points such as the lookout for the Pitons, the quaint port of Castries, and scenic waterfalls, beaches and inlets. It is so much more fun when you can share the delights and experiences with others. The *piece de resistance* was undoubtedly the visit to the well-kept Botanical Gardens, with its wonderful display of tropical plants, colourful foliage and dazzling flowers.

After a few days of socialising, we sailed out of the marina on *Lobea* and headed north towards the French island of Martinique. With steady easterly winds blowing, we hoisted the sails for what turned out to be 'a breeze' of a sail across to the island, as we again adjusted to the movement of *Lobea*. Our destination was the marina at Le Marin, a large inlet at the southern end.

"I will go to visit customs and immigration," Claude told us, as we handed him our European Union passports. It was strange to be on the other side of the Atlantic, yet once again under EU rules, on French soil.

Claude soon came back and told us we could go ashore for a stroll whilst he waited for the customs people to turn up. When we returned, he greeted us with a puzzled expression on his face.

"The customs people took your bags apart," he said. "They didn't touch ours at all."

Bjorn and I looked at each other. "That's strange. Could be our Maltese EU passports? They are unusual as Malta is such a small island," I said.

"On the other hand," Bjorn continued, "we have just travelled - practically zigzagged - through Central America. Perhaps all those stamps in our passports rang some alarm bells, and they thought we were smugglers or something."

If Claude had not mentioned it, I would not have known that

they had gone through my bag, so at least they must have been tidy officials. *Merci*!

We hired a car together and set out to drive around the island. Fort-de-France, the capital, set among steep hills, with narrow streets and ornate balconies, remnants of its colonial past was charming. The statue of Josephine, who was born on the island and was Napoleon I's wife, graces La Savane Park, in the middle of town. Our journey took us over the numerous hilltops in the southern part of the island. As in all the islands we had visited so far, the western coast proffered sheltered, idyllic beaches with white sand, palm trees and beautiful promenades, whilst the east coast was buffeted with strong breezes where wind and kite surfers took advantage of the still waters inside the outlying reefs.

We spent a lovely couple of days with Dominique and Claude exploring Martinique. The island's culture reflects a distinctive blend of French and West Indian influences. Martinique exuded more wealth than many of its southern neighbours. The towns and villages were modern and elegant, the promenades weed-free and tidily paved with neat shop fronts. There was less of the colourful, somewhat dilapidated yet charming character that we had experienced further south. That characteristic French 'chic' influence came through. I revelled in exploring the numerous boutiques and indulging in some retail therapy, especially in the smaller villages.

Our time in the Caribbean was drawing to a close, and Dominique and Claude offered to take us back on *Lobea* to St Lucia where we would board our plane back to Europe. Favourable winds helped us enjoy a final glorious sail across the waters. We returned to Rodney Bay Marina in time to for the colourful and lively food festival in the streets of Gros Islet, and a delicious farewell supper at one of the local speciality restaurants.

We had had a great taste of Caribbean cruising and a wonderful long and leisurely holiday to boot. It was with some sadness that we said *au revoir* once again to friends and to this part of the world, although we were sure that we would return, before long.

A Little Bit of MisChief

Local Fishermen at Gros Piton, St Lucia

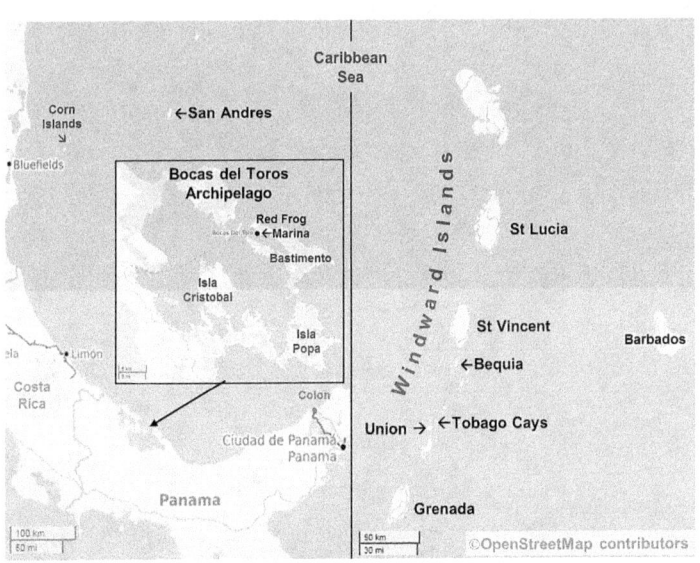

The Caribbean

Christina Gillgren

24
Dream the Dream

"Another cruiser!" Bjorn called out. He was standing on the balcony, back at our apartment in Malta, watching a boat sail into the bay. It was immediately recognisable as a long-term cruiser, with its telltale davits, wind generator and solar panels.

"Swiss flag," I said, joining him, as the self-focusing binoculars picked out the white cross amid the red. "There's a dolphin figure on the hull in the bow. I don't recognise it. Not someone we know."

The sea was in our blood. It can be a hard taskmaster and one you had better treat with respect. Yet time and again we were drawn to it like a magnet - an enduring love affair. Why, we couldn't even go to a restaurant without opting for one on the sea in preference to one inland.

We had the bug, and our Caribbean escapade had only served to confirm this.

"Sometimes I feel as though we moved too fast from Asia to the Med," Bjorn told me. "But had we not done so, we might not have been able to complete our journey across the Indian Ocean. So much has happened since we first set out: the rise of Arab Spring, and new countries embroiled in conflict."

"One thing I know for sure," I replied. "It is so much easier travelling in a boat from country to country, your boat serving also as your home. But I feel a bit jaded and exhausted with the never-ending packing and unpacking of suitcases over the last year or two. And you need time to take in all the new sights …And we still have our trip back to Perth to meet our new grandson."

"Remember the 'ABC?' Who told us about that? … not 'Another Bloody Church' or ruin or whatever is on offer for sightseers."

"I'm happy to spend a quiet summer sitting still for a while; swimming every day just outside our door, playing cards with friends, eating, drinking and generally making merry."

"I couldn't agree more. It has been an incredible eight years, magical, surreal. I can't quite find the right words to capture the wonderfully fulfilling spirit of our adventure."

"Remember what Clive used to say?" Clive was another cruiser on the boat *Jane G*. "We are living an adventure; when this finishes, we go on to a new adventure."

"What is it you used to say, Chris? Dream the dream …then go, make it happen. …Time to start dreaming again!" said Bjorn with a roguish twinkle in his eye.

"Yes…Yes!" I laughed back. "Whatever the future holds, there will always be a good doze of the 'naughty-cal' left in us. And wherever we go, we never leave anything behind, except perhaps friendship and happy memories. Hopefully people remember us with a smile, sprinkled with our very special blend of …a little bit of MisChief!"

A Little Bit of MisChief

Loki, the Norse God of Mischief's Drink.
Avengers Cocktails Series by The More I Arty
Lily Mitchell (2012)

◇◇CHEERS◇◇

A Special Request from the Author

Word-of-mouth is crucial for any author to succeed. If you enjoyed the book, please consider leaving a review wherever you bought the book. Even if it is only a line or two, it would make all the difference and would be very much appreciated.

Should you want to connect or learn more about the author you can do this at either FaceBook or Goodreads.

Facebook.com/ChristinaGillgrenAuthor
Christina Gillgren GOODREADS AUTHOR

Read on for more about sailing and for a few hints for how to get away and fulfil your dream - whatever it might be.

Christina Gillgren

A Little Bit of MisChief

The Weather Gods
Deities and Other Mythological Beings

Sailors are by nature a superstitious lot. And we were no exception. To be on the safe side we enlisted some 'divine' protection. Hopefully without upsetting anyone's sensibilities, here follows a light-hearted rendition of the different other-earthly planning aids that we enlisted on Sailing Vessel (SV) *Mischief*.

And they must have worked, as we never had more than some exuberant breezes during all the time we sailed. Or was it, I wonder, because we mostly enjoyed ourselves and couldn't be bothered fighting the elements when they did not co-operate: the best way to approach cruising!

As our family in Malta naturally thought we had taken leave of our senses setting out to sail around the world on large bodies of water in defiance of the elements - a not so uncommon 'take' on our adventure - they promptly provided us with a Saint Christopher pendant. Saint Christopher is the patron of travellers including sailors.

Saint Christopher

The Saint Christopher pendant was kept dry and comfortable in a prime position next to the navigation table. This is where all planning takes place on board *Mischief* when the weather is too inclement to sit in the cockpit. It usually follows on from a session with friends where we try to glean information over a glass of red wine. A caution here: we preferred friends that had actually been to where you are planning to go to avoid the "I have heard" version of information.

The Weather Gods

Well, this set the scene for an associated adventure: scouting out the deities we could call upon along the way. Let's say we weren't taking any chances.

The hunt began for Mediterranean deities. The Greek god Poseidon was mentioned of course as the protector of seafarers. But given his temper, he was decided against. Look what happened to poor Odysseus (Ulysses) who did not have much luck with him as protector. And who wants to have to be tied to a sheep's underbelly to escape a cranky landlord? It was enough contending with pirates on the high seas without also having to deal with warring, jealous or temperamental deities.

There were several Greek gods pertaining to violent seas. We thought it prudent to steer well clear of these!

We gave up on Neptune as well, as there was no appropriate spot to sacrifice bulls to this god on *Mischief*. Besides, our barbecue was not large enough.

With the Mediterranean dealt with, Bjorn thought it best to enlist a deity to cover the Atlantic. The Mediterranean deities were obviously no good, as some of their followers got so lost they thought they were in India when they landed in America. Bjorn reckoned that if the Vikings had managed to sail across to Vineland, and most importantly back again, this could only be a good thing.

And so, we started with Thor, but he is mainly known for mounting his wagon and causing thunder and lightning storms. Freyr, the god of the sunshine, rain, and fair weather, a proud sailor and owner of the magic ship *Skidbladnir* was discounted on the grounds that what he rides on is a giant boar, not quite the image we were after.

Aegir, the lord of the ocean, one of the giant Norse gods,

was next in the dock. His nine daughters, the 'billow maidens', are the spirits of the different waves and he is known for being a friend of all the gods, hosting elaborate parties for them: our sort of guy!

Aegir as depicted by Gustave Doré
Santine, X. B. La Mythologie du Rhin.
Paris: L. Hachette, 1862
(Internet Archive and Oxford University, Victorian Web)

Aegir, however, could be capricious and greedy, sometimes sinking ships laden with treasure in his lust for gold. The Vikings believed that this deity was close by when they encountered huge waves. In order to appease this fickle god, they would sacrifice prisoners on board to gain safe passage. I guess one could always substitute prisoners for passengers in our case. Being in charge of winds and waves, Aegir was appealing, especially as we carried no gold bullion to tempt him. Thus a picture of him was secreted away on board.

Next on our list was the Pacific. "How about Tiki?" our daughter, an ardent windsurfer and general wind aficionado, piped up.

It turns out that this god of winds and waves has wide support in Polynesia and the Pacific, where they are, and have been successful seafarers. In honour of this god, Tor Heyerdahl named his raft *Kon-Tiki*. Why not, we thought: if it was good enough for him and the Polynesians, why not for us?

Tiki is also the trademark logo for a major windsurfing brand, *Starboard*, and as result, their logo of Tiki was put up in the entry to the cockpit. From then on, it became a habit on board *Mischief* to rub Tiki's image every time we went in and out of harbour for good luck and weather.

Tiki - Starboard logo

We had addressed most of the oceans and seas we were about to cross, except for our own back yard. So for some affirmative action, we went to Chinese mythology to provide us with a guardian for the south-east Asia region. This came in the form of Mazu, a sea goddess and protector of seafarers, including fishermen and sailors. She is revered for heroic deeds, trying to save her father and those at sea. Definitely one for us!

When it came to the Indian Ocean, we decided to give Varuna the Hindu/Vedic god of the mighty ocean a miss. This was another member of a deity prone to violent rages, with the result that he was demoted and replaced by Indra, the god of war, and of thunder and storms (another NOT). Whilst this god liked a tipple, which made us give him five minutes' consideration, his other proclivities ruled him out.

Instead we opted for Samudra, goddess of the sea. The literal meaning of the name, 'gathering together of waters' sounded more benign for our purposes.

Amulets, Talismans and the Like

Bjorn's brother in Sweden, aware of our collection of deities, propelled us in a different direction. He sent us a picture of the Vegvisir: a magical runic compass, Icelandic in origin and

A Little Bit of MisChief

purportedly used by the Vikings (although there is no evidence either way). Literally translated the name means 'to show the way'. According to legends, this navigational tool would guide sailors through the worst of storms to their destination, even when the way is not known, or indeed, when they did not know where they were. Given that its presence on board ensured a safe journey, it was a talisman we definitely welcomed.

The Vegvisir - Viking Compass

Our collection of 'insurance' became a hobby as we sought out good luck symbols from wherever we visited. One of the most common representations was protection against the 'evil eye'.

In Turkey we came across the Nazar, an eye-shaped amulet whose prevalence is throughout the eastern Mediterranean and the Middle East. The Nazar is often set against various backgrounds, including being incorporated into religious themes, so that it was not uncommon to find a Christian icon with a Nazar attached.

Christina Gillgren

Nazar (Amulet)

In the central Mediterranean, there are more variations on this theme. Of course, being from the island of Malta, the eye to ward off evil and bad luck on the Maltese Luzzu stands out.

Maltese Luzzu

The eye symbol has a very long history. For example the guard towers on the bastions built to fortify the city of Valletta against invasion depict a carved the eye (and ear), this time to warn of dangers to the Maltese Islands.

Myths and legends abound - another world to explore. I leave it to you, dear reader, to follow up and enjoy!

A Little Bit of MisChief

The Weather
(For The Nautical Among You)

Part of what becomes important when you are at sea, especially on a sailing boat, is the weather. One of the fundamental points about sailing is that there needs to be some wind: enough to move the boat along at an acceptable speed but not so much that it becomes too lumpy at sea. For most pleasure sailors, unlike the racing variety, that tends to be somewhere between 13 to 20 knots, which is 24 to about 33 kilometres per hour for landlubbers. Additionally, cruisers prefer the wind to be 'over the shoulder'. This usually means a faster point of sail with the least effort and maximum comfort to reach your destination.

When you set out to sail around the world you quickly find that in planning to have enough, but not too much wind, you end up falling in line with sailing patterns of old, going back a couple of hundred years. Like the great explorers, you go with the seasonal trade winds, which is why it takes longer to circumnavigate the globe.

There are some excellent records collated by the British Admiralty. British ships, dating as far back as the square-riggers, were required to provide copies of their logbook. These recorded a treasure trove of information and included the daily weather and sea state observations according to geographic location and season. This information was then translated into maps and other voyage planning aids, today known as the British Admiralty Routeing Charts. With the help of these, you can plan your sailing to fit in with the best time and conditions to travel from one location to the next.

Before modern aids such as the Global Positioning System (GPS) the wisdom among sailors was that ships heading for India should leave England in late November and sail south until the butter melts. You would now be somewhere around Cape Verde, where you should turn right. When land next comes into sight, off the coast of Brazil, you should take a left turn to take advantage of the prevailing winds south of the Equator. Next time you see land, Africa, follow the coast and then go with the wind round Cape Horn. This circuitous route can still work of course. But there are more alternatives today, especially with the opening of the Suez Canal.

When it comes to weather reports, they are not all that hard to come by nowadays. Not only are they very good, as in 'accurate', for the first three to five days. But they also give you confidence in what to expect up to two weeks. Any seriously uncomfortable weather can easily be avoided on most passages, especially if you go with the trade winds. For most boats, only a couple of ocean passages would last longer: for example, Canaries to Barbados and Panama to the Galapagos.

On *Mischief*, we would go ashore and obtain a marine weather report over the internet, usually in a café over a coffee or such. When at sea, we would bring in a GRIB weather file (weather prediction models that give information such as wind, rainfall and swell) with the help of our SSB radio. This would then be fed to a clever PC package called *SailDocs*, which would then provide a synoptic chart for up to a week for both wind and wave. Some boats use a satellite phone. This would give us the forecasted weather at the boat location and the surrounding area asked for. This service and eMail is provided by *SailMail*: see - sailmail.com/category/weather/

It is probably a good idea to read up on meteorology and weather in general before setting out; it helps to understand the 'mechanics', the basic principles of how weather works.

A Little Bit of MisChief

The Boat: SV Mischief

When you go cruising, researching the choice of yacht is a bit like asking your friends what car to buy to go on a driving holiday. You get a lot of instant experts telling you what is essential, 'good to have', and of course the 'whatever you do'.

Having opened the floodgates, we suffered the result at the bar at the yacht club on numerous occasions. We listened carefully and patiently, but ended up more confused than ever. It came down to our own short list of 'must-haves': a sturdy, reputable ocean-going boat, big enough to live on comfortably, easy to handle, and a master cabin with a centreline bed (i.e. you can climb in on either side).

The one thing we did learn in our research was that you don't really sail all that much when cruising round the world. Most boats take about five to eight years getting around. Of that about just under a year is actually under sail: the rest you sleep, eat, lounge and entertain on board. To make it an enjoyable experience, the boat has to accommodate this, with a cockpit large enough for the regular sundowners.

Having looked at a lot of boats online it became apparent that a design with a centre cockpit and fore and aft cabins took care of the living bit. The sturdy and easy to handle part translated into a slightly more traditional design. My diminutive size and strength limited our search to the 38 to 45 foot range of yachts, if I was not to rely on powered winches. I felt confident I could handle this size of boat single-handedly in case of emergency. We made our list and started looking in earnest.

Sailing Vessel *Mischief* is a Moody 425, designed by the renowned English naval architect Bill Dixon, constructed to Lloyd's specifications and certified for North Atlantic crossing. The design become somewhat of a modern classic after it was first introduced in 1988. The biggest change was in the keel line, which deviated from the traditional true keel (keel going from around mast line to stern of boat as part of the hull) to a half-true keel that is approximately half the size and is bolted on to the boat. The rudder is protected by a partial skeg: sort of a little keel that the rudder is hinged on, which makes it much sturdier should it hit anything in the water. This was just what we wanted: tick!

She has a snug and safe centre cockpit and a clean functional deck layout. The simple but robust mast with in-mast furling made it easy to handle: tick!

It was promoted as a family cruiser that offers spacious accommodation. This included a huge master bedroom in the aft of the yacht (tick!), a good size double berth in the bow, and twin passage berths between the saloon and aft cabin, which can be closed off to form an additional guest cabin, if required: tick.

The galley (kitchen) was L-shaped and compact, so that cooking whilst at sea was safer, as you can hang on more easily in rough conditions: tick!

In reality, it is a boat version of a 3 bedroom, 2 bathroom, kitchen and lounge room floating apartment fitted into about 40 square meters (430 square foot).

Mischief was built and commissioned 1991 in Plymouth in England for the first owner and her first homeport was Mahon in Majorca. She was then acquired by a Swiss family and re named *Jomaro*, an amalgam of the owner's names. These owners sailed her from the Mediterranean through the Caribbean and the South Pacific ending up in Opua, Bay of Islands in New Zealand. That is where we found her.

We became the third owner in June 2007 when our adventure started. The yacht was rechristened *Mischief*. After many memorable miles, we reluctantly parted ways. As far as we are aware, the new owners took her to the Caribbean, still under the name of *Mischief*.

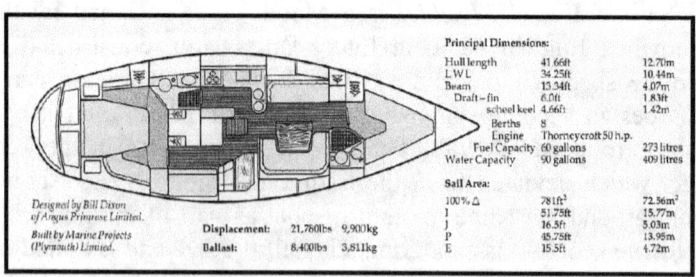

Moody 425 original sales brochure

A Little Bit of **MisChief**

Glossary of Nautical Terms

Anchor: what you throw into the water to stop the boat from drifting, preferably not following it in yourself.

Aground: when your boat gets stuck when it should be moving.

Autopilot: a hydraulic system (in our case) to steer the boat based on a course we set on our chartplotter, while I sipped a cup of tea.

Bilge: our wine cellar - below the inner flooring.

Bollard: short post on a wharf to tie boats up to or for dogs to pee against.

Boom: that long post to which the main sail is attached, handy for knocking you out if not careful.

Burgee: not a type of bird, but a small triangular flag, which identifies your sailing club.

Chartplotter: an expensive boat gadget showing where you are on the water using Global Positioning Service (GPS) as your smartphone does on land.

Cockpit: open area with seating where steering occurs, but usually better known as the sundowner deck.

Courtesy flag: flag of the country you are visiting, usually flown on the starboard spreaders.

Davit: a device for hoisting and lowering our dinghy: my salvation!

Dodger: aptly named shield against rain or spray in cockpit.

Genoa: I have no idea where the name originated from, but this is the large jib on front of boat.

Gybe: to change course by turning the bow away from the wind, resulting in shifting the boom to alternate side: for the non-nautical this is when you should keep your head down to

	avoid decapitation.
Halyard:	rope for hoisting and lowering sails
Hardstand:	(Also: on the hard) taking the boat out of the water and propping it up on shore, usually in a boat yard.
Helm:	boat's steering wheel.
Holding:	this refers to how well/secure your anchor rests on the seabed.
Jib:	small triangular sail forward of the mast, smaller than the genoa.
Mast:	a tall post that holds the main sail.
Nautical Mile:	1.15 miles or 1,852 metres.
Passerelle:	a board, plank or similar object used to get on and off boats when tied up: potentially your worst enemy after a night out!
Pen:	Mooring space/berth in a marina; this term is mainly used in Australia.
Port:	the left-hand side of a boat (facing forward): for the non-nautical, the reference to fortified wine is useful: remember port=red=left.
Pulpit:	rail at the front end, mainly utilised by birds to poop on your boat.
Pushpit:	handier rail at the back end of boat on which our barbecue sat.
Reef:	can be what you bump into when you don't want to, but in nautical terms, it refers to the act of reducing the sail area by rolling or folding part of it.
In-mast Reefing:	when the main sail rolls into the mast.
Shrouds:	Another curious name that in this case refers to the stainless steel wires (traditionally) from mast top to the side deck to hold the mast in place.
Spreaders:	horizontal support that stick out from the mast for the shrouds, making it a convenient place to fly your flags.

A Little Bit of MisChief

SSB Radio: Single Side Band Radio: A specialised long-distance (high frequency) radio used for communicating while at sea.

Starboard: the right-hand side of a boat (facing forward).

Stern: back part of a boat and nothing to do with discipline.

Stays: stainless steel wires (traditionally) from mast top to bow and stern to hold the mast in place.

Tacking: the manoeuvre of turning between starboard and port by bringing the bow into the wind.

Transom: the flat surface on the stern of a boat, handy for showering and for climbing back on board, usually via retractable steps.

VHF Radio: Very High Frequency Radio: A radio with a limited number of channels used for transmissions of up to 50 nautical miles.

Watch: what we gave up wearing when we went sailing; however in this case it refers to a short period of time when you have to keep a lookout and steer the boat.

Wind Self-steering: usually mounted on the transom and steers the boat with help of the wind, like an environmentally 'friendly' autopilot.

Windvane: an instrument at the top of the mast that shows the direction of the wind.

Vessel List

Name and Origin   **Crew**

Antares (New Zealand)..June and Pat
Billabong (Australia)..Caroline and Bill
Birvidik (UK).. Bob and Liz
Blue Gardenia (France)..?
Blue Marine (France) ....Marie-Christine and Yves
Bluesipp (Finland)... John and Petteri
Circe (Denmark) ....Birte and Jorgen
Cormorant (USA) ....Harry and Jane
Court Jester (Australia)................................... Sue and Wayne
Downshifting (Australia) .... Leighton and Julie
Dreamcatcher (Australia)................................. Helen and Joe
Eloise (Australia)... Tristan and Jas
Enrica (Italy).. Anna Fina and partner
Envy (Australia) ....Bruce and Audrey
Feijao (Australia) .... Gina and Lenny
Geronimo (New Zealand) .... Helen and Kerry
Imagination (Australia) .... ?
Interlude (USA)... Katie and Kurt
Jacqui Mac (Australia)Bernie, Roger and Dennis plus partners
Jandanooka (Australia) ....Lynne and Ralph
Jane G (Wales).. Clive and Jane
Kowekara (France) .... Alain and Marie-Joelle
Koza (Australia) ....Jim and Carola
Kristiane (Australia) .... Paddy and Carolyn
Little **Interlude** (USA) ....Linda and Frank
Lobea (France) ....Dominique and Claude
Mary Vorgan (France) .... Martine and Philippe
Mojo (Austria).. Gerlinde and Martin
Mr Bean (UK)..Malcolm and Linda
Nereid (Alaska) .... Judy and Ray
Orca Joss (New Zealand)..............................John and Jannine
Pampero (Australia).. Gus and Gabbi
Pegasus II (Australia) .... Kaye and Rob
Prism (USA) .... Dorothy and Ed

A Little Bit of MisChief

Purr (Australia)..Peter and Dorothy
Quilcene (UK)...Kit and Belinda
Sailaway Too (USA)... ?
Sandpiper (UK)...Margaret and Peter
Silver Fern (New Zealand).......................... Martha and Bryce
Sparrow (Holland)... John and Anne
Stefanija (Australia).. Gayle and Alec
Summer Wind (New Zealand).........................Alan and Holly
Sunburnt (Australia) .... Annie and Tony
Tangaroa (Australia) .... Helve and Rick
Te Ara (Monaco) .... Andi, Georges and Lea
Tulameen II (Canada) .... Frances and Bill
Vagabond (Malta)...Rolf and Wendy
Waterdrincker (Holland).........................Philip and Henriette
Westward II (Australia) .... Selena and Steve
Wraith (UK) ....Vicki and Jeff

<>The Very End<>

Christina Gillgren

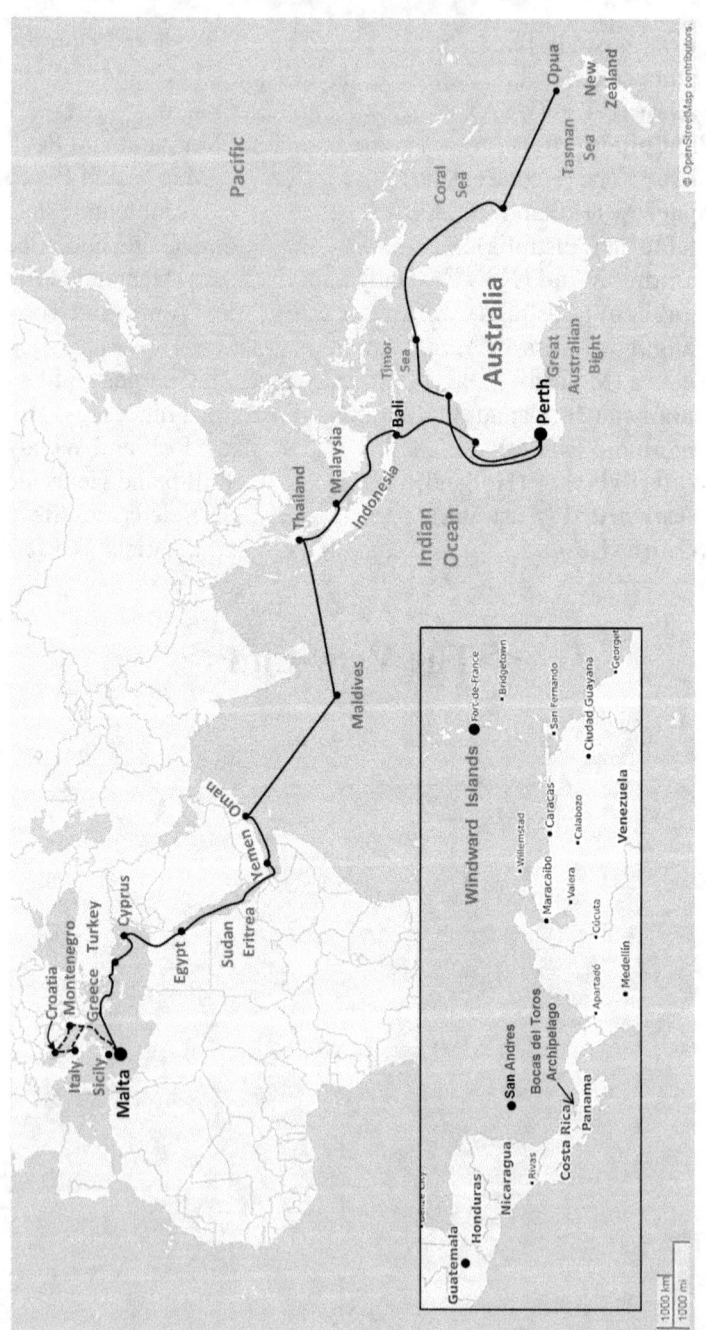

www.ingramcontent.com/pod-product-compliance
Lightning Source LLC
Chambersburg PA
CBHW071855290426
44110CB00013B/1155